MW00800183

Routine Emergency

Julia Chaitin • Sharon Steinberg
Elad Avlagon • Shoshana Steinberg

Routine Emergency

The Meaning of Life for Israelis Living Along the Gaza Border

palgrave
macmillan

Julia Chaitin
Sapir College
Doar Na Ashkelon, Israel

Elad Avlagon
Tel Aviv, Israel

Sharon Steinberg
Kaye Academic College of Education
Be'er Sheva, Israel

Shoshana Steinberg
Department of Conflict Management
Ben-Gurion University of the Negev
Be'er Sheva, Israel

ISBN 978-3-030-95982-1   ISBN 978-3-030-95983-8   (eBook)
https://doi.org/10.1007/978-3-030-95983-8

This Palgrave Macmillan imprint is published by the registered company Springer Nature Switzerland AG.
The registered company address is: Gewerbestrasse 11, 6330 Cham, Switzerland

This book is dedicated to all the innocent people who have suffered and continue to suffer from the "intractable" Israel-Hamas conflict.

Preface

Figure Preface 1 Rami—Flowers in the "Gaza Space" (2020)
vs.

Figure Preface 2 Tamar—Incendiary Balloons in *Otef Aza* (2019)

On December 18, 2019, Adele Raemer from Kibbutz Nirim, located less than three kilometers from the Gaza Strip, addressed the UN Security Council about Israeli life along the Gaza Border. Adele said:

> Have you ever had to run for your life? Literally? When I hear the Red Alert early warning system for incoming rockets, I know that I have between five to ten seconds to get to someplace safe, regardless of where I am in my little kibbutz house. From my kitchen, I can sprint to the safe room in about three seconds. If it catches me in the shower, I'm out of luck. There's no way I can jump out and make it to the safe room before impact without slipping. If I'm out walking my dogs, I either throw myself down next to the wall or just lie down wherever I am and cover my head and hope that whatever falls, doesn't fall too close.

Adele, like the nearly 250,000 Israeli residents who live in the region that is nicknamed *Otef Aza* (literally, the Gaza Envelope, located in the

Western Negev), have known 21 years of war. They have experienced over 26,000 mortar shell and rocket attacks, four wars, the violent hostilities on the fence, termed the March of Return that began in March 2018, and thousands of fires from incendiary balloons and kites.

This book presents and analyzes residents' life stories, collected through narrative and in-depth interviews, YouTube videos, and postings on Facebook pages that residents of the region have created and written. Our research asked: (1) What are the experiences of residents of *Otef Aza*, in the context of the ongoing war between Israel and the Hamas regime? (2) How do these residents perceive the concept of patriotism, in general, and Israeli patriotism, in specific? (3) How do the residents understand the ideology of Zionism? (4) How do *Otef Aza* residents perceive the Gazan "other"? (5) What do they think will happen in the region in the next five years?

Before we turn to our in-depth, multi-layer, and multi-method discussion on and answers to these issues, it is important for us to explain why our study solely focused on Jewish-Israelis living near the border with the Gaza Strip, and did not include Palestinian voices. We will first clarify why our study did not include Arab citizens of Israel and then explain the reasons for not including interviews with Palestinians from the Gaza Strip.

As will be detailed in Chap. 1, the Israeli-Palestinian and the Israeli-Arab conflict are two (related) conflicts that have bloodied the region for approximately 120 years. These conflicts center on hostile relations between Jews and Arabs (mainly Muslim, but also Christian Arabs). While *within* Israel, approximately 21% of the 9.3 million citizens of the country are Arabs, for the most part, Jews and Arabs do not live in the same geographical region.[1] The significance of this sad fact of physical separation (Robinson, June 14, 2021) (which also connects to deep social-psycho-political divides)—in the context of our research—is that there are almost no Palestinian citizens of Israel who live in the region that our study covered: the area in which residents have no more than 30 seconds to find cover when rockets are launched from the Gaza Strip into

---

[1] The exceptions are Jews and Arabs who live in what are officially designated "mixed cities" (Akko [Acre], Haifa, Lod, Ramle, and Jaffa [the southern part of Tel Aviv-Jaffa] (Mixed Cities in Israel, n.d.).

Israel. For that reason alone, we did not include this population in our research.

With this said, while our study did not elicit Arab citizens' voices, we have no doubt that it is important to learn how Arab citizens of Israel view and think about Israel-Gaza relations, in additional studies. We will return to this point in our Epilogue, especially given that a number of Palestinian citizens of Israel have relatives in the Gaza Strip.

The second population, which was not part of our research, are Palestinians living in the Gaza Strip. So, why didn't our study include this population? After all, their lives have been severely harmed by the wars and military operations, as well as the Israeli blockade, all major factors, which have contributed to the dangerous humanitarian crisis that exists there. This makes it very important to hear how Gazans live with this ongoing life-threatening situation.

Our reason concerning the inclusion of this population is depressing, but simple. Due to the war relations that exist between Israel and the Hamas, there is no direct channel of communication between the two governments. As a result, very few Palestinians receive permits to enter Israel, and Israelis are not allowed into the Gaza Strip. Furthermore, the Hamas is opposed to relationships between Israelis and Gazans, seeing such relations as acts of collaboration and such Gazans as traitors. Therefore, it is usually physically dangerous for Gazans to be in contact with Israelis—even when this contact is virtual, through Facebook, WhatsApp, text messages, Zoom meetings, or phone. This physical separation between the peoples, which has been going on for decades, is an almost total separation, which also has multiple negative, psycho-social-political consequences. This means that Israeli researchers have almost no access to Gazans and, thus, are unable to interview them and/or publish their findings.

For these reasons, while we were, and remain, extremely interested in learning the Palestinian-Gazan perspectives on the issues we raised, at this time, such a study is not possible.

This book, thus, focuses on the Jewish-Israeli side: it discusses the meaning of the intractable war for Jewish-Israeli individuals, families, and communities. We wanted to give voice to ordinary people who live near the border with the Gaza Strip, have children and/or grandchildren, and, who for years, have lived in a region characterized by a war that shows no signs of being resolved. We wanted to gain a deep understanding of what it means for adult men and women, from different backgrounds, with diverse personal and family histories, with varied political and religious orientations, who live in different kinds of communities, to live such a life.

In *Otef Aza* lingo—Jewish-Israelis living near the border with the Gaza Strip live lives of שגרה חירום and שגרת חירום—*cherum shigra and shigrat cherum*—emergency routine and routine emergency. This means that they are constantly poised "for the other shoe to drop." They move (seemingly) easily between war and quiet—though, as our analyses will show, this back and forth is far from easy. They know what to do when there is a צבע אדום—*tzeva adom* (red alert) signaling an incoming rocket. There is no moment in their lives when somewhere, in the back of their minds, they are not thinking and worrying about the next rocket attack, or incendiary and explosive balloons. Moreover, this is not only true of the adults; it is true of the children, who have never known a life without war.

To reach deep understandings of what it means to live such a life, we used three main methods of data collection—personal narrative interviews, photographs from our interviewees—that they either took or chose—and analyses of Facebook posts and YouTube videos written/created by *Otef Aza* residents. In addition to wanting to learn residents' stories, we also wanted to explore issues missing from the academic literature. We wanted to learn how they understand concepts of patriotism—that is, love of and attachment to country—and how they perceive Zionism—the ideology that states that Israel is the homeland of the Jewish people—given the context of their lives in a warzone. We were also interested in learning from residents how they perceive the Palestinian-Gazan "other" and what they think will happen in the region in the coming years. In the following chapters, we present many examples from these interviews, photos, posts, and videos that reflect the essence of what it means to live in this intractable warzone.

Why was it important for us to undertake this study? While numerous psycho-social studies have focused on the traumatic aspects of life in the *Otef Aza* region and how people cope (or not) with this trauma, little research has focused on the life stories of the residents, in the context of living in this warzone. To the best of our knowledge, no research has explored residents' postings and videos made for social media. It wasn't that we thought that researching trauma, coping mechanisms, and resilience is unimportant. It was/is that we wanted to better understand the larger significance of life in the region, for people who have experienced the four wars[2] of Cast Lead (2008–2009), Pillars of Defense (2012), Protective Edge (2014), and Guardians of the Walls (2021), the myriad operations and terror attacks, the incendiary and explosive kites and balloons, and the March of Return, by exploring issues that are understudied in this context. Therefore, we wanted to gain insights into how residents see and experience life in the *Otef*, without assuming an a priori framework of trauma and victimhood and by expanding the topics that connect to life in Israel, in specific, and in the *Otef Aza* region, in specific. We believe/d that these stories and voices warranted a study in and of themselves.

Before we delve into the issues addressed in our study, however, it is important to understand who we—the authors—are.

Julia, a social psychologist and qualitative researcher, is a resident of *Otef Aza*. She has lived on a kibbutz in the area since 1973 and has had many harrowing experiences connected to the rocket attacks, wars, and incendiary balloons. While she felt safe enough to volunteer in the area during Cast Lead, helping people suffering from the trauma of the war, during Pillars of Defense, she was traumatized, because of her experiences, and looked to escape from the area. Over the years, she has more or less learned to live with the situation, though it causes her great stress and sadness whenever there is an escalation in the hostilities.

In terms of professional work, Julia is a recently retired faculty member from the School of Social Work at the Sapir College—located next to Sderot and directly across from the Gaza Strip—the hardest hit area of the *Otef*. She has also been involved in peace activism for many years that connects Israelis and Gazans and is a prominent member in Other Voice—a local grassroots organization that strives for a non-military

---

[2] While, officially, the Israeli government defines these as "military operations" and not "wars" (mainly due to economic obligations of the country to its citizens during and after wars), for all intents and purposes they are wars and the residents of the area perceive them as such.

solution to the Israel-Hamas hostilities. (In Chap. 6, we present one of her Facebook postings from Other Voice's page). In short, this research was not only an academic undertaking for her, but also a very personal one.

Sharon lives in Be'er Sheva. Even though this city is not within *Otef Aza*, long-range rockets have targeted the city mainly during combat operations. In fact, Be'er Sheva has come under heavy attack during the wars. During Operation Protective Edge, Sharon worked in Tel Aviv. During the first three weeks of the war, because of the heavy missile attacks on Be'er Sheva, and on cities between Be'er Sheva and Tel Aviv, she stayed home with her children, because of the war. Sharon felt that her co-workers, who lived in the country's center, lived a parallel life, since the events did not appear to affect their daily lives. This experience interfered with her working outside the Negev and, eventually, this was one reason she decided to make a career change and work close to home. These experiences helped her identify with *Otef Aza* residents, who spoke about the frustration resulting from living in a parallel region, as if it was a different country. In addition, experiencing the wars, as a mother of two children, made it easy for her to identify with experiences and feelings that concerned the interviewees, who were parents. Sharon is a senior lecturer at the Kaye Collage of Education, where she teaches research courses.

Elad—a social worker, who obtained his degree from the Sapir College—was the main interviewer in our study. During the research, Elad lived in the village Ashalim, located 40 kilometers south of Be'er Sheva. However, he has lived in Tel Aviv most of his life. The interviews left a significant mark on him and opened a window for him into *Otef Aza* residents' life experiences. As a result, his interest increased, making him an integral part of the research team. As the study progressed, Elad also obtained a deep understanding of the fact that people from outside the area have difficulty understanding the life experiences of the residents there. Moreover, he was in reserve duty during two Gaza wars. Thus, he did not only have insights into and professional expertise working with people who have experienced trauma, but also has had up-close war experiences in the Gaza Strip.

Shoshana lives in Be'er Sheva. She holds a doctorate in Social Psychology and was a long-term faculty member at the Kaye College. Shoshana has been a lecturer in the Conflict Management undergraduate and graduate programs at Ben Gurion University for 15 years, due to her expertise in work on Palestinian-Israeli narratives and dialogue between the two groups. For years she worked as a research observer and evaluator of a joint Palestinian-Israeli project with PRIME (The Peace Research Institute in the Middle East), in which Israeli and Palestinian teachers developed a history textbook that includes both groups' narratives of the historical events of Palestine-Israel, presented side by side. Shoshana's deep interest in the topic of narratives in this context, and commitment to helping Jewish-Israeli young adults understand the significance of the different historical perspectives in the Israeli-Palestinian conflict, as one "bottom-up" step toward peace-building between the peoples, has been highly integrated into her academic and educational work.

Because we were four researchers working on the study, who brought to the project different personal and academic/professional backgrounds and experiences, we were able to reach understandings that we would not have reached if each one of us had worked alone. The analyses presented in this book reflect our three years of joint work that included our individual and joint analyses, and ongoing discussions and reflection in face-to-face meetings, WhatsApp conversations, phone calls, and, during the COVID-19 crisis, hours of Zoom meetings. What we present in this book is our joint understandings of the meaning of life for adult residents in *Otef Aza*, understanding that, since our work was based in a qualitative, interpretive paradigm, there are additional ways to understand the texts, photographs, posts, and video clips that we collected.

In order to provide a "road map" for the reader, our book is organized into four parts. Part I—*Introduction to the Study, History of the Region, and Methodology*—is comprised of Chaps. 1 and 2. This part "sets the stage" for the study, laying out the history and context of the region and detailing the methods we used in our research. Chapter 1 presents the background to the *Otef Aza* region, the Israeli-Arab/Palestinian conflict, in general, and the Israel-Hamas conflict, in specific. Chapter 2 presents an overview of the methodological framework of our study.

Part II—*Psycho-social Aspects of Living with the War and the Meaning of This Life for Otef Aza Residents*—is comprised of Chaps. 3–7. Chapter 3 presents an overview of academic-empirical psycho-social literature that has focused on continuous and post-trauma coping and resilience in the *Otef Aza* region, as well as psycho-social concepts connected to intractable conflicts, in general, and to the Israeli-Palestinian conflict, in specific. This chapter, then, provides the psycho-social context of our work and information about what we know so far, from an academic-empirical aspect, about *Otef Aza* residents. Chapters 4–7 present the four major themes that we found in our analyses of the interviews, photographs, and Facebook and YouTube posts and videos that we collected and studied.

Part III—*Patriotism and Zionism, Our Interviewees' Perceptions of Self and Gazan Other*—covers Chaps. 8–10. Here we explore how *Otef Aza* residents understand and relate to patriotism and Zionism—topics that have yet to been examined in this population in the psycho-social academic literature. In order to understand how *Otef Aza* residents understand these belief systems and ideologies, this Part, beginning with Chap. 8, offers a concise overview of the academic literature on patriotism—in general, and in relation to Israel, in specific. Chapter 8 also briefly presents the main streams of Zionism—a multi-faceted ideology that, while often embraced by Jewish-Israelis, is also often denigrated by others, both inside and outside Israel. This chapter, thus, aims to provide an outline of Zionism's different streams, given that, overall, Zionist ideology remains one of the bedrocks of Jewish-Israeli social-political life.

In Chap. 9, we present our findings concerning patriotism and Zionism, based on analyses of the interviews. In Chap. 10, we move on to the next question we explored—how *Otef Aza* residents perceive the Gazans. Part III, therefore, presents and analyzes residents' understandings of ideologies connected to national belonging, as well as their understandings and perceptions of the "other," the "enemy."

The final part—Part IV—*Summary and Conclusions—Tying It All Together, Implications for Living with Intractable Conflicts and Thoughts About the Future*—is comprised of Chap. 11 and the Epilogue. Chapter 11 summarizes the main research results and combines these with the lenses of the psycho-social concepts presented in Chap. 3. We weave together our findings with previous conceptualizations, in order to offer a multi-layered theoretical understanding of the meaning of life for people in the *Otef Aza* warzone. In this chapter, we also briefly tie our findings to other intractable conflicts, placing our study in a larger context. In doing so, we expand our focus a bit, in order to demonstrate the psycho-social commonalities that different intractable conflicts have on ordinary people, who live in such regions.

In the Epilogue, we present information on events that occurred in the first part of 2021 and our thoughts concerning ideas for future research and work on the ground. This is based mainly on extremely troubling events that unfolded in the Jewish-Arab and Israeli-Palestinian contexts that occurred after we finished the actual work on our study.

Before we begin, however, we would like to extend our deepest thanks to all our interviewees. They opened not only our minds, but our hearts as well, and gave us the opportunity to gain in-depth understandings of the complexity, significance, sadness, and joy of living in *Otef Aza*. They showed us—and hopefully, you, the reader, as well—the richness to be found in the people from the *Otef.*

Doar Na Ashkelon, Israel	Julia Chaitin
Be'er Sheva, Israel	Sharon Steinberg
Tel Aviv, Israel	Elad Avlagon
Be'er Sheva, Israel	Shoshana Steinberg

Praise for *Routine Emergency*

"A micro-geopolitical study on Jewish-Israeli experiences of living along the tense border with Gaza, the so-called Otef Aza region. It is a much needed, multi-layered analysis of interviews with Jewish residents about their fears and hopes in a contested political environment and ongoing military conflict. Interspersed with photo and social media evaluations, this book provides a richly textured canvas on the complex negotiations of people caught between security needs and justice values, including their love for and criticism of their country."
—Björn Krondorfer, Regents' Professor and Director of the *Martin-Springer Institute, Northern Arizona University, USA*

"I sincerely want to commend this piece of work. It is an excellent piece of scholarly research. However, the word research does not do this work justice, as it brings us up close and personal, to the pain of division, the trauma of war, the loss of hopes, dreams and aspirations of a future for all our children and grandchildren. Read it slowly, hear the human voices, picture the faces and take a step or maybe two, deep into their lives, it could just change your life also."
—Rev. Dr. Gary Mason, MBE, BA, Dip.Th, D.D. Phd.

"Chaitin, Steinberg, Avlagon, and Steinberg bring to the reader the experience of living in a place where the potential for incoming rockets means that life cycles through the lulls between the panic. Through the use of personal life stories drawn from interviews, photographs, and an examination of social media, the authors are able to bring those typically distant realities of protracted civil conflict to the forefront. The perspective of Jewish Israelis living in the Otef region along the Gaza Strip is presented in crisp detail. What transpires is an interesting mix of trauma and also solidarity leading to resilience. Through the words and pictures of those included in the study, we are better able to see and feel their experience and how they view their neighbors in Gaza, which itself is quite varied from sympathetic to blaming. The authors themselves lament about the inability to examine the life experiences from the perspective of those living in Gaza, who must also feel the 'routine-emergency.' Such interactions between even Israeli and Palestinian researchers, however, are strongly discouraged, demonstrating just how polarized the Israeli-Palestinian conflict has become over time. With this in mind, the authors call for a resolution that addresses the needs for all people in the region, on both sides of the border."

—Marie Olson Lounsbery, Professor of Political Science, Director of *International Relations Undergraduate Programs, East Carolina University, USA*

"This book is must reading for anyone interested in how war affects the emotional lives and thinking of civilians caught up in it. The authors have come up with a unique study. Using non-conventional research methods, they report on a relatively neglected group of people: Israeli residents who live near the border with Gaza, a Palestinian territory with which Israel has been at war. The authors use interviews, photos and social media material to provide insights not only into the trauma that residents have experienced but also their life stories, their ideologies, their hopes and their resilience in the face of a decades-long intractable conflict. This is truly a view from the inside. For the first time, we have an account of the ways people, including the authors, live with the contradictions, in their words, of "working for peace while being bombed and burned." While Gaza residents have borne the brunt of the conflict with far more casualties, the authors show how understanding the lives of these Israelis under constant stress may help in understanding how people retain their humanity and work to end a seemingly hopeless conflict."

—Charles W. Greenbaum, James Marshall Emeritus Professor of Social Psychology, *The Hebrew University of Jerusalem, Israel.*

"This book presents the routine emergency of daily life for Israeli residents living near the Gaza Strip. The success of the book is in its ability to capture moments— usually considered normal for people throughout the world—but, in the residents' reality, become extremely difficult, often unbearable. Routine Emergency lets us peek into the lives of a quarter of a million people and the everyday difficulties they face, caused by the ongoing war between Israel and the Gaza Strip, which has lasted for over two decades. Nonetheless, residents live full and normal lives, in a reality that is so abnormal. We find people who are victims of a harsh and complex reality, who also demonstrate the will to live, and to carry on with routine life. The book is written in a flowing style and not too 'academic', making it a book that people who wish to learn about these residents' complex lives will be able to easily read. Routine Emergency serves as an important document for understanding the complexity of the lives of Israeli residents living near the Gaza border. From 1885 to 1891, Theodor Herzl covered the French Parliament, the Palais Bourbon. He described the politicians—"who once lived and had a quarter of an hour of fame"—a sentence attributed to Andy Warhol in 1968. This book presents the lives of hundreds of thousands of people via the prism of interviewees, who deserve all the fame in the world. Residents of the region have up to '15 seconds of fame', concentrated in one book. It is important that everybody reads about them."

—Dr. Moti Gigi, Chair of the Communications Department,
Sapir College, Israel

Contents

List of Figures

List of Tables

Part I

Introduction to the Study, History of the Region, and Methodology

In this first Part of the book, in Chap. 1, we begin with a presentation of the Otef Aza region—its history, demographic characteristics, and basic information—that provides the social-cultural-political-economic context of the region that was the focus of our research. We then present a short overview of the Israeli-Arab/Israeli-Palestinian conflicts. We begin with the end of the British Mandate in 1947 over Palestine and the establishment of the State of Israel in 1948, which exacerbated the hostilities between Jews and Arabs that had begun in the dawn of the twentieth century, when Jewish Zionists began immigrating to the region. We then focus on the Israel-Gaza hostilities, by presenting the history of this specific conflict that has—so far—rocked the region for over 20 years. In Chap. 2, we present our methodology. Here the reader will find detailed information on all the facets of the research process, including the ethical issues we faced.

Therefore, Part I presents the background and context of our study, and sets the stage for the exploration of the psycho-social understandings of the meaning of life for residents of the Otef Aza region.

1

Otef Aza, the Israeli-Arab/Palestinian Conflict, and the War Relations with the Hamas Regime in the Gaza Strip

This chapter opens with an overview of the *Otef Aza* region. We then present a brief synopsis of the Israeli-(Arab) Palestinian conflict, beginning with the end of the British Mandate over Palestine. The last section of this chapter focuses on the relations between *Otef Aza* and the Gaza Strip over the years.[1] This chapter, thus, provides the context for understanding the narratives and social media materials of Jewish-Israelis, who live near the border with the Gazans.

A Brief Overview of the *Otef Aza* Region

Otef Aza (Gaza Envelope) has become the popular name for the Western Negev (desert), due to its proximity to the Gaza Strip and the violent hostilities that have characterized the area for over 20 years. In this region, residents have between 0 and 30 seconds to take cover when rockets or mortar shells are fired from the Gaza Strip into Israel. The area includes four regional councils (along with some parts of other regional

---

[1] There are numerous books on the Israeli-Arab/Palestinian conflict. Here, we do not cover this entire social-political history, since our focus is on the Israel-Gaza border region.

© The Author(s), under exclusive license to Springer Nature Switzerland AG 2022
J. Chaitin et al., *Routine Emergency*, https://doi.org/10.1007/978-3-030-95983-8_1

councils)—*Eshkol, Sha'ar Hanegev, Sdot Negev,* and *Hof Ashkelon*—which are comprised of 103 communities, *kibbutzim, mosahvim,*[2] and villages, and the three cities of Sderot, Netivot, and Ashkelon. The regional councils and the towns were established in the beginning of the 1950s, although some of the *kibbutzim* and *moshavim* were established before Israel's independence and three villages (comprised mainly of Jewish-Israelis, who were evacuated by the Israeli government from their settlements in *Gush Katif,* in the Gaza Strip, in 2005) were established within the last decade.

The population is approximately 245,000 people (Israel Central Bureau of Statistics, 2019). As noted in the Preface, this region is almost exclusively comprised of Jewish-Israelis, since Jews and Arabs tend to be geographically separated in terms of residence in Israel.

The *Otef Aza* region has one hospital (in Ashkelon) and two major public colleges (Ashkelon College and Sapir College, the latter located next to Sderot). There is a Cinemateque (in Sderot) and important ultraorthodox institutions in Netivot (the tomb of Yisrael Abuhatzeira [the Baba Sali], one of Morocco's most renowned rabbis, is a major pilgrimage site in Netivot that attracts hundreds of thousands of people every year [Netivot, 2020]).

In general, more so in the beginning, the development towns and *moshavim* were comprised mainly of religiously observant *Mizrachi* immigrants, while the *kibbutzim* were mainly comprised of secular people from *Ashkenazi* origins (Gigi, 2018). The *Mizrachi* immigrants, who came mainly from Muslim countries, were often sent to newly constructed towns after their arrival in Israel, in peripheral, undeveloped areas. Such was the case of Ashkelon, Netivot, and Sderot and the *moshavim* in the *Otef Aza* region. Over the years, the region developed and acquired a diverse population of old-timers and new immigrants from North and South America, countries of the former Soviet Union, and Ethiopians. In terms of religious background—10% of the population in the *Otef Aza* rural communities and about 14% in the urban

---

[2] *Kibbutzim* and *moshvim* are small rural settlements that have traditionally been based on agriculture and are characterized by communality and mutual aid.

centers are Orthodox Jews, which is similar to the percentage found in all of Israel (Vinrab, 2021).

According to the Israel Central Bureau of Statistics' (CBS) (1) socio-economic ranking, on a scale of 1–10 (10 is the top decile, 1—the lowest), which measures household income and expenses, combined with data on education, of all the communities in Israel, the cities in the *Otef* are in the 3–6 range and the rural communities in the 3–9 range, with many of the latter having a ranking of 7–9. Furthermore, over the years, in comparison to other parts of the country, the cost of building a home in the region was very low—a strategy that aimed to entice people to come live in the *Otef*, in spite of the danger (Neuman, April 9, 2020).

While many of our interviewees and people in the region talk about the beauty and charm of the area, most people in Israel equate *Otef Aza* with *Kassam* rockets and with the *Hamas* and Islamic splinter groups' ongoing violence, often thinking of it as a very distant place. Unfortunately, from discussions we have had with people over the years, we have also learned that many Israelis do not know where *Otef Aza* is geographically located, although the country itself is quite small. The area borders the Gaza Strip (bounded by the Mediterranean Sea to the west, surrounded by Israel to the north and east, and Egypt to the south) and extends approximately 20 kilometers in the different directions into Israeli territory.[3]

Below we turn to a short presentation of the Israeli-Arab/Palestinian conflict. However, it is first important for us to note three things that connect to our presentation of the history and to the issue of Zionism, which was one major focus of our research that connects to the history of the conflict.

Firstly, while our historical overview begins with the end of the British Mandate over Palestine (in 1947), the establishment of the State of Israel, and the Palestinian *al Naqba* in 1948, this conflict has its roots in ancient history that began approximately in 1200 BCE and ended approximately 135 CE, when the Jews were exiled from their ancient homeland. This led to Jewish dispersion in the diaspora for two millennia, in which Jews

---

[3] For more information and links to maps, see Range of Fire from Gaza (Israel Ministry of Foreign Affairs: https://mfa.gov.il/MFA/AboutIsrael/Maps/Pages/Range-of-Fire-from-Gaza.aspx)

suffered persecution and genocide throughout time. This period ended officially with the establishment of Israel, which was/is an independent Jewish state (Jarus, August 16, 2016).[4] However, since it is beyond the scope of this book to present all of this history, we begin with this modern time period, which holds the seeds of the current wars.

Secondly, while we concentrate here on the modern history, it is important to note that Zionism—the umbrella ideology that supports the belief—and often realization—that Jews need a state of their own and should live in their ancient homeland, Israel—appeared centuries ago, well before Israel's declaration of independence. In its modern version, it gained traction during the nineteenth century (Tyler, 2011). Therefore, this ideology, which includes numerous streams and understandings of what Zionism is and what it means to be a Zionist, is an issue that is central to Jewish-Israeli society. For that reason, we asked our interviewees to share their understandings of this ideology with us. When reading the following historical overviews of the Israeli-Arab, Israeli-Palestinian, and Israeli-Hamas conflicts, it is important to keep in mind that, for the most part, the underlying ideology of Israel's official institutions, government, and Israeli Defense Forces (IDF) has reflected some form of Zionism (more on this in Chaps. 8 and 9).

The third important point to remember is that the Israeli-Palestinian conflict is a classic example of an intractable conflict (Coleman, 2006). This conflict is characterized by highly entrenched, polar positions of issues, opposing ideologies, religious contention, and contradictory narratives of why the conflict started, who is to blame, who has the rights to the land, who is the victim, and who is the aggressor. Furthermore, since this conflict began over 100 years ago, generations of Israelis and Palestinians have experienced great loss and trauma. Taken together, these factors have created a conflict characterized by deep distrust between and separation of the peoples, who hold extremely negative emotions (Chaitin, 2011). Thus, we have a highly complex conflict that is multi-level and multi-generational.

---

[4] The interested reader can find information on ancient Israel at *Ancient Israel: A Brief History* at LiveScience: https://www.livescience.com/55774-ancient-israel.html

All of this means that it is almost impossible to write an objective overview of the conflict, given that the Israelis and the Palestinians hold very different narratives of the historical "truth" and different, conflicting ideologies (Adwan et al., 2012). Since we were aware of this difficulty, and since we—the authors—are all Jewish-Israelis, we used numerous references written by a variety of authors and sources, that came from Jewish, Israeli, Arab, Palestinian, and international scholars and organizations, in order to present, as best as possible, the history via the different perspectives. With this caveat in mind, we now begin.

A Brief Overview of the Israeli-Arab/ Palestinian Conflict

After 30 years of control—characterized by violence and numerous political complications—of the area known as Palestine, in early 1947, the British government, which had been awarded the mandate to govern Palestine in 1917, turned the problem of Palestine over to the United Nations (UN) for resolution (Morris, 2001). On November 29, 1947, the UN General Assembly voted to partition Palestine into two states — one for the Jews and one for the Palestinian-Arabs, and to turn Jerusalem into an international enclave under UN trusteeship. The Jewish Zionist camp, headed by David Ben-Gurion, who became Israel's first prime minister, accepted the plan. The Palestinian Arabs and the surrounding Arab states rejected it (Bickerton & Klausner, 2017).

On May 14, 1948, Israel declared its independence. The following day, Egyptian, Jordanian, Iraqi, Syrian, and Lebanese forces declared war, beginning their attacks. After eight months of bloody warfare, armistice agreements were reached; however, peace treaties were not signed (Morris, 2001). The outcome of this war, termed the War of Independence by the Israelis and *al Naqba*—the Catastrophe—by the Palestinians, who lost their homeland, had many results. For the Israelis, the saddest result was that over 6000 Israelis were killed—almost 1% of the total population (About the War of Independence, 2006). One good result, from Israel's standpoint, however, was that the country gained more land than allotted in the original partition plan.

Another tragic outcome was the creation of the Palestinian refugee issue (Rabinowitz & Abu-Baker, 2002). During that war, Jordan annexed the West Bank and Egypt assumed control of the Gaza District (Bickerton & Klausner, 2017) although it did not extend citizenship to the Gazan population (Goldberg, 1996). While there is not always consensus on the number of Palestinians who became refugees, the estimate adopted by the United Nations was 711,000. This number included Palestinians, who were either forced out of their homes by the IDF or fled, based on orders from Arab leaders, who believed that the exodus would be temporary (General Progress Report and Supplementary Report of the United Nations Conciliation Commission for Palestine, 1951).

According to the definition of the United Nations Relief and Works Agency for Palestinian Refugees in the Near East (UNRWA),[5] "Palestine refugees are people whose normal place of residence was Palestine between June 1946 and May 1948, who lost both their homes and means of livelihood as a result of the 1948 Arab-Israeli conflict" (Palestine refugees, para. 1). Today, UNRWA has over 5.5 million registered refugees (the original refugees and their patrilineal descendants), who are eligible for their services. Approximately 20% of the refugees live in the Gaza Strip (UNRWA in figures, May 2019). More on this below—in the section that focuses on the Israeli-Hamas conflict.

Since 1948, Israel has had numerous wars and military hostilities with the Palestinians and its Arab neighbors. These have included: the Sinai Campaign of 1956 (with Egypt); the Six Day/June War of 1967 (Egypt, Syria and Jordan); the 1969–1970 War of Attrition (Egypt); the Yom Kippur/October War of 1973 (Egypt and Syria); the First Lebanon War (1982); the First *Intifada* (1987–1993); the First Gulf War (Israel was attacked by Iraq, in 1991); the Second *Intifada* (which began in September 2000); the Second Lebanon War (in 2006, with the *Hezbollah*); the third "knife" *Intifada* (from 2015); four wars on the Gazan front (detailed

---

[5] The organization was created in 1950 to provide assistance and advocacy for Palestinian refugees.

below, in late 2008/early 2009, 2012, 2014, and 2021[6]); violent hostilities that began with the Gaza March of Return (beginning in March 2018). In between these hostilities, there have been myriads of Israeli operations and assassinations in the Palestinian territories, Lebanon, and Syria. There have also been myriads of Palestinian militant incidences of injuring, killing, and kidnapping of Israeli soldiers and attacks against Israeli civilians (Bickerton & Klausner, 2017).

While the 1948 war was, and remains, pivotal in the Israeli-Palestinian context, the 1967 war was a key event in the region's history, as it resulted in Israel's occupation of the West Bank, East Jerusalem and the Old City, the Gaza Strip and the Sinai, and the Golan Heights (Shlaim, 2001). The issue of Israeli occupation over the Palestinians—who have not achieved independence—has remained central to this day.

In order to create an entity to represent the Palestinian people in the world, the Palestine Liberation Organization (PLO), an umbrella political organization, was formed in 1964. The PLO, thus, centralized the leadership of the different Palestinian groups that had been operating as separate resistance movements. After the 1967 war, through the early 1990s, the PLO engaged in a guerrilla war against Israel, until it entered into peace negotiations with Israel (The Palestine Liberation Organization, 2020). In 1974, the Arab League formally recognized the PLO as the sole, legitimate representative of the Palestinian people. King Hussein of Jordan followed suit in 1988, when he recognized the PLO as the Palestinian's representatives and handed over the West Bank to the PLO and to the Palestinian people (Nusseibeh, 2009).

Even though the PLO agreed to enter into a peace agreement with Israel in 1993, the different groups, which comprise the organization, do not always see eye to eye with one another concerning the PLO's vision and objectives. Hence, there have been many internal disagreements. There are 11 factions within the PLO (Mapping Palestinian Politics, November 4, 2019). The major PLO factions, or those associated with it, have included *Fatah* (the Arabic acronym for the National Liberation Movement, which became the leading faction within the PLO), the

---

[6] We completed our research in mid-2020, but during the writing of this book, another war took place in May 2021.

Popular Front for the Liberation of Palestine (PFLP), and the Democratic Front for the Liberation of Palestine (DFLP). While there are radical factions that call for the destruction of Israel, there are also moderate factions, which are interested in negotiating a settlement.

Up until his death in 2004, Yasser Arafat, from *Fatah*, was the Chairman of the PLO. Since 2004, Mahmoud Abbas, also from *Fatah*, became the PLO Chairman. In early 2005, Abbas became the Palestinian president of the State of Palestine and the Palestinian National Authority (PNA) (Mahmoud Abbas, 2020).

While no progress on the peace front was made between Israelis and Palestinians during the first 30 years of Israel's existence, Israel's Prime Minister Menachem Begin and the Egyptian President Anwar Sadat signed a peace agreement in 1979, facilitated by the US president of the time, Jimmy Carter. This was the first Israeli-Arab treaty. Israel returned the Sinai Peninsula to Egypt, pulling out its citizens and pulling down their settlements (Carter, 2006). However, the return of the Gaza Strip was not part of this agreement; Egypt was uninterested in regaining jurisdiction over this territory and gave it to the Palestinian people. A second peace treaty was signed between Jordan and Israel in 1994. While both agreements produced a "cold peace," there have been no wars between the states since they signed their treaties.

Over the years, Israeli-Palestinian relations continued to deteriorate. After the 1967 war, the Israeli government sanctioned—indeed, even encouraged—Jewish-Israelis to settle in the West Bank and Gaza, building neighborhoods in East Jerusalem and the Old City and settlements throughout the territories. According to the CIA World Fact Book (2018), there are approximately 633,000 Israeli citizens residing in settlements over the Green Line.[7] Of these, over 215,000 Israelis live in areas in the West Bank that Israel annexed to the municipal jurisdiction of Jerusalem, and 418,600 live throughout the rest of the West Bank.

The expansion of the settlements and the tightening of the Occupation on the Palestinian population were two major factors that led to the eruption of the first *Intifada* (rebellion/uprising) in December 1987. This *intifada* was triggered by a traffic incident in Gaza, seen by Israelis as an

---

[7] The armistice line from 1949.

accident and by Palestinians as a purposeful killing (Intifada begins on Gaza Strip, December 7, 2020).

> In … the Gaza Strip, the first riots of the Palestinian *intifada* …began one day after an Israeli truck crashed into a station wagon carrying Palestinian workers in the *Jabalya* refugee district … killing four and wounding 10. Gaza Palestinians saw the incident as a deliberate act of retaliation against the killing of a Jew in Gaza several days before, and on December 9 they took to the streets in protest, burning tires and throwing Molotov cocktails at Israeli police and troops. At *Jabalya*, an Israeli army patrol car fired on Palestinian attackers, killing a 17-year-old and wounding 16 others. The next day, crack Israel paratroopers were sent into Gaza to quell the violence, and riots spread to the Israeli-occupied West bank. (Intifada begins on Gaza Strip, December 7, 2020, para.1)

The Intifada lasted until approximately 1993, when Israelis and Palestinians officially considered peace negotiations (Hudson, 2002).

During this time, the Palestinian National Council (PNC)[8] proclaimed that it would establish an independent Palestinian state on land occupied after the 1967 war. The PLO agreed to recognize and make peace with Israel, and Israel recognized the PLO as the legitimate voice of the Palestinian people (Bickerton & Klausner, 2017; Morris, 2001). These events opened the way to the Declaration of Principles on Interim Self-government for the Palestinians (the Oslo Accords), which were signed on September 13, 1993, by Prime Minister Rabin and the Palestinian leader Arafat at the White House (Bickerton & Klausner, 2017).

Further agreements followed. The 1994 Agreement on the Gaza Strip and the Jericho Area ("the Cairo Agreement"), transferred control over the Gaza Strip and a 65-square-kilometer area encompassing Jericho to the PNA (Morris, 2001). The Oslo II Agreements were signed in 1995, which gave Palestinians more civil and administrative control over other regions in the West Bank, including many of its cities (Shlaim, 2001).

---

[8] The PNC is the legislative authority within the PLO, responsible for formulating the organization's policies. It acts as a parliament that represents all Palestinians, except for those who are Israeli citizens. The PNC has 747 members, who represent Palestinians in Palestine and in the diaspora. Despite not being members of the PLO, representatives from the *Hamas* and the Islamic *Jihad* are invited to attend PNC meetings as observers (Mapping Palestinian Politics, November 14, 2019).

Unfortunately, however, the peace process ran into many problems, due to violent actions undertaken by Palestinian and Israeli national, religious fundamentalists, who tried to derail the process by striking terror into the other side (Bickerton & Klausner, 2017). For Israel, the darkest moment came when Yigal Amir, a religious Zionist nationalist, who believed that Rabin's peace actions betrayed the Jewish people, assassinated the prime minister on November 4, 1995 (Cohen & Susser, 2000).

Despite this, after Rabin's murder, more agreements were reached between the PNA and Israel. The Hebron Agreement of 1997 divided the city into two parts—H1 under Palestinian control and H2—under Israel security and control (Protocol Concerning the Redeployment in Hebron, January 17, 1997). Furthermore, the 1998 Wye River Agreements led to Israel's withdrawal from 2% of the West Bank (Morris, 2001).

In July 2000, President Clinton, Prime Minister Barak, and Chairman Arafat and their negotiation teams met at Camp David for a summit meeting, with the aim of reaching a final peace treaty. The topics included the Palestinian refugees, the status of Jerusalem, the borders, the Israeli settlements, and water supplies and pollution (Morris, 2001). However, due to the deterioration in relations that had occurred since Rabin's assassination, and to both sides seeing the other as not living up to their side of the bargain, the talks failed.

On September 28, 2000, Ariel Sharon, the newly elected head of the *Likud*[9] party, toured the Temple Mount/*al Haram al Sharif* (where the Dome of the Rock and *Al Aqsa* Mosque are located). Sharon was surrounded by large numbers of Israeli police—an act perceived by Palestinians and Israelis as a way to solidify Israel's claim to the site (Morris, 2001) and as triggering the *Al Aqsa Intifada* (Said, 2001). The violence escalated two days later, when TV crews filmed a 12-year-old boy in Gaza, Muhammad al Durra, being shot and killed, seemingly by Israeli soldiers, when he tried to hide behind his father. Two Israeli reservists were lynched and murdered in Ramallah on October 12th, when they mistakenly entered Palestinian territory (Muravchik, 2003). These events, and more, which were highly covered by the media, signaled the end of the "peace era."

---

[9] The National Liberal party—considered to be a right-wing party.

Nevertheless, another attempt was made at reaching resolution when the sides met at *Taba* (Sinai) in early 2001 (Matz, 2003). The process failed; after Ariel Sharon was elected prime minister a month later, he blamed Arafat for the failure (Isseroff, 2005). In 2001, militants in Gaza began firing *Kassam* rockets into Israeli communities located near the border. The first rocket hit Sderot, a town of approximately 20,000 people, located two kilometers from the Gaza Strip (Rockets from Gaza, 2009). Below, in the section that focuses on the *Otef Aza*-Gaza region, we provide details of the years of escalation of the rocket attacks that began that year.

In March 2002, The Arab League, led by Saudi Arabia, initiated the first pan-Arab plan for peace. They offered to normalize relations with Israel in exchange for a withdrawal from the Occupied Territories, creation of an independent Palestinian state with East Jerusalem as its capital, and the return of the Palestinian refugees (The Arab Peace Initiative, 2002). This initiative was never formally addressed by Israel. In the same month, Operation Defensive Shield—launched by Israel after a *Hamas*-backed suicide bomber killed 29 Israelis at their *Pesach seder* (Passover's festive meal) in a Netanya restaurant—resulted in the reoccupation of much of the West Bank. In Ramallah, the Israeli army targeted all the major ministries and infrastructure. In Bethlehem, fighting went on for days at the Church of the Nativity, where fighters and others had taken refuge (Operation Defensive Shield, Israel Ministry of Foreign Affairs, March 29, 2002).

Mahmoud Abbas became prime minister of the PNA in early 2003. A month later, the United States, under President George W. Bush, published the "Road Map," which outlined a peace process that he hoped would culminate in the creation of an independent Palestinian state by 2005. In June 2003, Israel began construction of the security fence/wall/barrier between the country and the West Bank. This construction has been a further source of numerous arguments, court cases, and violent and non-violent protests, by some Israelis and many Palestinians, as it cuts into and usurps Palestinian land in a number of places (Separation Barrier, n.d.). During this period, prominent Palestinian and Israeli politicians, experts, and cultural figures, outside of the official channels, held meetings in which they drafted a peace accord, hoping that it would be a foundation for future negotiations. This proposal, called the Geneva Initiative, was co-signed at a ceremony in 2003 (The Geneva Initiative, n.d.).

In 2004, Prime Minister Ariel Sharon gained approval from the Knesset to disengage from the Gaza Strip and to dismantle all the Jewish settlements located in the *Gush Katif* area, which had been established after the 1967 war. The 21 Jewish settlements, in which approximately 8000 Israelis lived, were evacuated in August 2005 (Special Update: Disengagement, August 2005). In early 2006, Sharon suffered a massive stroke, went into a coma, and eventually died in early 2014. Ehud Olmert became the prime minister after Sharon's stroke.

In January 2006, parliamentary elections were held in the PNA. As of this writing (2021), these were the last elections held there. The majority vote went to the *Hamas* (the Islamic Resistance Movement),[10] a party which challenged the *Fatah*'s and the PLO's ideology and mandate, and gave the party the right to form the cabinet under the PNA's president, Abbas (Wilson, January 27, 2006). The Israeli elections, which followed in late March, brought the new *Kadima* party into power, headed by Ehud Olmert.

Olmert started the Second Lebanon War in the summer of 2006. This war aimed to cripple the *Hezbollah*[11] infrastructure and military arm that was firing rockets into Israel, and that had captured and killed two Israeli soldiers. According to UN statistics, the war had bloody and destructive consequences for Lebanon and Israel, though Lebanon bore the brunt of the destruction, injuries, and death (Report of the Commission of Inquiry on Lebanon, November 23, 2006).

Despite these hostilities, in November 2007, President Bush convened the Annapolis Peace Conference in which leaders from Israel and the PNA agreed to work toward a peace pact, based on the Road Map (Text of Bush's remarks at Annapolis, November 27, 2007). However, this conference did not lead to concrete results and the peace process hit yet another roadblock.

---

[10] The US Department of State defines the *Hamas* as a foreign terror organization (*Country Reports on Terrorism 2017 – Foreign Terrorist Organizations: Hamas*, September 19, 2018). See: https://www.refworld.org/docid/5bcf1f4aa.htm

[11] A *Shia* Islamist political party and militant group based in Lebanon.

Since 2008, there has been no Israeli-Palestinian peace process. Benjamin Netanyahu, who was prime minister from 2009 until mid-2021 (All Governments of Israel, 2020), along with the right-wing coalition governments that he led, did not renew talks with the Palestinians.[12]

In 2009, due to pressure from the past US President Obama, who attempted to rejuvenate the peace process (Obama, June 4, 2009), Netanyahu put out a public call to Abbas to enter into negotiations (Address by PM Netanyahu at Bar-Ilan University, 14 June 2009). However, nothing came of this call, and the PM later backtracked on the statement. Furthermore, given the split in the PNA—between the *Fatah* and *Hamas* (described below)—the idea and practicalities of peace have become more complex, as there are now at least three players in the field, all of whom appear to hate the other (Kurz, 2015).

Before turning to a presentation of *Otef Aza*-Gaza relations and the specific context of this study, we will note that in Netanyahu's last year as prime minister, due to the brokerage of the Trump administration, Israel signed the Abraham Accords with the United Arab Emirates (Baker et al., August 13 2020) and with Morocco (Morocco latest country to normalize ties with Israel in US-brokered deal, 2020, December 10). While the Israelis were excited about these agreements, the Palestinians perceived them as a slap in the face, as these deals were neither contingent on finding a solution to the Israeli Occupation, nor redressing Palestinian grievances.

Otef Aza-Gaza Relations over the Years

As noted above, from 1948 to 1967, the Gaza Strip was mainly under Egyptian jurisdiction and military administration (Goldberg, 1996). Due to the 1948 war, between 190,000 and 200,000 Palestinians became refugees in the Gaza Strip (Final Report of the United Nations Economic

---

[12] Naftali Bennet, from the right-wing *Yemina* Party, became prime minister in June 2021, after forming a unity government. His government has not yet engaged in peace negotiations with the Palestinians.

Survey Mission for the Middle East, 28 December 1949), who came from the Jaffa, Be'er Sheva, and Gaza districts (Masiryeh-Hazboun, 1994). This region, often referred to as the most densely populated piece of land in the world, is also home to one of the world's poorest populations (Gaza Emergency, 2019). The Gaza Strip is 360 square kilometers; it has eight refugee camps and a population of nearly 2 million people (Gaza Strip, The World Factbook, 2018)—of which over 1.4 million are considered refugees by UNRWA (the United Nations Relief and Works Association—UNRWA in figures, June 2020) . According to Gaza Strip Demographics Profile (September 18, 2021), the median age in the Gaza Strip is 18 years of age, with 63% under the age of 25. Hence, one characteristic of the Gaza Strip is its very young population. Approximately 77% live in urban areas—mainly Gaza City in the north. Seventy-four percent of the Gazans are registered refugees (2019 OPT Emergency Appeal) in the Gaza Strip: over 919,000 Palestinians receive food assistance, over 581,000 live in abject poverty, and the unemployment rate is 55%.

After the 1948 war, the relations between Gaza and Israel were hostile relations. For example, from the end of the 1940 through the early 1950s:

Destitute and often starving refugees [snuck] back to their villages across the border to attempt to reclaim possessions and harvest crops. In the early 1950s, some 10000–15000 instance of "infiltration" occurred annually, with 2,700–5,000 Arab "infiltrators" (the vast majority unarmed) killed by the IDF between 1949 and 1956. By the mid-1950s, "infiltrations" gradually fell to about 4,500 annually as the IDF's shoot-on-sight policy increasingly had a deterrent effect. (A Gaza Chronology, 1948–2008, 2009, p. 99)

However, in 1968, Israel opened its markets to Palestinian labor, allowing in workers from the Gaza Strip. At least 45% of the Gaza workforce was working in Israel by the 1980s. Furthermore, many Israeli goods were imported to the Gaza Strip, while Palestinian exports, to Israel and to foreign markets, were controlled by Israel. The economic changes led to a clear rise in the standard of living in Gaza (A Gaza Chronology, 1948–2008, 2009).

During the first years of occupation, Israel integrated Gaza's water supply into its water network and connected the territory to its national electricity grid. In addition, the Occupation and open border also led to a situation, in which many Israelis, who lived close to the Gaza Strip, became acquainted and friends with Gazans when they went to their shops, restaurants and the beach, and when thousands of Gazans came to work in Israel—mainly in agriculture and in construction (Mandell, 1985). However, this did not equalize power relations between the Israelis and Gazans: the Israelis were the occupiers, and the Gazans were stateless and occupied. Nevertheless, numerous personal ties developed between the people, which, over time, as will be detailed below, gradually disappeared.

Another result of the 1967 war was that the Israeli government approved establishment of Jewish settlements in Gaza, in what became known as *Gush Katif*. The first settlement, *Kfar Darom*, was founded in 1970 (A Gaza Chronology, 1948–2008, 2009); 20 additional communities were eventually developed. In order to ensure these settlers' safety, Israel established a strong military presence there. Furthermore, in late 1981, Israel established the Civil Administration (CIVAD) that took charge of the non-security sectors, such as health, education, and welfare—a move that was met with resistance and unrest by Gazan professionals (A Gaza Chronology, 1948–2008, 2009).

The Gazan population did not passively accept Israel's occupation. Two armed resistance groups emerged—the *Hamas*, which grew out of the Muslim Brotherhood, and the *Islamic Jihad*, whose manifest aim was to destroy Israel. These organizations engaged in numerous attacks against Israeli soldiers and citizens. In 1984, Israel arrested Sheik Yassin—the head of the *Hamas* in Gaza—along with 12 members of the group, which had been outlawed by the Israelis. Yassin was sentenced to a long prison sentence. However, he was released in 1985, as part of a prisoner exchange (A Gaza Chronology, 1948–2008, 2009).

Due to the first *Intifada* and increased terror attacks, the number of Israelis who visited Gaza decreased, and, over the years, more restrictions were placed on Gaza workers. Furthermore, Israel allowed more Jewish-Israelis to join/establish settlements in *Gush Katif*, thus increasing IDF presence in Gaza. However, as noted above, in 2005, the Israeli government ordered the evacuation of the settlers and the army (Bickerton & Klausner, 2017). On September 12, 2005, the last group of Israeli soldiers left the Gaza Strip, ending 38 years of Israeli military presence inside the area (Shany, 2005). However, since then, Israel has retained control over Gaza's land, sea and air space, on the east side, while Egypt retains control over the southern border.

The Oslo Accords (in the 1990s) had defined Gaza and the West Bank as a single territorial unit—the Palestinian Authority—within which freedom of movement would be permitted. However, over the years, Israel gradually closed off and isolated the Gaza Strip (Gisha, 2020), which culminated in a full closure/blockade in 2007 (discussed in more detail below). Therefore, since that time, there has been very little movement and direct contact between Palestinians in the Gaza Strip and the West Bank. This has also, of course, seriously decreased encounters between Palestinians in Gaza and Israelis in the *Otef Aza* region.

As noted above, in 2006, the PNA held elections that were internationally recognized as being free and fair. The *Hamas* won 72 seats in the 132-member parliament. For the first time since 1968, *Fatah* was replaced as the central force in Palestinian politics (Usher, 2006).

The relations between the two Palestinian movements were never good. Things came to a head during the *Al Aqsa Intifada*, when the two had a full-fledged split (Kurz, 2015). After the 2006 elections, the animosity between the parties became extremely toxic, when President Abbas refused to accept the loss of his party's dominance. In June 2007, he fired the *Hamas*-led government in the West Bank and installed an emergency government, in order to reassert his authority. *Hamas* dismissed this government as illegitimate (Kessler, June 15, 2007) and, after bloody battles, overthrew the *Fatah* in Gaza (Shanzer, 2008). Since then, relations between the two political parties have been extremely strained and hostile, although many efforts have been made to bring about national reconciliation. None of them, however, have borne fruit.

In terms of Israel-*Hamas* relations, no formal relations exist between the two sides, who are in a state of armed conflict. In addition to the rocket and mortar attacks that began in 2001, *Hamas* also constructed tunnels, as one of their military strategies. These tunnels, which have cost many millions of dollars, were often financed with the help of Iran

(Watkins & James, 2016). The military purpose of these tunnels is to kidnap Israeli soldiers and/or to infiltrate border communities in order to take Israeli hostages or kill/injure them (Al Mughrabi, August 19, 2014; Pelham, 2012; Watkins & James, 2016). Over the years, from the *Hamas* perspective, the tunnels became an important strategy, especially after the instigation of the 2007 blockade from the land, sea, and air. The tunnel industry has caused much fear among Israeli residents of the region, since tunnel attacks do not have prior warning, as do rocket attacks (Rubenstein, 2014; Stein et al., 2018),

Israel's first recorded discovery of a tunnel was in 1983. At the beginning, they imported food and goods, and later served as channels for importing large appliances and cars. As time passed, the tunnels began serving many purposes, such as transferring and storing weapons, as launching pads for rockets, and for the facilitation of underground border crossings (below the security fence that Israel had installed). They also function as war-rooms and as safety corridors for top leaders in the organization, affording them and their families' mobility and sanctuary (Al Mughrabi, August 19, 2014).

By the eve of Operation Cast Lead in December 2008, it was estimated that there were at least 500 tunnels. By the end of 2010, after *Hamas* rebuilt and added more tunnels, it was estimated that their number had risen to 1100 (Pelham, 2012). At the end of Protective Edge (August 2014), Israel reported that it had destroyed 30 tunnels leading into Israel (Watkins & James, 2016). In order to combat the tunnels, in early 2019, Israel began construction of an upper barrier, which runs along the lines of the underground barrier on the border with Gaza. The barrier was planned to be 60 kilometers in length and reach a height of six meters (Israeli Ministry of Defense, February 3, 2019).

As noted above, *Hamas* militants, who were later joined by other militant groups, began firing homemade rockets into Israeli civilian communities located near the border. From 2001 through late 2021 (the time of this writing), between 20,000 and 26,000 rockets and mortar shells were fired into Israel (based on a plethora of sources that give different information: Ahronheim, December 31, 2018; December 1, 2019; Israel under Fire, 2014; Kubovich, January 7, 2018; Operation Protective Edge: Israel under Fire, IDF Responds. Israel Ministry of Foreign Affairs,

August 26, 2014; Rocket Fire from Gaza and Ceasefire Violations after Operation Cast Lead, March 16, 2016; Rockets from Gaza, 2009). Over the years, the rockets became more sophisticated, causing increased damage, and reaching communities much farther than the border communities. In order to fight this danger, in 2010, Israel adopted the Iron Dome—a mobile air defense system—which has had a success rate of approximately 90% (Gross, January 12, 2020).

To date, there have been four wars in the region. The First Gaza War/Cast Lead, began in late December 2008 and ran for a few weeks until a unilateral ceasefire, announced by Israel, was achieved (Israel agrees to Gaza ceasefire, BBC News, June 18, 2008). According to the UN Fact Finding Mission on the Gaza Conflict—popularly known as the Goldstone Report (September 23, 2009)—it was estimated that 1400 Palestinians were killed and thousands more wounded—most of them innocent civilians. On the Israeli side, four Israeli citizens and nine soldiers were killed. The report further noted that in the *Otef Aza* region, 72%–94% of the civilian population was found to be suffering from post-traumatic symptoms, due to the large number of rockets that had been fired over the years. In the war, thousands of Palestinian homes and buildings were destroyed and the Gaza infrastructure was severely damaged.

The Second Gaza War took place in November 2012 and was given the name Operation Pillar of Defense by Israel. According to Saressalo (1), this operation was the result of *Hamas'* and other factions' escalation of attacks against Israel during that year, alongside Israeli air force's strikes. One *Hamas* prominent leader, Ahmad al-Jabari, was assassinated by the IAF (on November 14th). The Israeli military attacked over 1500 targets in Gaza, including military arsenals, manufacturing plants, tunnels, and rocket launch sites. It was estimated that 1500 rockets and mortar round attacks were launched against Israel. The war ended on November 21st, when Israel and *Hamas* agreed upon the ceasefire, which had been brokered by Egypt and the United States. Between 140 and 167 Palestinians and six Israelis were killed during this war (Human Rights Violations during Operation Pillar of Defense, Btselem, May 9, 2013).

It did not take too long until the hostilities resumed and another war ensued. On June 12, 2014, three Israeli teenage boys were abducted and murdered in the West Bank. Israel blamed the *Hamas* since PM Netanyahu and the IDF averred that they had proof that *Hamas* was involved (Sharon, September 25, 2014; Israel IDs 2 main suspects in teens' disappearance, June 26, 2014). While *Hamas*' political chief, Khaled Meshal, neither confirmed nor denied the kidnapping of the Israeli teenagers, he congratulated the abductors (Eldar, June 29, 2014). This, along with rocket fire and retaliatory air strikes from Israel's air force, was the background to Operation Protective Edge.

Protective Edge lasted 51 days: it began on July 8th and ended with a ceasefire on August 26th (Cohen et al., 2017; Saressalo, 2019). Over 2100 Palestinians were killed in the Gaza Strip; 66 Israeli soldiers and seven civilians were killed in Israel. According to IDF reports, *Hamas* fired approximately 4600 rockets toward Israel during the period, while Israeli forces hit approximately 5300 targets in Gaza, including UN buildings, in which Palestinians were often sheltering inside (Gaza Crisis: Toll of Operations in Gaza, September 1, 2014). In 2014, mouths of *Hamas* tunnels were found by the IDF to be under hospitals, schools and civilian buildings. This made it difficult not to kill and injure innocent children and civilians (Globes, July 27, 2014). In addition to the Iranian funding, the money from Qatar that was given at the time, and intended for rebuilding, passed to the *Hamas* and was used for building tunnels (Sadeh, July 26, 2014).

According to the OCHA—The UN's Office for the Coordination of Humanitarian Affairs (Protection of Civilians, OCHA, June 23–29, 2015), approximately half a million Palestinians in the Gaza Strip (28% of the population) were displaced during the war, 2251 Palestinians, including 1462 civilians—551 of whom were children—were killed, and 11,231 Palestinians were injured. This number included 3436 children and 3540 women. Furthermore, 18,000 housing units were completely or partially destroyed and 73 medical facilities and many ambulances were damaged. According to the Palestinian Ministry of Endowments and Religious Affairs, 203 mosques were damaged during the war and 73 were destroyed. Israel maintained that since the *Hamas* military used mosques for weapon storage, tunnel entrances, training, and gathering of militants, they were legitimate military targets (Cohen, August 26, 2014).

As OCHA noted, on the Israeli side, approximately 1600 Israelis were injured, including 270 children. Direct damage to civilian property in Israel amounted to almost $25 million. Palestinian armed groups fired 4881 rockets and 1753 mortars toward Israel; the IDF uncovered 32 tunnels, 14 of which extended into Israel. An estimated 5000–8000 Israeli citizens temporarily fled their homes due to the threat of rocketry from Gaza. Furthermore, the bodies of two soldiers, Oron Shaul and Hadar Goldin, who were killed in the war, were taken through tunnels by *Hamas*, during the war (Harel & Cohen, August 8, 2014).[13]

Both the *Hamas* and Israel were condemned for their use of violence against citizens on the enemy side. However, due to the massive destruction in Gaza and high number of Palestinian civilians, including children, who were injured and killed during Protective Edge, Israel received most of the blame by the international community (Report of the independent commission of inquiry established pursuant to Human Rights Council resolution S-21/1, June 24, 2015).

The fourth war took place from May 10 to May 21, 2021—after completion of our research. However, since this demonstrates that the conflict is far from over, we present some information about it here. According to the IDF (Operation Guardian of the Walls, 2021), the operation began when terror organizations in Gaza fired rockets toward Jerusalem. Over the next 12 days, *Hamas* and the *Islamic Jihad* fired almost 4400 rockets at Israel, targeting Israeli civilians. The IDF struck over 1500 terror targets in the Gaza Strip, including launch sites, command and control centers, weapons' storage sites and kilometers of *Hamas'* tunnels. Furthermore, the IDF reported that it killed hundreds of *Hamas* and *Islamic Jihad* terror operatives.

According to Human Rights Watch (Gaza: Apparent war crimes during May fighting, July 27, 2021), Israeli military attacks killed 260 Palestinians, including at least 129 civilians, of whom 66 were children. The Gaza Health Ministry stated that Israeli military forces injured nearly 1950 Palestinians, including 610 children, while Israeli authorities stated

---

[13] As of this writing, their bodies have not yet been returned.

that rocket and mortar attacks killed 12 civilians, including two children, one soldier, and injured "several hundred" people.

In addition to the wars, another aspect of the Israeli-*Hamas* hostilities, which has been the source of violence, is the blockade on Gaza. On March 12, 2006, while *Hamas* was negotiating with the *Fatah* in order to form a unity government, Israel closed the (passenger/pedestrian) *Erez* terminal to Gazan laborers in Israel, who once constituted 70% of Gaza's workforce (Pehlham, 2012). In 2006, the *Hamas* captured an Israeli soldier, Gilad Shalit, who was held in captivity until 2011, when he was freed in a prisoner exchange (Gilad Shalit Exchange, 2011). In reaction to the abduction and to the *Hamas* takeover of the Gaza Strip, Israel placed a total blockade on Gaza in 2007, which remains to this day. Almost no Palestinians can obtain permits—usually only for humanitarian reasons—to leave the Gaza Strip and enter Israel and Israelis are not allowed into Gaza (Gaza Blockade, n.d.).

The decision concerning the blockade, published by the Prime Minister's office on September 19, 2007 (Security Cabinet Declares Gaza Hostile Territory, September 19 2007), states:

> The Hamas organization is a terror organization that has taken control of the Gaza Strip and turned it into a hostile territory. This organization undertakes hostile actions against … Israel and its citizens … it was decided to adopt the recommendations … put forth by the defense department and experts, that include continuing military actions and thwarting the terror organization. Furthermore, additional limitations will be put on the Hamas regime, so that the transport of goods into the Gaza Strip will be limited, there will be a reduction of the provision of gas and electricity, and there will also be a limitation on movement of people to and from the Gaza Strip. These limitations will be applied after the decision is examined from the legal standpoint and will also take into consideration the humanitarian aspects that exist in the Gaza Strip, with the intention of avoiding a humanitarian crisis.

It is not surprising that OCHA has a different perspective on the blockade (Gaza Blockade, n.d.). According to this UN agency, Israel began imposing movement restrictions on the Gaza Strip in the early

1990s with the 2007 blockade being one more extreme step in the process. As OCHA notes, the Gazans remain locked in, denied free access to the outside world. Some of the outcomes of the blockade include a drastic decrease in living conditions, and economic and social fragmentation from the Palestinians in the West Bank and East Jerusalem. The isolation of Gaza has been exacerbated by restrictions imposed by the Egyptian authorities on Rafah, the single border from which Gazans can cross into Egypt.

Despite Israel's insistence that the blockade would not cause a humanitarian crisis, UNWRA has reported devastating effects that the closure has had on the region: a severe blow to the economy, serious environmental concerns, the worsening of health conditions, and disruptions in education (2019 OPT Emergency Appeal, 2019). According to the Israeli NGO, *Gisha* (Gaza Up Close, 2019), for years the Gazans only had electricity for up to fours a day; today, they have electricity between 8 and 14 hours a day. Furthermore, as von Medeazza (January 10, 2019) notes, only one in ten Gaza households has direct access to safe water. The reasons are that pollution has made the aquifer's water unfit to drink, and the infrastructure to purify and desalinate the water cannot work, due to lack of electricity to run the plants. Limited access to clean water also has also affected the area's hygiene, leading to risks of disease, especially among children. One result of the sewage treatment plants' inability to operate fully is that approximately 70% of Gaza beaches are contaminated. In recent years, Qatar has provided money for the Gazan civilian population, and has been used to meet humanitarian needs (Khoury & Lis, 2021).

The humanitarian crisis, alongside the lack of freedom of movement for the Gazans, were the main impetuses for the March of Return, which began on March 30, 2018—nearly 70 years after the *Nakba*. According to OCHA (Protection of Civilians Report, January 7–20, 2020; January 23, 2020), Israeli military has killed 213 Palestinians, and injured 36,134 people since the demonstrations began.

On the Israeli side, the March of Return is perceived as a dangerous stream of violent demonstrations and ongoing Palestinian attempts to infiltrate Israel, kill, and harm citizens and soldiers, and destroy Israeli land. One of the main tactics used by the demonstrators is incendiary and explosive kites and balloons. Although there are no official reports on the numbers of kites/balloons that have been released from Gaza to Israel, Adele Raemer (one of our interviewees), has been recording the number of fires set off by these devices. According to her mapping (as of December, 2021), there have been at least 2400 fires, which she estimates to be about 85% of the actual fires. Since these fires appear next to/in the communities near the Gaza border, they have not only caused physical destruction, but also left people in the area living in black clouds of suffocating smoke.

When we summarize the conflict that characterizes the *Otef Aza*—Gaza region, we can only agree with Cohen (August 3, 2017) that since neither Israel nor the *Hamas* has succeeded in defeating the other, the solution to the hostilities does not appear to be war. The frightening and dangerous fighting continues, harming people on both sides of the border, who see no end in sight to this dangerous life. Furthermore, given the almost total separation between Jewish-Israelis and Gazans, relations between the peoples have not just deteriorated; they have ceased to exist.

As noted above, as Israeli researchers, we could not undertake a study that focused both on Gazans and Israelis, *due* to this conflict and separation. Therefore, we concentrated on understanding how Jewish-Israelis, living near the Gaza Strip, see their lives, how they perceive patriotism and Zionism, the Palestinians in Gaza, and what they think will happen in the coming years. In the following chapter, we describe the methodology that we used in our research.

References

2019 OPT Emergency Appeal. (2019). UNRWA. https://www.unrwa.org/sites/default/files/content/resources/2019_opt_ea_final.pdf

A Gaza Chronology, 1948–2008. (2009). *Journal of Palestine Studies, 38*(3), 98–121. https://doi.org/10.1525/jps.2009.xxxviii.3.98

About the War of Independence. (2006). The Knesset. https://knesset.gov.il/holidays/eng/independence_day_war.htm

Address by PM Netanyahu at Bar-Ilan University. (2009, June 14). Israel ministry of foreign affairs. https://mfa.gov.il/MFA/PressRoom/2009/Pages/Address_ PM_Netanyahu_Bar-Ilan_University_14-Jun-2009.aspx

Adwan, S., Bar-On, D., & Naveh, E. (2012). *Side by side: Parallel histories of Israel-Palestine.* Peace Research Institute in the Middle East.

Ahronheim, A. (2018, December 31). *IDF annual report: 1,000 rockets fired at Israel from Gaza in 2018.* Jerusalem Post. https://www.jpost.com/Arab-Israeli-Conflict/IDF-1000-rockets-fired-at-southern-Israel-from-Gaza-over-the-past-year-575871

Ahronheim, A. (2019, December 1). *Israel struck by over 2,600 rockets and mortars over past two years.* Jerusalem Post. https://www.jpost.com/Arab-Israeli-Conflict/gaza-news/Israel-struck-by-over-2600-rockets-and-mortars-over-past-two-years-609544

Al Mughrabi, N. (2014, August 19). *Exclusive: Hamas fighters show defiance in Gaza tunnel tour.* Reuters. http://www.reuters.com/assets/print?aid= USKBN0GJ1HS20140819

All Governments of Israel. (2020). *The Knesset.* https://knesset.gov.il/govt/eng/GovtByNumber_eng.asp?govt=32

Arab Peace Initiative. (2002, March 28). *The Guardian.* https://www.theguardian.com/ world/2002/mar/28/israel7

Baker, P., Kirschner, I., Kirkpatrick, D. D., & Bergman, R. (2020, August 13). *Israel and United Arab Emirates strike major diplomatic agreement.* New York Times. https://www.nytimes.com/2020/08/13/us/politics/trump-israel-united-arab-emirates-uae.html

Bickerton, I. J., & Klausner, C. L. (2017). *A history of the Arab–Israeli conflict* (8th ed.). Routledge.

Carter, J. (2006). *Palestine: Peace not apartheid.* Simon and Schuster.

Chaitin, J. (2011). *Peace building in Israel and Palestine: Social psychology and grassroots initiatives.* Palgrave Macmillan.

Cohen, A., & Susser, B. (2000). *Israel and the politics of Jewish identity: The secular-religious impasse.* John Hopkins University Press.

Cohen, G. (2014, August 26). *Mosques used for military operations, say Hamas POWs.* Haaretz. https://www.haaretz.com/.premium-mosques-used-for-military-ops-say-hamas-pows-1.5261217

Cohen, R. S. (2017, August 3). *Five lessons from Israel's wars in Gaza.* RAND. https://www.rand.org/blog/2017/08/five-lessons-from-israels-wars-in-gaza.html

Cohen, R. S., Johnson, D. E., Thaler, D. E., Allen, B., Bartels, E. M., Cahill, J., & Efron, S. (2017). *From cast lead to protective edge: Lessons from Israel's wars in Gaza.* RAND Corporation. https://www.rand.org/pubs/research_reports/RR1888.html

Coleman, P. T. (2006). Intractable conflict. In M. Deutsch, P. T. Coleman, & E. C. Marcus (Eds.), *The handbook of conflict resolution: Theory and practice* (2nd ed., pp. 533–559). Jossey-Bass.

Eldar, S. (2014, June 29). *Accused kidnappers are rogue Hamas branch*. The Pulse of the Middle East. https://web.archive.org/web/20140630191535/http://www.al-monitor.com/pulse/originals/2014/06/qawasmeh-clan-hebron-hamas-leadership-mahmoud-abbas.html#

Final Report of the United Nations Economic Survey Mission for the Middle East. (1949, December 28). United Nations. https://unispal.un.org/UNISPAL.NSF/0/C2A078fc4065D30285256DF30068D278

Gaza Blockade. (n.d.). United Nations office for the coordination of humanitarian affairs. https://www.ochaopt.org/theme/gaza-blockade

Gaza Emergency. (2019). UNRWA. https://www.unrwa.org/gaza-emergency

Gaza Crisis: Toll of Operations in Gaza (2014, 1 September). *BBC*. https://www.bbc.com/news/world-middle-east-28439404

Gaza Strip. (2018). *The world factbook*. Central Intelligence Agency. https://www.cia.gov/library/publications/the-world-factbook/geos/gz.html

Gaza Strip Demographics Profile. (2021, September 18). Indexmundi. https://www.indexmundi.com/gaza_strip/demographics_profile.html

Gaza Up Close. (2019). Gisha. https://features.gisha.org/gaza-up-close/

Gaza: Apparent war crimes during May fighting. (2021, July 27). Human Rights Watch. https://www.hrw.org/news/2021/07/27/gaza-apparent-war-crimes-during-may-fighting

General Progress Report and Supplementary Report of the United Nations Conciliation Commission for Palestine. Covering the period from 11 December 1949 to 23 October 1950. (1951). United Nations General Assembly. https://web.archive.org/web/20110822123836/http://unispal.un.org/unispal.nsf/b792301807650d6685256cef0073cb80/93037e3b939746de8525610200567883?OpenDocument

Geneva initiative. (n.d.). Geneva Accord Organization. http://www.geneva-accord.org/

Gigi, M. (2018). Relations between development towns and kibbutzim. Sderot and Sha'ar Hanegev. *Israel Studies Review, 33*(3), 121–139.

Gilad Shalit Exchange. (2011). IDF. https://www.idf.il/en/minisites/wars-and-operations/gilad-shalit-exchange-2011/

Gisha. (2020). https://gisha.org/updates/10866

Globes (2014, July 27). Hamas. Crazy: You won't believe where the IDF found an opening of a terror tunnel. *Globes*. Retrieved December 6, 2021, from https://www.globes.co.il/news/article.aspx?did=1000958356

Goldberg, J. E. (1996). *How has the Gaza Strip influenced the Israeli-Palestinian conflict? An historical encyclopedia of the Arab-Israeli conflict*. Procon.org. https://israelipalestinian.procon.org/view.answers.php?questionID=000503

Gross, J. A. (2020, January 12). *Decade after 1st interception, new Iron Dome boasts 100% success rate in trials*. The Times of Israel. https://www.timesofisrael.com/decade-after-1st-interception-new-iron-dome-boasts-100-success-rate-in-trials/.

Harel, A., & Cohen, G. (2014, August 8). *What happened in Gaza's Rafah on 'Black Friday.'* Haaretz. https://www.haaretz.com/.premium-what-happened-in-rafah-on-black-friday-1.5258612

Hudson, M. C. (2002). The transformation of Jerusalem 1917–2000 A.D. In K. J. Asali (Ed.), *Jerusalem in history* (pp. 249–286). Olive Branch Press.

Human Rights Violations during Operation Pillar of Defense, 14–21 November, 2012. (2013, May 9). Btselem. https://www.btselem.org/press_releases/20130509_pillar_of_defense_report

Intifada Begins in Gaza Strip (2020, December 7). History. https://www.history.com/this-day-in-history/intifada-begins-on-gaza-strip

Israel Agrees to Gaza Ceasefire. (2008, June 18). *BBC News*. http://news.bbc.co.uk/2/hi/7460504.stm

Israel Central Bureau of Statistics. (2019). https://www.cbs.gov.il/he settlements/Pages/default.aspx?subject=%D7%AA%D7%A4%D7%A8%D7%95%D7%A1%D7%AA%20%D7%92%D7%90%D7%95%D7%92%D7%A8%D7%A4%D7%99%D7%AA

Sadeh, S. (2014, July 26). Tunnels, donations, taxes and "collection of money from everything that moves": The way the Hamas economics work. *The Marker*. Retrieved December 6, 2021, from https://www.inss.org.il/he/wp-content/uploads/sites/2/systemfiles/SystemFiles/%D7%9E%D7%A0%D7%94%D7%A8%D7%95%D7%AA,%20%D7%AA%D7%A8%D7%95%D7%9E%D7%95%D7%AA,%20%D7%9E%D7%A1%D7%99%D7%9D%20%D7%95%D7%92%D7%91%D7%99%D7%99%D7%AA%20%D7%9B%D7%A1%D7%A4%D7%99%D7%9D%20-%20%D7%9B%D7%9A%20%D7%A2%D7%95%D7%95%D7%93%D7%AA%20%D7%94%D7%9B%D7%9C%D7%9B%D7%9C%D7%94%20%D7%A9%D7%9C%20%D7%94%D7%97%D7%9E%D7%90%D7%A1%20%20%D7%A6%D7%99%D7%98%D7%95%D7%95%D7%A9%D7%98%20%D7%A9%D7%9C%20%D7%99%D7%95%D7%90%D7%9C%20%D7%92%D7%95%D7%96'%D7%A0%D7%A1%D7%A

7%D7%99%20''%D7%93%D7%94%20%D7%9E%D7%-A8%D7%A7%D7%A8".pdf
Israel IDs 2 main suspects in teens' disappearance. (2014, June 26). *CBS News.* https://www.cbsnews.com/news/israel-ids-2-main-suspects-in-teens-disappearance/
Israel under Fire. (2014). Israel defense forces. https://web.archive.org/web/20140804022213/http://www.idfblog.com/facts-figures/rocket-attacks-toward-israel/
Israeli Ministry of Defense and Security. (2019, February 3). *The construction of the upper barrier on the Gaza border has begun.* https://www.mod.gov.il/Defence-and-Security/articles/Pages/3.2.19.aspx
Isseroff, A. (2005). *Biography—Ariel Sharon: Prime Minister of Israel.* MidEastWeb for Coexistence. http://www.mideastweb.org/bio-sharon.htm
Jarus, O. (2016, August 16). Ancient Israel: A brief history. *LiveScience.* https://www.livescience.com/55774-ancient-israel.html
Kessler, G. (2007, June 15). *Takeover by Hamas illustrates failure of Bush's Mideast vision.* Washington Post. http://www.washingtonpost.com/wp-dyn/content/article/2007/06/14/AR2007061402098.html
Khoury, J., & Lis, J. (2021, August 19). *Qatar, Israel announce agreement on stalled aid money for Gaza families.* Haaretz. Retrieved December 6, 2021, from https://www.haaretz.com/middle-east-news/palestinians/qatar-israel-announce-agreement-reached-on-transferring-aid-money-to-gaza-1.10133936
Kubovich, Y. (2018, January 7). *2017 saw highest number of rockets launched from Gaza since 2014 War, Israeli army says.* Haaretz. https://www.haaretz.com/ israel-news/.premium-idf-2017-saw-highest-number-of-gaza-rockets-since-14-war-1.5729601
Kurz, A. (2015). A conflict within a conflict: The Fatah-Hamas strife and the Israeli-Palestinian political process. In G. Sher & A. Kurz (Eds.), *Negotiating in times of conflict.* Institute for National Security Studies. https://www.inss.org.il/publication/a-conflict-within-a-conflict-the-fatah-hamas-strife-and-the-israeli-palestinian-political-process/
Mahmoud Abbas. (2020). Encyclopedia Britannica. https://www.britannica.com/biography/Mahmoud-Abbas
Mandell, J. (1985). Gaza: Israel's Soweto. *Middle East Research and Information Project, Inc.* (MERIP) Reports, No. 136/137, 7–19+58.

Mapping Palestinian Politics. (2019, November 14). European council on foreign relations. https://www.ecfr.eu/page/-/Mapping_Palestinian_Politics_Word_file_for_PDF_200618_%281%29.pdf

Masriyeh-Hazboun, N. (1994). *The resettlement of the Palestinian refugees of the Gaza Strip*. Doctoral dissertation. University of Leeds.

Matz, D. (2003). Trying to understand the Taba talks (Part I). *Palestine-Israel Journal of Politics, Economics and Culture, 10*(3). http://www.pij.org/details.php?id=32

Morocco latest country to normalize ties with Israel in US-brokered deal. (2020, December 10). BBC. https://www.bbc.com/news/world-africa-55266089

Morris, B. (2001). *Righteous victims: A history of the Zionist-Arab conflict 1881–2001*. Vintage Books.

Muravchik, J. (2003). *Covering the Intifada: How the media reported the Palestinian uprising*. Washington Institute for Near East Policy. file:///C:/Users/Julia/Documents/Otef%20Aza%20Book%20October%202020/CoveringtheIntifada.pdf.pdf.

Netivot. (2020). *Jewish Virtual Library*. https://www.jewishvirtuallibrary.org/netivot

Neuman, E. (2020, April 9). *The apartments here are cheaper and the take-home pay is higher. Where is it really worthwhile for you to live?* The Marker (in Hebrew). https://www.themarker.com/realestate/.premium-MAGAZINE-1.8750949?lts=1634968968896

Nusseibeh, S. (2009). *Once upon a country: A Palestinian life*. Halban Publishers.

Obama, B. (2009, June 4). *The President's speech in Cairo: A new beginning*. https://obamawhitehouse.archives.gov/issues/foreign-policy/presidents-speech-cairo-a-new-beginning

Operation Defensive Shield. (2002, March 29). Israel ministry of foreign affairs. https://mfa.gov.il/MFA/MFA-Archive/2002/Pages/Operation%20Defensive%20Shield.aspx

Operation Guardian of the Walls. (2021). IDF. https://www.idf.il/en/minisites/operation-guardian-of-the-walls/operation-guardian-of-the-walls/

Operation Protective Edge: Israel under Fire, IDF Responds. Israel Ministry of Foreign Affairs. (2014, August 26). https://mfa.gov.il/MFA/ForeignPolicy/Terrorism/ Pages/Rise-in-rocket-fire-from-Gaza-3-Jul-2014.aspx

Palestine Liberation Organization. (2020). Encyclopedia Britannica. https://www.britannica.com/topic/Palestine-Liberation-Organization

Pelham, N. (2012). Gaza's tunnel phenomenon: The unintended dynamics of Israel's siege. *Journal of Palestine Studies, 41*(4), 6–31.

Protection of Civilians. (2015, 23 29 June). United Nations Office for the Coordination of Humanitarian Affairs. https://www.un.org/unispal/document/auto-insert-208239/

Protection of Civilians Report, 7–20 January, 2020. (2020). OCHA. https://www.ochaopt.org/publications

Protocol Concerning the Redeployment in Hebron. (1997, January 17). Israel ministry of foreign affairs. https://mfa.gov.il/mfa/foreignpolicy/peace/guide/pages/ protocol%20concerning%20the%20redeployment%20in%20hebron.aspx

Rabinowitz, D., & Abu-Baker, K. (2002). *Hador hazakoof. (the stand tall generation)*. Keter.

Report of the Commission of Inquiry on Lebanon Pursuant to Human Rights Council, Resolution S-2/1. (2006). https://digitallibrary.un.org/search?

Report of the independent commission of inquiry established pursuant to Human Rights Council resolution S-21/1. (2015, June 24). Human rights council—The United Nations. https://www.ohchr.org/EN/HRBodies/HRC/CoIGazaConflict/ Pages/ReportCoIGaza.aspx

Rocket Fire from Gaza and Ceasefire Violations after Operation Cast Lead. (2016, March 16). Israel ministry of foreign affairs. https://mfa.gov.il/MFA/ForeignPolicy/Terrorism/Pages/Palestinian_ceasefire _violations_since_end_Operation_Cast_Lead.aspx

Rockets from Gaza: Harm to civilians from Palestinian armed groups' rocket attacks. (2009). Human rights watch. https://www.hrw.org/sites/default/files/reports/ ioptqassam0809webwcover.pdf

Rubenstein, D. (2014). *Hamas' tunnel network: A massacre in the making*. Jerusalem Center for Public Affairs. http://jcpa.org/hamas-tunnel-network/

Sadeh, S. (2014, July 26). Tunnels, donations, taxes and "collection of money from everything that moves": The way the Hamas economics work. *The Marker*. Retrieved December 6, 2021, from https://www.inss.org.il/he/wp-content/uploads/sites/2/systemfiles/SystemFiles/%D7%9E%D7%A0%D7%94%D7%A8%D7%95%D7%AA,%20%D7%AA%D7%A8%D7%95%D7%9E%D7%95%D7%AA,%20%D7%9E%D7%A1%D7%99%D7%9D%20%D7%95%D7%92%D7%91%D7%99%D7%99%D7%AA%20%D7%9B%D7%A1%D7%A4%D7%99%D7%9D%20-%20%D7%9B%D7%9A%20%D7%A2%D7%95%D7%91%D7%93%D7%AA%20%D7%94%D7%9B%D7%9C%D7%9B%D7%9C%D7%94%20%D7%A9%D7%9C%20%D7%94%D7%97%D7%9E%D7%90%D7%A1%20%

20%D7%A6%D7%99%D7%98%D7%95%D7%98%20
%D7%A9%D7%9C%20%D7%99%D7%95%D7%90%D7%9C%20
%D7%92%D7%95%D7%96'%D7%A0%D7%A1%D7%A
7%D7%99%20''%D7%93%D7%94%20%D7%9E%D7%-
A8%D7%A7%D7%A8".pdf
Said, E. W. (2001). Palestinians under siege. In R. Carey (Ed.), *The new intifada: Resisting Israel's apartheid* (pp. 27–44). Verso.
Saressalo, T. (2019). Israel Defense Forces' information operations, 2006–2014, part 2. *Journal of Information Warfare, 18*(1), 103–116.
Security Cabinet Declares Gaza Hostile Territory. (2007, September 19). Israel Ministry of Foreign Affairs. https://mfa.gov.il/mfa/foreignpolicy/terrorism/pages/security%20cabinet%20declares%20gaza%20hostile%20territory%2019-sep-2007.aspx
Separation Barrier. (n.d.). B'tselem: The Israeli information center for human rights in the occupied territories. https://www.btselem.org/topic/separation_barrier
Shany, Y. (2005). Faraway, so close: The legal status of Gaza after Israel's disengagement. *Yearbook of International Humanitarian Law, 8*, 369–383.
Shanzer, J. (2008). *Hamas vs. Fatah: The struggle for Palestine.* St. Martin's Press.
Sharon, A. (2014, September 25). *Failure in Gaza.* The New York Review of Books. https://www.nybooks.com/articles/2014/09/25/failure-gaza/
Shlaim, A. (2001). *The iron wall: Israel and the Arab world.* W.W. Norton & Company.
Special Update Disengagement. (2005, August 15). Israel ministry of foreign affairs. http://www.mfa.gov.il/MFA/History/Modern+History/Historic+Events/Disengagement+-+August+2005.htm
Stein, J. Y., Levin, Y., Gelkopf, M., Tangir, G., & Solomon, Z. (2018). Traumatization or habituation? A four-wave investigation of exposure to continuous traumatic stress in Israel. *International Journal of Stress Management, 25*, 137–153.
Text of Bush's Remarks at Annapolis. (2007, November 27). *New York Times.* https://www.nytimes.com/2007/11/27/world/middleeast/27cnd-prexytext.html
Tyler, A. (2011). Encounters with Zionism: A ripened vision for peacemaking? *International Journal on World Peace, 28*(1), 67–84.
UNRWA in figures. (2019, May). Communications division—UNRWA headquarters. https://www.unrwa.org/resources/about-unrwa/unrwa-figures-2019-2020

UNRWA in figures. (2020, June). https://www.unrwa.org/sites/default/files/content/resources/unrwa_in_figures_2020_eng_v2_final.pdf

Usher, G. (2006). The democratic resistance: Hamas, Fatah, and the Palestinian elections. *Journal of Palestine Studies, 35*(3), 20–36.

Vinrab, A. (2021). *The south of Israeli demographic and social profile.* Taub Center for Research of Social Policy in Israel. Retrieved December 2, 2021, from https://www.taubcenter.org.il/research/a-sociodemographic-profile-of-the-south-heb/

von Medeazza, G. (2019, January 10). *Searching for clean water in Gaza.* UNICEF. https://blogs.unicef.org/blog/searching-clean-water-gaza/

Watkins, N. J., & James, A. M. (2016). Digging into Israel: The sophisticated tunneling network of Hamas. *Journal of Strategic Security, 9*(1), 84–103.

Wilson, S. (2006, January 27). *Hamas sweeps Palestinian elections: Complicating peace efforts in Mideast.* Washington Post. http://www.washingtonpost.com/wp-dyn/content/article/2006/01/26/AR2006012600372.html

2

Methodology

Our research, which ran from 2018 through 2020, asked the following questions: (1) What are the experiences of residents of *Otef Aza*, in the context of the ongoing war between Israel and the *Hamas* regime? (2) How do residents perceive the concept of patriotism, in general, and Israeli patriotism, in specific? (3) How do they understand the ideology of Zionism? (4) How do *Otef Aza* residents perceive the Gazan "other"? (5) What do they think will happen in the region in the next five years? We used a combination of different qualitative methods: (1) a mixture of narrative and phenomenological traditions (Chaitin, 2004; Josselson, 2013), (2) photographs, and (3) discourse analysis (Chaitin et al., 2017) of Facebook posts and YouTube videos. In this chapter, we present information on our sample, the methods of data collection and analysis, and ethical issues we faced.

© The Author(s), under exclusive license to Springer Nature Switzerland AG 2022
J. Chaitin et al., *Routine Emergency*, https://doi.org/10.1007/978-3-030-95983-8_2

Our Sample

We aimed to reach a diverse population in order to hear a variety of voices (see Table 2.1). We looked for interviewees who had lived in the region since at least 2009 (the first Gaza War), in order to reach people who had experienced the three wars in the region and the myriad hostile events over the years. We interviewed 34 Jewish-Israel men and women (21 years or older—after completion of military/national service). Each one was asked to self-identify, in terms of their political orientation, placing themselves on the continuum from the extreme right to the extreme left, and concerning their religiosity.[1] Nine defined themselves as left-wing, nine as left-center or center-left, nine as center, two as center-right, four as right-wing, and one said that he did not think of himself in such terms and could not label himself. We interviewed 16 men and 18 women, of which 26 people identified as secular and 8 people identified as holding religious beliefs. Twelve of our interviewees lived in *mosahvim* and villages, 12 in *kibbutzim*, and 10 in Sderot, Netivot, or Ashkelon. Seven interviewees grew up in the area; 27 came from the outside.

When we talked to potential interviewees about what the research would entail, so that they could decide if they wanted to participate, we asked the person to place her/himself on a continuum that ranged from extreme right-wing to extreme left-wing, in terms of political views. We attempted to reach equal percentages of people with different political orientations. However, in the end, we found more people with left-wing views than with right-wing views, who agreed to be interviewed, while most of participants placed themselves in the center. Furthermore, we interviewed more secular people than religious. As in the case of political orientation, after trying numerous times and avenues to find more religious people for our study, we did not have as high of a success rate as we

---

[1] Since we looked for residents with diverse political orientations, labels of "left" and "right" need to be clarified in the Israeli context. However, it is important to remember that political orientation is complex and dynamic, making assignation of political labels difficult (Zhitomirsky-Geffet et al., 2016). In Israel, religiosity and right-wing political beliefs are often conflated, as are secularity and left-wing sentiments (Dalsheim, 2010). The latter usually supports peace processes, while the former tends to support continued Israeli control and jurisdiction over the Green Line. These groups usually appear as binary opposites: left versus right, secular versus religious.

Table 2.1 Our interviewees—demographic characteristics

Name	Sex	Age	Religious Belief	Political Orientation	Residence	Originally from Region/ Outside
Zohar[a]	Male	65	Secular	Left	Sderot	Inside
Ziona	Female	71	Secular	Center-right	Moshav	Outside
Yoram	Male	51	Secular	Center	Kibbutz	Outside
Tamar[a]	Female	50	Secular	Center	Kibbutz	Outside
Asher[a]	Male	73	Secular	Center	Moshav	Outside
Daniel	Male	68	Religious	Left	Kibbutz	Outside
Avi	Male	48	Religious	Right-center	Sderot	Outside
Ofra[a]	Female	58	Secular	Center-left	Moshav	Inside
Adele[a]	Female	65	Secular	Center-left	Kibbutz	Outside
Sarah	Female	49	Religious	Extreme right	Village	Outside
Ovadia[a]	Male	78	Secular	Center	Moshav	Outside
Orna	Female	50	Secular	Center-left	Moshav	Outside
Roni[a]	Female	75	Secular	Left	Moshav	Outside
Adva	Female	43	Secular	Left	Netivot	Outside
Shuki	Male	55	Secular	Right	Sderot	Outside
Tali	Female	50	Secular	Center-left	Kibbutz	Inside
Yael	Female	21	Secular	Left	Sderot	Inside
Channa	Female	32	Religious	Right	Village	Outside
Sa'ar[a]	Male	47	Secular	Left-center	Kibbutz	Outside
Noa	Female	36	Secular	Left-center	Sderot	Outside
Hila	Female	40	Believer	Left-center	Moshav	Outside
Yoni[a]	Male	36	Religious	Right	Village	Outside
Rami[a]	Male	61	Secular	Left	Kibbutz	Inside
Sigal	Female	65	Secular	Center	Kibbutz	Outside
Eli[a]	Male	65	Secular	Left	Kibbutz	Outside
Arieh[a]	Male	55	Secular	Center-left	Sderot	Inside
Alice[a]	Female	80	Traditional[b]	Center	Sderot	Outside
Shalom[a]	Male	46	Secular	Center	Moshav	Outside
Tamara	Female	73	Secular	Center	Sderot	Outside
Ronit[a]	Female	46	Secular	Center-left	Kibbutz	Outside
Gal[a]	Female	35	Secular	Center	Ashkelon	Outside
Micha[a]	Male	55	Traditional	Left	Moshav	Inside
Ronen	Male	60	Secular	Moderate left	Kibbutz	Outside
Haim[a]	Male	62	Secular	Refused to categorize himself politically	Kibbutz	Outside

[a]The interviewees who asked to keep their real names and details
[b]"Traditional" indicates people who believe in God, keep *kashrut*, and tend to observe Shabbat, but are not considered Orthodox

would have liked. Five of the interviewees (three women and two men) had never been married or were divorced/widowed; the others were married. All but one woman had children and/or grandchildren. The age range of the participants was 21–80 years old.

We used a snowball (Babbie, 2004) and purposive sampling approach (Creswell, 2017), based on our personal and professional connections. We began by talking to people we knew, who held a variety of political and religious orientations, who came from different communities in the region, and from different professions. Often, participants suggested further potential interviewees, and thus our pool of candidates grew over time. Since we were four researchers, we were able to reach a wide variety of interviewees.

Data Collection

The Interviews

All of our interview questions were in-depth, open-ended, and often narrative questions (Josselson, 2013). We began by asking the interviewees to share their life stories, in the context of life in *Otef Aza*. They were told that they were free to speak about whatever they choose, and that we would not interrupt them at all during this narrative. The interviewees were then asked follow-up questions, based on what they had shared. For example, when an interviewee said, "the situation really angers me," without explaining what he meant, we asked if he could define anger and/or provide an example of when he felt angered by the situation. Alternatively, when a person only talked about the security situation in her narrative, we would ask if she could also talk about her life, in general, in the region. The purposes of using this method were: (1) to document Jewish-Israeli stories in this context, and (2) to have the context of the interviewees' lives, which also helped us better understand their perceptions of patriotism, Zionism, the Israeli-Hamas conflict, the Gazan "other," and what they thought would happen in the coming years in *Otef Aza*.

After this part, which generally lasted from 45 to 60 minutes, we asked the participants questions that were open-ended and mainly phenomenological. These queries tapped understandings and experiences specifically concerning the research topics. (1) When you think about the concept, "patriotism," how do you understand it? (2) In your opinion, what are the aspects of Israeli patriotism? (3) Do you consider yourself a patriot? If so, please give us an example from your life that explains this and, if not, please explain why not. (4) How do you understand the ideology of Zionism? (5) Do you see yourself as a Zionist? (The remaining questions on this topic were similar to the questions on patriotism.) (6) What connections, if any, do you see between Zionism and patriotism? (7) How do you perceive the Gazans? (8) What do you think will happen in the area in the next five years? Finally, all interviewees were asked if there was anything else they wanted to add.

The average length of the interview was 90 minutes—the shortest was 50 minutes and the longest was three hours. All the interviews were audio-recorded, so that they could be transcribed, word for word, in order to carry out the analyses. The interviews were one on one and carried out in a private place that was comfortable for both the interviewee and the interviewer (usually the participant's home).

Photographs

In addition to the interviews, we asked each participant to take 3–4 photographs that represented either patriotism or life in the area. In the beginning, we asked for photos that reflected their understanding of patriotism; however, as the research proceeded, we learned that some people did not connect to the concept and so we gave them the option of taking photos that represented their lives. Furthermore, most preferred to share photographs that they had taken before and wished to use. Finally, a few chose photos from the internet. We accepted whatever the interviewees gave us, since we believed that whatever photos they chose were meaningful for them.

After the first two parts of the interview, we asked the interviewee to share each photo with us, one at a time, and to describe what was in the photo and why s/he had chosen it. They then sent us the photos (by WhatsApp or by e-mail). This part of the interview took between 10 and 15 minutes.

Transcription of the Interviews

After we transcribed the interviews, word for word, we sent them back to the interviewees to read over and see if there was something we had misunderstood, or that they wanted to delete or to add. In this way, we ensured that the interviewee saw and agreed that the transcript could be used for the analysis. After we received their approval, we began analyzing the interview.

Postings from Facebook and Youtube Videos

Since many people in the *Otef Aza* region use social media to share their experiences and understandings with the wider Israeli (and sometimes, international) public, we decided to collect a sampling of these as well, in order to see if we could gain additional insights into how residents see their lives in the warzone. Altogether, we collected 54 Facebook postings, videos from YouTube and op-ed articles that had been posted online in different media outlets between early 2018 and late 2020. All these materials were written/created by residents of the region or completely focused on them and their experiences.

Data Analysis

Analyses of the Interviews and Photographs

In the beginning, each author read the interviews from beginning to end, in order to get a *holistic sense* of the interviews and interviewees. We also looked specifically at the different parts of the interview, writing down our first understandings. We then met together to discuss what we had found. Together we analyzed three of the interviews. At the end of these two group sessions, we decided upon the final steps of analysis for all the interviews. Then, three of us—Julia, Elad, and Shoshana—divided up the interviews and carried out the same steps of analysis. Every few weeks, we (also with Sharon) met together to share what we had found in the analyses and to hear if another researcher had ideas to add, since we all read all of the interviews, even those that we did not personally analyze. When the COVID-19 pandemic struck, we continued meeting via Zoom meetings.

These were the steps of analysis:

1. Each researcher read the entire transcript. Then s/he wrote a *global analysis*, which was a summary of the interview. This analysis described both the topics of the interview and the style of talk. This stage provided an overview of the entire interview.
2. We then noted the *major themes*—topics that appeared to be of major significance in the interviewee's life (Chaitin, 2004) found in the interview. Each analyst gave the theme a name and wrote one to two sentences that described the theme. There were between two to four themes for each interview.
3. The main narrative of the interview was then reread in order to create an *I-poem* (Gilligan, 2015). According to Gilligan, the I-poem accomplishes the following (p. 71):

> Listening for the I, tunes the ear of the researcher to the voice of the other and specifically to the "I," the first-person voice as it speaks of acting and being in the world. Listening for the I signals a clear departure from other approaches to qualitative research. The procedure itself is straightforward: choose every I statement (pronoun and verb with or without the object) in a given passage or text and list them in order of appearance.

Since we were working in Hebrew, in which the "I' can be manifestly stated or reflected in the verb itself, we created the poem based on these two versions. We created the I-poem from the main narrative, since this was the part of the interview that was uninterrupted by the interviewer and thus reflected the "pure" voice of the interviewee.

As we interpreted the interviews, we had the idea to extend our analyses, triggered by what we found in the creations of the I-poem, by also producing what we called a *We-poem* and a *They-poem*. *We-poems* reflected the places in the entire interview where the person referred to the collective "we" (as opposed to the family)—that is, when speaking about the *kibbutz/moshav*, the community, the unit in the army, and so on. We concentrated on the collective "we," since we were focusing on not only how residents understood their personal lives, but also how they perceived the social-cultural frameworks that comprise a major part of their lives. Regarding the *They-poems*—here we focused on the "they" of the Palestinians and mainly the Palestinian Gazans—since these could be thought to be the ultimate "other"—given that the intractable conflict in our context is between Israel and the Gaza regime. We created these two poems from the entire interview, since often they were not mentioned in the main narrative.

After the creation of each poem, we read the poem from beginning to end at least twice and wrote an analysis of each of the three poems.

4. Each researcher then reread the interviews, concentrating on *patriotism*. Here we extracted quotes that focused on patriotism and listed the understandings concerning patriotism in the eyes of the interviewer and the characteristics of Israeli patriotism that s/he denoted. We also classified the type of patriotism exhibited by the interviewee. We first based our decisions on the classifications found in the literature—*blind, conventional, constructive patriotism, constitutional,* and *environmental,* and its opposite—*cosmopolitanism.* However, since we found types and nuances that did not fit the academic classification, we created new categories that extended the existing types.

5. We carried out a similar analysis concerning Zionism. We extracted quotes that expressed the interviewee's understandings of the ideology, created a summary list of the main points, and designated whether the person saw him/herself as a Zionist, and, if so, what kind of Zionist, or if s/he did think of her/himself in this way. As in the case of patriotism, we found new conceptualizations of this ideology.

6. We then summarized the content concerning *how the person envisioned the next five years* in the region—in terms of the conflict.
7. *Analyses of the photographs* was based on Wang and Burris' (1997) photovoice methodology. We analyzed what the interviewee told us about her/his photograph (who/what is in the photo, why did the person choose/take the photo, what does it mean for them?) and then we looked at each photograph separately and noted what we saw. For example, did the photo include mainly people (e.g., the person, her children, co-workers, soldiers, etc.), animals (e.g., birds of the region, sheep, etc.), objects (e.g., the Israeli flag, a *Kassam* rocket, Iron Dome, etc.), or landscape (e.g., a photo of the community, a nature reserve, a burning field, etc.)? Did the photo include the interviewee? Was the photo of an inside or an outside space? Did the photos appear to be similar or different from one another? We also noted whether the photos appeared to reflect the themes discerned in the interview, expressed something different, or contradicted what the person had already shared.
8. In addition to our analyses, Sharon entered the interviews into Atlas.ti 8.4 version. The software was used both for manual coding and for automatic coding. She extracted quotations from each interview, which reflected the themes we had previously found, helping us carry out further analyses of themes and comparisons between the interviews. This aided us in better defining the themes that emerged from the texts, and gain an overview of all the interviews, seeing which ones were similar/different from one another and in which ways.
9. Based on this information, we reached understandings that could explain the connections between the themes, categories of patriotism and Zionism, and the interviewees' perceptions of the Palestinian Gazans and the future.

Analyses of the Posts, Videos, and Op-eds

We analyzed these texts using one method of discourse analysis (DA), in the following way. We constructed five questions for DA, based on recommendations made by Alvesson and Skoldberg (2000) that uncovers how people construct the social world. As researchers interpret different kinds of texts, they focus on understanding how the writer/creator expresses different attitudes, how utterances are constructed, and the functions they fulfil. The five questions were: (1) What is actually written? (2) What are the structures and metaphors in the texts being interpreted? (3) What nuances, vagueness, and contradictions are in the texts? (4) What values, beliefs, and meanings appear to lie behind the actual text? (5) What is the overall message of the text?

Taken together, these analytical steps helped us gain deep understandings of how our interviewees from *Otef Aza* understand their lives, how they perceive patriotism, Zionism, and the Gazans, and what they think will happen in the future. Furthermore, they ensured triangulation of analysis methods, hence resulting in trustworthiness of our results.

Ethical Issues

In our research, we faced different ethical considerations.

To begin with, the research topic was a very sensitive one, since the *Otef Aza* region has been embroiled in a violent political conflict for 20 years. This means that all our interviewees have had direct experiences of *Kassam* rocket/mortar shell attacks, burning fields, explosive balloons and kites and wars. When a war begins, the entire area turns into a huge military base. The roads become clogged with tanks, army vehicles and soldiers; overhead there is the constant drone of fighter planes and helicopters, as well as uncountable booms from our/their rockets. Sirens and *tzeve adom*—"red alerts"—continually are sounded. Schools are closed, only people who work in jobs classified as "essential" (e.g., medical staff and paramedics, fire and police departments, psychological services) go to work; others remain home. People are often told to stay indoors, in or near their safe rooms or to go to public bomb shelters. Furthermore, in times of intense conflict, thousands of people, who have where to go (family in other parts of the country, for example) leave the region, becoming internal refugees in the country, without knowing when they will be able to return home. In other words, regular life ends, and the war routine begins for an unknown and frightening period of time.

The implications of this for our research were that since our interviewees were asked to talk about their life in the region, this, of course, could easily bring up traumatic memories, causing them distress. Since the most basic tenet of ethics in research is do no harm (Vanclay et al., 2013), we had to do our best to ensure that our interviewees would not be negatively impacted by agreeing to participate in our study. This we did by promising them that they were free to answer only what they chose to answer, however they chose to do so, and that they could stop the interview/end their participation in the study at any time, until we submitted the draft of the manuscript to a publisher. None of our interviewees refused to answer any of our questions and none rescinded their participation in the research.

All participants signed an informed consent form that detailed the purpose of the research, the questions to be asked, and the potential risks involved (e.g., bringing up traumatic memories). They did this before we commenced with the interview. A copy of the signed consent form was left with the interviewee and the interviewer took one as well for our records. This ensured that the interviewees understood what the research was exploring and that they chose to participate of their own free will. The interviewees were also given the choice to remain anonymous—and thus we promised to do our best to conceal any details that could expose who they were, working to ensure (to the best of our ability) their privacy and confidentiality. However, the interviewees also had the opportunity to choose to use their own names, for those participants who wanted the readers/public to know who they were (Vanclay et al., 2013).

After we had written all of the chapters that cited texts from the interviewees, we returned to the interviewees for a final check to see if they still agreed to be quoted in the book, have their names used, and/or use their photographs. We received permission from everyone. Two people changed their minds about using their real names, so we changed those, doing our best to alter details in the text that might suggest who they were. All the interviewees gave their final approval to be included in the book.

In terms of the social media materials, we only cited posts and video clips that appeared and had been shared in the public sphere.

Another important ethical aspect in our study was respect of our participants (Vanclay et al., 2013), especially since we did not always agree with the political and/or social values that the person expressed. Therefore, throughout the entire process, we endeavored to keep open minds, refrain from being judgmental, and bracketing our subjective and pre-research and current perspectives (Josselson, 2004). This was done so that we would not "find" what we wanted/expected to find, thus disrespecting the interviewee, as well as calling the authenticity of the entire project into question. In this way, we were able to employ both hermeneutics of faith and hermeneutics of suspicion during the analyses—in order to reach underlying meanings that were not always discerned on the manifest level (Josselson, 2004).

This leads us to our final point—reflexivity (Josselson, 2004). As noted in the Preface, we brought to this research different life experiences and political views connected to the Israel-Hamas conflict. When we undertook this study, we had to remain aware of our subjective views, in order to avoid placing them on our interviewees. We endeavored to remain true to their words and understandings, to give them voice, remain empathetic (even when we disagreed), and not to exploit our positions as researchers vis-à-vis our participants (Shlasky & Alpert, 2007). While this was not always easy—especially given that we are all Jewish-Israelis and far from neutral concerning the issues we studied—we used one another as checks and balances. We also did our best to remain aware of our own emotions and perceptions so that we would neither judge the interviewee nor reach an understanding that could not be backed up by the text.

We now turn to Part II, which reviews the academic literature on the psycho-social impacts of living in a warzone and the four major themes we discerned in analyses of the materials.

References

Alvesson, M., & Skoldberg, K. (2000). *Reflexive methodology: New vistas for qualitative research*. Sage Publications.

Babbie, E. (2004). *The practice of social research* (9th ed.). Wadsworth.

Chaitin, J. (2004). My story, my life, my identity. *International Journal of Qualitative Methodologies, 3*(4).

Chaitin, J., Steinberg, S., & Steinberg, S. (2017). Polarized words: Discourse on the boycott of Israel, social justice and conflict resolution. *International Journal of Conflict Management, 28*(3), 270–294.

Creswell, J. W. (2017). *Qualitative inquiry and research design: Choosing among five approaches*. Sage Publications.

Dalsheim, J. (2010). On demonized Muslims and vilified Jews: Between theory and politics. *Comparative Studies in Society and History, 52*(3), 581–603.

Gilligan, C. (2015). Introduction. The listening guide method of psychological inquiry. *Qualitative. Psychology, 2*(1), 69–77.

Josselson, R. (2004). The hermeneutics of faith and the hermeneutics of suspicion. *Narrative Inquiry, 14*(1), 1–28.

Josselson, R. (2013). *Interviewing for qualitative inquiry: A relational approach*. The Guilford Press.

Shlasky, S., & Alpert, B. (2007). *Ways of writing qualitative research. From deconstructing reality to its construction as a text*. Machon Mofet. (in Hebrew).

Vanclay, F., Baines, J. T., & Taylor, C. N. (2013). Principles for ethical research involving humans: Ethical professional practice in impact assessment part I. *Impact Assessment and Project Appraisal, 31*(4), 243–253. https://doi.org/1 0.1080/14615517.2013.850307

Wang, C., & Burris, M.A. (1997). Photovoice: Concept, methodology, and use for participatory needs assessment. *Health Education & Behavior, 24*(3), 369–387. https://doi.org/10.1177/109019819702400309

Zhitomirsky-Geffet, M., David, E., Kippel, M., & Uzan, H. (2016). Utilizing overtly political texts for fully automatic evaluation of political leaning of online news websites. *Online Information Review, 40*(3), 362–379.

Part II

Psycho-social Aspects of Living with the War and the Meaning of This Life for *Otef Aza* Residents

Part II includes an overview of the main psycho-social aspects of life in the *Otef Aza*-Gaza Strip warzone that appear in the academic literature, as well as the four major themes we discerned from our analyses of the participants' interviews and photographs, and the social media materials produced by area residents that we collected.

Chapter 3—the first chapter in this Part—reviews the existing psycho-social research on *Otef Aza* residents—that mainly centers on trauma, coping, and resilience. It also includes a brief overview of the psycho-social literature tied to intractable conflicts, in general, and to the Israeli-Palestinian conflict, in specific, based mainly on the work of Daniel Bar-Tal concerning the Ethos of Conflict.

The first theme we found, presented in Chap. 4, focuses on the transitions made by residents between routine and emergency and back to routine, and how the borders between war and quiet have blurred over time. Furthermore, it presents and analyzes the mechanisms that residents have devised for coping with the dangerous situations. The interviewees also noted serious concerns about their children and grandchildren, at times expressing guilt about putting them at risk of being injured or killed. The second theme, presented in Chap. 5, includes the strong sense of community and belonging, and mutual care and volunteerism that were often discussed by the interviewees. We learned that care for others appears to play a major role in their lives, from their perspective. The third theme, presented in Chap. 6, reflects the feeling of many residents that people from outside the *Otef Aza* region do not/cannot understand what life is like for people in this warzone. The interviewees and the social media materials stressed that residents often feel abandoned by their government, other Jewish-Israelis, and mainstream media. These experiences, then, often leave residents feeling "invisible." The last chapter in this Part, Chap. 7, presents the theme of the paradoxes and internal conflicts of living in *Otef Aza*, which also tied the previous themes together. The participants present in their photographs and narratives the two major paradoxes: (1) feeling stressed/traumatized, while also averring that the war does not affect them and (2) their ongoing internal conflict of wanting to leave, while feeling that there is no other place they want to be. Finally, the chapter presents the quandary of peace activists from the region, who are, simultaneously, victims of the war and advocates for the people in Gaza—"the enemy"—which, at times, complicates their relations with other *Otef Aza* residents and with Jewish-Israelis from other parts of the country.

These five chapters, therefore, serve as the main foundation for understanding the psycho-social meaning of life for the *Otef Aza* residents, which later will be seen to intertwine with their perspectives on patriotism, Zionism, and the Gazan other, explored in Part III.

3

Psycho-social Aspects of Living with the War

In 2019, Yigal Tzachor, whose background is in Israeli political science and history, published a book in Hebrew, titled *Life in the Shadow of the Conflict*, based on his collection of family interviews, during 2017–2018. Tzachor spoke to people from 40 multi-generational families, who live in *kibbutzim* and *moshavim* in *Otef Aza*, in order to document their experiences in these different kinds of communities, over the generations/years, including their experiences tied to life in the warzone.

In connection to the focus of our book, one of Tzachor's major findings was that his interviewees had a deep desire "to illustrate to what extent life in the *Otef* is abnormal." They noted that "every simple act is accompanied by the fear that, all of a sudden, there will be an alert" (p. 273). In addition, Tzachor learned that family members felt that they had been abandoned by "Israeli governments and Israeli citizens [who] accept … this terrible situation" (p. 275). Residents felt that people in the center of the country do not know, or, perhaps worse, are apathetic to what is happening in *Otef Aza*, *even* during rocket attacks. Tzachor also notes that when residents escaped and became temporary refugees in other parts of Israel, because of the escalation in attacks, they were alarmed to learn that people in the center of the country were continuing

© The Author(s), under exclusive license to Springer Nature Switzerland AG 2022
J. Chaitin et al., *Routine Emergency*, https://doi.org/10.1007/978-3-030-95983-8_3

on with their normal lives, not understanding that life in the *Otef* was anything but normal. Residents told Tzachor that they were very frustrated by the apathy expressed by most Israeli citizens to their plight.

Moreover, Tzachor found that parents of small children were highly fearful about the threat and the traumatic experiences they and their children were feeling, due to the ongoing rocket attacks. They discussed the difficulty in being expected to return quickly to routine, after the rocket attacks temporarily subsided. Finally, he noted that while many of the young people and children were receiving psychological therapies in the area's resilience centers, interviewees reported that they did not believe that these treatments were helping enough.

Tzachor's study, which proceeded ours by about one year, is a good place to start this chapter. While our foci were on different aspects, different frames of reference, and employed different methodologies, Tzachor began the important process of bringing *Otef Aza* voices into the Israeli public sphere. In our Summary, Discussion, and Conclusions chapter, we will return to Tzachor's findings, seeing how they compare to what we found, including the importance of bringing *Otef Aza* voices out of the *Otef* and into the world.

Since the residents of *Otef Aza* have known war for 21 years, it is not surprising that the trauma and stress they experience was present in all the interviews (albeit some to a greater degree and some to a lesser degree). While this book's focus is *not* the psychological trauma, coping mechanisms, resilience, and/or post-traumatic growth exhibited by people in connection to life in this warzone, it would be ludicrous—and even callous—to ignore the negative psychological effects that the rockets, tunnels, incendiary and explosive balloons, and the fires have had on the region's residents. Therefore, we begin with an overview of research that has explored these issues among adults from the region.[1]

After this section, we look at three other psycho-social conceptualizations that aided us in our analyses of the interviews, photographs, and social media materials: the concept of intractable conflict, Bar-Tal's

---

[1] Here we focus on the traumas and coping patterns connected to the Israel-Hamas conflict and do not present an overview of these issues in relation to other aspects of the Israeli-Palestinian/Arab conflict.

conceptualization and categorization of societal beliefs for coping with intractable conflict—the Ethos of Conflict (EOC) and cognitive dissonance.

Trauma and Life in the *Otef*

At the end of 2019, a joint study of the Eshkol Resilience Center and Ben-Gurion University (Boker, November 17, 2019) was undertaken. The research sampled 1000 residents of the Eshkol Regional Council, finding that 52% of the respondents felt that their families were in danger, with 37% feeling that they could not protect them. A third of the sample experienced outbursts of rage and nearly the same percentage suffered eating disorders. Forty-eight percent reported psychological fatigue and felt that they did not have the ability to cope with life's challenges. However, despite these figures, 81% of the interviewees stated that they wanted to continue to live in the region, because of the quality of life and community resilience and support the area offers. These results demonstrate that even though life in this warzone is so difficult for many residents, the majority believe that life is good. Therefore, they do not want/ choose to live somewhere else—two simultaneously opposite stances/ feelings. In the following chapters, we will relate to these complex understandings; however, we begin with the literature.

Psychological Effects of Living in an Ongoing Warzone

For over a decade, research has explored the effects of the ongoing war and security tensions on Israeli citizens who live close to the Gaza Strip. Since these residents have been exposed to a prolonged armed conflict, it makes most sense to relate to them as experiencing *continuous* or *ongoing trauma* (CT or OTS) although many studies employ terminology of post trauma (PTSD—post-traumatic stress disorder/PTSS—post-traumatic stress symptoms), which can occur when people have been exposed to an objective, external, life-threatening event.

Continuous/ongoing trauma differs from one-time occurrences in terms of its cumulative effects and the way it affects perceptions of risk or feelings of insecurity, as well as the ways that people cope with the situation (Regev & Nuttman-Shwartz 2016). Research has found that continuous exposure can produce opposite reactions: it may lead to a greater vulnerability, with severe traumatization (Somer & Ataria, 2015), or it can result in accommodation and habituation to stress, and thus promote resilience (Stein et al., 2018). Furthermore, PTSD may not be relevant for the trauma faced by *Otef Aza* residents, since avoidance—one PTSD symptom—is impossible as long as they continue to live in the area, and arousal—another hallmark of PTSD—may be adaptive in this context, since this keeps people tuned to incoming dangers (Diamond et al., 2013). Since residents do not have respite from the conflict and know that the violence can explode at any moment, they are governed by the physiological reactions of fright or flight, are hypervigilant, and/or use avoidance to control feelings of dread, fear, and sadness (Somer & Bleich, 2005).

Furthermore, since the region's entire population is exposed to the same traumatic events and stressors, social support, usually considered crucial for good coping with trauma/stress, may actually *deepen* the distress, rather than reduce it. This is because social networks, in such a case, can create an environment of fear and worry, and reinforce heightened fear (Hobfoll & London, 1986; Nuttman-Shwartz & Dekel, 2009). For example, in their study of *Otef Aza* residents, Bayer-Topilsky et al. (2013) learned that since all their respondents had directly or indirectly experienced terror events, this evoked a change in the relationships between individuals and their environment and generated a continuous uncertainty in daily life.

Given that the academic literature has explored both PTSD and continuous trauma, we present an overview of these studies here.

There are three factors important to the onset of PTSD (Friedman et al., 2007; Vogt et al., 2007): (a) pre-traumatic factors—the predisposing vulnerability that exists before the traumatic exposure, such as prior psychiatric problems, personality traits, biological vulnerability, and demographic variables (Vogt et al., 2007); (b) peri-traumatic factors: closeness to the traumatic event, the enormity of the event, level of physical injury, and subjective appraisal of what occurred (e.g., Johnson et al., 2009), and the appearance of acute stress disorder (ASD) symptoms—three days to one month after exposure to a traumatic event (American Psychiatric Association, 2013). Finally, there are (c) post-traumatic factors, which characterize immediate/long-term reactions and the coping abilities of the victims and others in the victim's social group (e.g., Ballenger et al., 2000). These stages are clearly relevant for *Otef Aza* residents.

Psycho-social quantitative and qualitative research on people/communities in the region concerning trauma and coping have had different foci. Studies have explored: (a) personal factors that increase risk of CT/PTSD and protective factors that decrease the potential, during escalations and between wars. These include variables such as age, specific populations (e.g., mothers of small children, access to safe rooms, etc.), (b) kind of community (development towns versus rural communities), and (c) geographical location (comparisons of communities from close to the border to farther away).

Personal Factors That Increase/Decrease Potential of Experiencing CT or PTSD

Greene et al. (2018) reviewed 28 quantitative articles on psychopathology in the *Otef Aza* adult population, who were exposed to continuous trauma, covering the years 2005–2014. The review examined quantitative evidence on clinical reactions to CT, in order to investigate risk and protective factors for such trauma. The meta-analysis found that residents reported moderate levels of probable PTSD, depression, and other psycho-pathological reactions during low-intensity periods, which rose sharply during escalations in the conflict. In the studies that explored residents' responses during "routine" times (between the wars), PTSD rates ranged from 6% to 35%. These wide differences appeared to stem from risk factors that included current exposure, overall exposure level, and low socio-economic status. The researchers further found that depression and distress rates doubled during escalations, in comparison to "routine" life, thus, concluding that psychopathology was much higher during intense escalations than between the wars. The analysis further showed that personal/objective exposure to rocket attacks positively related to probable PTSD, depression, anxiety, stress symptoms, and lower levels of functioning.

In a survey study, Shahrabani et al. (2019) examined differences in responses to the 2012 war between three groups of 540 Jewish-Israeli students living in *Otef Aza*. There were those who left the area, residents who wanted to leave, but were unable to do so for different reasons, and residents who chose to remain. The researchers explored differences in the levels of perceived risk, sense of anxiety and a feeling of national identity, in connection to residents' decisions to remain or leave. The results showed that while the average fear and anxiety levels were relatively high in all groups, the highest levels were found among the respondents who wanted to leave, but could not do so, followed by the group who left. Those who wanted to leave, but could not, expressed the highest perception of risk of being harmed, among the groups. The majority of those who left the area during the escalation lacked easy access to a shelter, which could explain their high levels of fear and anxiety and their decision to leave. However, the majority of those who wanted to leave, but could not, *did* have easy access to a secure room. Therefore, the researchers could not conclude that this group's negative emotions and risk perceptions related to lack of access to easily available shelter. Other interesting findings were that the group that left expressed the lowest level of perceived risk and that participants with higher national identity showed higher levels of fear, anxiety, and perceived risk from terrorism.

In sum, the results of this study highlight the complex interactions between objectively having a safe room, perception of risk, anxiety, sense of national identity, and decision-making concerning whether to remain or leave *Otef Aza* during escalations in violence.

Litvak Hirsch et al. (2015) undertook a study, which also explored the choice of remaining or leaving the area during extremely tense times. The researchers found, in their study on Sderot mothers' attachment to their homes, that "home" could be a resource for coping with the wars.

According to the women, deciding to remain, as opposed to leaving the area, helped them maintain routine, feel a sense of responsibility and belonging to their families and community, and gave their lives a sense of meaning—of being able to appreciate the good things they had in life. These factors, thus, reduced feelings of stress and trauma.

Studies that explored other protective factors against stress and trauma have focused on different issues. For example, Braun-Lewensohn and Rubin (2014) found that *a sense of coherence*—a sense that life is manageable, understandable, and meaningful—can help decrease distress. Furthermore, in two studies on college students living near the Gaza Strip, hope, optimism, and self-esteem, were all negatively related to PTSD levels (Besser & Zeigler-Hill, 2014), as was a sense of belonging (Nuttman-Shwartz & Dekel, 2009). Other protective factors found to negatively relate to PTSD, depression, anxiety, and stress include acceptance and positive reframing (Dickstein et al., 2012) and life satisfaction (Besser & Neria, 2012).

On the other side, factors that tended to associate with negative emotional states and PTSD include a tendency to use alcohol and/or medication and the seeking of psychological help (Nuttman-Shwartz & Dekel, 2009). In their study of 250 non-clinical *Otef Aza* residents during Protective Edge (2014), Besser et al. (2015) found that the severity of PTSD symptoms was positively associated with severity of exposure to trauma. However, this was moderated by individual differences in intrapersonal resilience: residents who expressed low levels of intrapersonal resilience reported more PTSD symptoms than those with high levels of intrapersonal resilience in the regions in which individuals were exposed to low and high levels of rocket fire. Another factor, found to be connected to post-traumatic symptomology, is age. Dekel and Nuttman-Shwartz (2009) and Avidor et al. (2017) found, in their studies of residents over the age of 50, that these residents exhibited high levels of traumatic symptoms.

In sum, research has shown that numerous intrapersonal and personal variables influence levels and symptoms of trauma, experienced by residents of the *Otef Aza* region, thus, highlighting the complexity of factors that can lead to or mitigate trauma.

Trauma and Coping in Different Kinds of *Otef Aza* Communities

Two studies, which compared *kibbutzim* and *moshavim* to Sderot—a development town, with a history of being socially and economically in the periphery—found that the rural communities fared better than the town dwellers (Gelkopf et al., 2012; Stein et al., 2013). In the Gelkopf and colleagues' study, only 1 out of 140 participants met PTSD criteria, while over 25% of the Sderot participants reported symptom rates exceeding the threshold for probable PTSD. Furthermore, over 75% of the population reported re-experiencing and arousal symptoms. Stein et al. (2013) found that while 70% of Sderot and rural communities had suffered rocket attacks, the odds of Sderot residents having PTSD were eight times higher than that of people from the *kibbutzim* and *moshavim*. The researchers concluded that the differences might connect to the level and types of community solidarity, strength, and community resources at their disposal. That is, the rural communities had many more of these than did Sderot had.

Stein et al. (2018) undertook a four-year longitudinal study (2010–2014) that assessed Israeli populations exposed to high and medium intensities of rocket fire in urban and rural communities, at four assessment points: prior to, close to, during, and after a major escalation of violence. The researchers asked if continuous exposure promotes habituation and greater resilience or more traumatization, while focusing on the contribution of environmental, intrapersonal, and interpersonal resources to resilience. Results indicated that greater exposure prior to escalation was associated with more resilience during high-intensity shelling, thus suggesting a habituation effect to continuous traumatic stress. However, various indicators of personal exposure revealed that more exposure was predictive of more symptomatology. Moreover, contrary to previous studies (Stein et al., 2013), the urban population exhibited more resilience than the rural population, as indicated by less post-traumatic symptoms.

Trauma Responses, Coping, and Geographical Location

Eshel and Kimhi's (2016) study compared 260 northern residents (out of rocket range from the Gaza Strip) to 250 southern residents (within rocket range), four months after the end of the 2014 war. The researchers explored individual, community and national resilience, sense of danger, recovery from adversity, distress symptoms, wellbeing, and sense of coherence. They found that successful adaptation, positive functioning, or community competence were not enough to guarantee its resilience, without consideration of its level of vulnerability. The researchers concluded that these results indicate that studying CR, in terms of strength, without concurrently considering its vulnerability components, may result in a loss of information, crucial for understanding the multidimensional nature of communities' responses to adversities and traumas.

In a longitudinal study, Gil et al. (2016) examined the association between *DSM–5* PTSS symptoms and PTSD risk factors. The researchers assessed 160 Israelis, from different geographical locations, who had all been impacted by rocket attacks, at two points in time during Protective Edge: one week after the war began, when they examined ASD symptoms, and one month later, when they investigated PTSS. The researchers found that ASD symptomatology was the hallmark risk factor for development of PTSS. However, they were surprised to learn that proximity to the Gaza Strip was *not* associated with PTSS. Gil and colleagues' explanation for this finding was that since large areas of Israel had been under frequent rocket attack during this war, this created uncertainty and a shared threat, regardless of variations in distance. Thus, even though *Otef Aza* residents had been exposed to terrorist/war threats to a greater degree than most Israelis had, in the 2014 war, which was longer than the previous two wars, many Israelis from different areas reacted similarly. This supported the assumption that a prolonged terrorist threat is a unique type of trauma.

Another interesting finding was that social support was high at both assessment points: it exhibited neither significant change over time, nor association with PTSS. The authors hypothesized that the widespread uncertainty and shared threat neutralized social support as a coping resource.

Resilience in the *Otef*

Even though studies on the psychological health of *Otef Aza* residents paint a bleak picture, the news is not all bad. Studies conducted in communities near the Gaza border have shown that over the years, alongside more reports of residents suffering anxiety and post-traumatic stress reactions, there is also evidence of personal and community growth and resilience (Dekel & Nuttman-Shwartz, 2009).

According to the Resilience Research Center (n.d.), in the context of exposure to significant hardship, resilience (paragraphs 2–3)

> is both the capacity of individuals to navigate their way to the psychological, social, cultural, and physical resources that sustain their well-being, and their capacity individually and collectively to negotiate for these resources to be provided in culturally meaningful ways.

This definition shifts our understanding of resilience from an individual concept … to a more relational understanding of well-being embedded in a social-ecological framework. Understood this way, resilience requires individuals have the capacity to find resources that bolster well-being, while also emphasizing that it's up to families, communities and governments to provide these resources in ways individuals value.

In their ten-year mixed-methods study, Padan and Elran (2019) explored the differences in societal resilience between six *Otef Aza* communities—*kibbutzim, moshavim*, and Sderot—in order to discern whether and how each community's character influenced its level of societal resilience. Their major findings showed that (1) the communities demonstrated high resilience in the face of the security challenges, with the highest level of societal-community resilience found in the *kibbutzim*. However, individual *kibbutz* residents tended to report anxiety, albeit at varying levels, especially during the wars, and less so after and between rounds. (2) The national and local leaderships were found to be crucial for enhancing societal resilience. Residents saw local leaders as creating and strengthening their communities, as they made decisions quickly and led their communities toward recovery and growth following the wars. Local leaders, who were in ongoing contact with national decision-makers, succeeded in receiving support for physical infrastructures, for increasing community preparedness for new rounds of violence, and for physical/psychological recovery. Furthermore, the leaders noted that since they understood that the ongoing rounds of political violence had a serious psychological impact on residents, they found it important to keep their communities up to date concerning the objective level of threat, in order to help lower stress. (3) The continuous attacks from 2006 to 2016 created a growing sense of attrition among the population, leading some residents to question their decision to continue to live in *Otef Aza*. Thus, despite the generally high level of resilience, individuals paid an emotional price for continuing to live in the war-torn environment.

On the other hand, the study also demonstrated that the communities' success in meeting the repeated security threats contributed to their sense of empowerment, and residents recognized their capacity to endure. This positive phenomenon raised the communities' societal resilience. (4) Social capital was found to be the most important contributor to the attainment and sustainment of community resilience—a resource found in all three kinds of communities. The *kibbutzim* exhibited high socio-economic capital, mostly due to their tightly woven network of social horizontal and vertical bonds (with national leadership). These traits, together with their ideology of mutual responsibility, and organizational collective/volunteer structure, helped the *kibbutzim* cope successfully. (5) Sderot, which had undergone revitalization over the years, also demonstrated resilience during and after Protective Edge.

Another research focus, which has compared older residents and younger ones, have yielded mixed results. For example, some researchers found resilience among older residents (e.g., Chaitin et al., 2013; Stein et al., 2018), while others found that younger residents coped better with the tenuous security situation and wars than older residents (Nuttman-Shwartz et al., 2015).

In their research on the aftereffects of the 2014 war, Nuttman-Shwartz and Regev (2018) found four main themes in their focus groups, attended by older residents: (a) *moral issues* centered on decisions to leave their homes during the war or to remain; (b) *emotional issues*, such as fear of death and pain, loneliness and alienation among residents who had left the region during the war, and anger and frustration toward younger people/families who had left; (c) *intergenerational issues*—the older generation felt that they valued commitment to the community, and collectivism versus individualism more so than the younger generation; and (d) *resilience* in the face of the ongoing hostilities, including thoughts about the future.

The researchers found a range of resilience levels. On one pole were people who stated that they could fend for themselves; on the other, people expressed a lack of control and dependence upon others (e.g., family members, the army). However, interestingly, the individuals on the dependent pole expressed major disappointment with the army. For example, when residents from Nahal Oz returned home after the army announced that it was safe to do so, a small child was killed from a mortar bomb. This shook confidence in government institutions, which, in turn, reduced residents' sense of resilience. Nuttman-Shwartz and Regev (2018) concluded that efforts to organize at the individual, interpersonal and family levels strengthened the participants and their families and enabled them to cope successfully with the security threats. However, at the community and system-wide levels, the participants' sense of resilience was undermined.

Post-traumatic Growth (PTG) Among *Otef Aza* Residents

Studies on the *Otef Aza* population have also documented instances of PTG—a "positive psychological change experienced as a result of the struggle with highly challenging life circumstances that represent significant challenges to the adaptive resources of the individual" (Tedeschi & Calhoun, 2004, p. 1). Calhoun and Tedeschi's (2006) model of PTG includes five domains: (a) a greater appreciation of life and a changed sense of priorities, (b) a more intimate relationship with others, (c) a sense of increased personal strength, (d) recognition of new possibilities, and (e) spiritual and existential development.

In Litvak-Hirsch and Lazar's (2012) study that explored coping and PTG among 52 mothers from *Otef Aza*—all of whom had been exposed to rocket attacks and had at least one child under the age of 18 living at home—the researchers found that the mothers used different coping strategies. These were: the use of optimism and humor, belief in Zionist ideology, denial of threat, and maintaining routine. In-depth interviews conducted with 16 of these mothers showed that they expressed PTG, felt less vulnerable, more able to take responsibility, and more prepared to manage future adversarial situations. Furthermore, the mothers reported a change in their relationships with others: some reported more positive relationships with family members and experienced a tighter bonding with their community. Others also reported feeling more empathy toward the Palestinian civilians, especially women and children in Gaza. This finding, of developing a sense of empathy toward "the enemy," surprised the researchers, since it contradicted previous research on Israeli victims' perceptions of the Arab "enemy" (Hobfoll et al., 2006).

In sum, the research on the psychological effects of the ongoing war between Israel and Hamas, played out in the *Otef Aza* region, shows that many factors are involved in the exacerbation and decrease of traumatic symptoms. The intrapersonal, interpersonal and community expressions of stress, trauma, coping, resilience, and post-traumatic growth demonstrate how complex these factors and levels are. One thing is clear, however: there is no resident who has not been impacted by the war and terror, and it is a basic component of life in the *Otef*.

Intractable Conflict and Societal Beliefs for Dealing with Such Conflict

According to Bar-Tal (2013), intractable conflicts are protracted and violent. They are perceived as having a zero-sum nature and as being unsolvable. Such conflicts are total and central, and, as such, the sides in the conflict have an interest that they will continue. In terms of their psycho-social nature, they are demanding, stressful, painful, exhausting, and costly both in human and in material terms. Furthermore, intractable conflicts have an imprinting effect on the individual and on collective life. Since they continue to preoccupy people affected by the conflict, they lead to the development of beliefs, attitudes, emotions, values, motivations, norms, and practices that are functional in coping with the challenges posed by the conflict (Bar-Tal et al., 2014).

According to Bar-Tal (2017) and Kriesberg (1998), intractable interethnic conflicts have seven characteristics. They are: (1) total, in terms of essential goals, needs and/or values, and regarded as indispensable for the society's existence; (2) perceived as irresolvable; (3) violent; (4) perceived of as being zero-sum interactions; (5) central in the lives of the individuals and their society; (6) demanding of extensive monetary and psychological investment; and (7) protracted—lasting for at least a generation. Furthermore, as Coleman (2006) states, intractable conflicts tend to be connected to a history of social-political injustice, periods of rapid change, dialogic poles, opposing ideologies, destructive relations between the conflict sides, polarized identities, intense negative emotionality, protracted trauma, and normalization of hostilities (pp. 535–536). As a result, these long-term complexities and violence make it almost impossible for people and their leaders to imagine that a solution is possible.

Bar-Tal et al. (2014) drew our attention to another reason why intractable conflicts are so difficult to solve:

> A culture of conflict develops in the societies involved that transforms both collective and individual life into part of the conflict. This culture normalizes and sustains the conflict and inhibits a peaceful resolution … on one of the mechanisms of the culture of conflict—routinization—which transforms an intractable conflict into part of everyday experience.

In order to cope with intractable conflicts, Bar-Tal conceptualized that people, and their societies, embroiled in intractable conflicts, adopt beliefs—an Ethos of Conflict (EOC)—that helps them live with their ongoing wars. He concentrated on the Jewish-Israeli case and identified societal beliefs that Jewish-Israelis have adopted to "cope" with the intractable Israeli-Arab/Palestinian conflict. We now turn to an overview of these beliefs.

Bar-Tal's Ethos of Conflict and Societal Beliefs

Since 1998, Bar-Tal, alone and with colleagues, has discussed and researched societal beliefs that he perceives as mechanisms for "helping" Jewish-Israelis cope with the intractable Israel-Arab/Palestinian conflict (e.g., Bar-Tal, 1998, 2000, 2007, 2013; Bar-Tal et al., 2012; Rosler et al., 2020). These are beliefs held by individuals that are bolstered by social and cultural mechanisms that reinforce these beliefs on the personal and collective level.

> Societies engulfed by intractable conflict develop a particular type of worldview, [...] defined as the ethos of conflict (EOC). EOC is defined as a configuration of central, shared societal beliefs that provide a particular dominant orientation to a society and give meaning to societal life under conditions of intractable conflict. (Bar-Tal et al., 2012, pp. 40–41)

Furthermore, Bar-Tal et al. (2012, p. 42) averred that EOC can be viewed as a type of ideology, since it

> represents a coherent and systematic knowledge base that provides a major rationale for explaining the present state of affairs, directs the decisions of the society's leaders, and serves as a guide to the coordinated behavior of society members, development of the societal system, and its functioning [...] it serves as a prism through which society members process new information and judge particular situations that appear periodically throughout the long years of intractable conflict. It is a conservative ideology because its orientation strives to preserve the existing order of continuing the conflict [...] [However], it is important to emphasize that EOC may change with time, as ideologies are also altered as a result of long-term changes in the societal conditions.

As Bar-Tal noted (2007), on the one hand, societal beliefs help people cope with the conflict and, thus, perhaps, help reduce trauma and despair.

On the other hand, however, since they involve serious psychological investment, they also contribute to the conflict's prolongation.

The eight beliefs, which comprise the EOC, are as follows: (1) the justness of one's goals, (2) importance of security, (3) delegitimization of the enemy, (4) positive self-image, (5) an identity rooted in victimization, (6) patriotism, (7) unity, and (8) the belief that only one's side wishes for peace. Furthermore, Bar-Tal and his colleagues propose that in societies involved in intractable conflict, these beliefs are interrelated and "combine to form a single holistic and coherent ideological worldview that distinguishes these societies from others" (2012, p. 43).

In *justness of goals*—the society believes not only that its goals are diametrically opposed to the goals of the enemy group, but that they are the social-historical-politically correct goals, and necessary for survival. Therefore, individuals become committed to their attainment. In the Israeli-Palestinian case, the goal is to keep Israel a Jewish state in order to ensure the survival of the Jewish people. This goal is based on the historical narrative that the Holy Land was promised to the Jews, and that Jews have been the victims of millennia of persecution, in the diaspora. Therefore, now, the Jewish people are rejuvenating their ancient homeland. Its continued existence is perceived as being threatened by the Palestinian "others" whose goal is the destruction of Israel.

Security becomes one of the all-important topics, since in intractable war, there are numerous and dangerous situations of violence (i.e., wars, terror attacks). As a result, societies invest huge resources in national security, and people are often worried about their personal and country's security. In the Israeli-Palestinian case, due to the belief in the need to highlight security, militarism and the army are sanctified: it is a taboo to criticize them. *Delegitimization of the enemy* occurs when the "other" is related to as less-than-human, irrational, and bloodthirsty, who does not have justice on its side. This belief keeps the conflict going since it only "makes sense" to continue to fight such an immoral enemy. In the Israeli-Palestinian conflict, the Palestinians are delegitimized and their "rights" or "claims" are perceived as being false and unworthy of consideration.

The fourth societal belief, *a positive self-image*, is necessary to keep the group and its members feeling good about themselves. People perceive themselves as being moral and holding desirable values. They distinguish themselves from the "other" and solidify the "us vs. them" belief that we are not only different from the enemy; we are better (Waller, 2002). This belief is also very evident in the Israeli-Palestinian case and reiterated in the common statement, "We want peace—but there is no partner." *Victimization* is another important societal belief. People in a society in an intractable conflict believe that they alone are the victims of the enemy, who is immoral, dangerous, and murderous. The other holds immoral and unjust goals and is completely responsible for the physical and psychological harm. In the Israeli-Palestinian context, Jewish-Israelis perceive themselves as the sole victim in the conflict and the Palestinians as the terrorist perpetrators.

Patriotism becomes another bedrock belief. As will be discussed in detail in Chap. 8, love of and attachment to country becomes central to people whose country is embroiled in an intractable conflict. People are socialized to believe that their country deserves complete dedication, at times, even to the point of being willing to personally sacrifice oneself— or one's children—for the country. In the Israeli-Palestinian conflict, there is the widespread belief that dying for one's country is of the highest value.

The next belief is *unity*. A country cannot successfully fight an enemy without national *unity*, solidarity, and cohesion. This belief finds expression in Israel in the following way:

> During the first Lebanon war, the journalist, Amiram Nir, wrote an article with the following headline, "Silence! We're shooting". The article presented the simple argument: during war … silence is necessary, silence that provides a space of action free from punctilious criticism. According to Amiram Nir, during the war: "There is no opposition. There is no Likud or Labor. There are no religious or secular people, rich or poor, Ashkenazim and riffraff. We are all one people, in uniform. And now, we are shooting. Silence!" Th[is] message … during the Lebanon war, became a symbol of ridicule and mockery for the Israeli left. The expression—"Silence! We're shooting"—became a description of a dictatorship in the making, a situation in which needed criticism is run over by the wheels of the government. (Koppel, March 2, 2015)

The final societal belief, held by people in an intractable conflict, is the belief that it is only their side that wants peace. As a result, people and governments convince themselves that they are peace-loving and gentle, and it is only because the *other* is insatiable and bloodthirsty, that peace remains elusive.

In conclusion, according to Bar-Tal, these beliefs help Jewish-Israelis feel good about themselves and their country, while also prolonging the conflict that is hazardous to their personal and collective lives. As a result, what "helps" continues to hurt, as people remain unaware (consciously? unconsciously?) that holding onto these beliefs fashions and cements one version of "reality" that appears rational, obvious, justifiable, and inevitable. In such a way, the intractable conflict goes on and on and on and on.

Cognitive Dissonance

The final psycho-social notion presented here is *cognitive dissonance*. The reason for presenting this concept is because, in our interviews, we found instances in which people's behaviors and/or attitudes and values appeared to highly contradict one another. As a result, we saw this concept as helping us understand the complexity of how residents perceived their experiences.

Leo Festinger (1957) defined cognitive dissonance as the psychological discomfort that occurs when an individual or a group (Moghaddam, 2014) experiences two mutually inconsistent elements of cognition concerning what a person/group knows about themselves, about their behavior, and about their surroundings (Festinger, 1957, pp. 9–10). The cognitive elements represent one's emotions, pains, desires, and attitudes. They also represent the environmental and causal states concerning the world in which one lives or what causes what. Festinger called this knowledge, *a map/mirror of reality*. According to the researcher, there can be relations of consonance or dissonance between all pairs of these elements. When people keep their maps/mirrors "responsive to reality"—by means of actively reducing dissonance—this helps them understand and survive in the world (p. 11).

Festinger emphasized that when people experience dissonance, they feel pressure to align the "appropriate cognitive elements into correspondence with that reality" (p. 3). Cognitive dissonance, therefore, is a motivator. Since dissonance is psychologically uncomfortable, the individual is motivated to reduce the dissonance. Four strategies can achieve this.

Firstly, the person can change her/his behavior. For example, if a person experiences dissonance when eating the chocolate she loves (since she knows that chocolate is bad for one's teeth and health), she can stop eating it. Secondly, the person can change or distance him/herself from a social cognitive element that leads to dissonance. For example, if a person often finds herself acting belligerently, even when among kind people, she can seek out belligerent people. In the third strategy, the person adds new cognitive elements, if the dissonance cannot be eliminated: (a) by *focusing on supportive beliefs*—such as seeking out information that can reduce the dissonance (e.g., "Studies show that drinking wine is good for your heart—the stuff about alcoholism is blown out of proportion"); (b) by *adding cognitive elements*, which "reconcile" two dissonant cognitive elements. This tactic involves engaging in self-justification (e.g., "More people die from obesity than from smoking, so it's not so bad to smoke— it keeps me thin"). (c) Finally, the individual can *change conflictive cognitive elements*, for example, change one's beliefs, attitudes, or values (e.g., "It's not so bad to keep Blacks/Jews [etc.] out of the neighborhood; the neighbors here get along fine"). The fourth strategy is to avoid the dissonance altogether (or as much as possible).

Since Festinger's early studies, the concept has been widely discussed and researched (e.g., Aronson, 1997; Moghaddam, 2014; Neuman & Tabak, 2003). As Aronson (1997, p. 129) stated:

Dissonance theory is more than simply a theory about consistency. It is essentially a theory about sense-making: how people try to make sense out of their beliefs, their environment, and their behavior—and thus try to lead lives that are (at least in their own minds) reasonable, sensible, and meaningful.

If cognitive dissonance arises from people trying to make sense of their lives, then it makes sense that scholars have approached the concept not solely from an intrapersonal standpoint. For example, Billig (1987) averred that cognitive dissonance occurs in dialogue, rhetoric, and argumentation. Therefore, it is not inconsistency that is disruptive, but the interpersonal *criticism of inconsistency* that leads the individual to engage in defensive justification (Billig, 1987, p. 192). In other words, Billig presented cognitive dissonance as an *interactional problem*, rather than as an intrapersonal *cognitive problem*. This led him to propose that we should: "look at the ways people resolve or dismiss inconsistency without any fundamental changes of belief" (Billig, 1987, p. 194).

Since we will be referring to instances of cognitive dissonance found in our analyses of materials and interviews of *Otef Aza* residents, in Chap. 7, which focuses on the theme of life as conflictual and paradoxical, it is also worthwhile to briefly mention some studies that have explored cognitive dissonance in the context of the Israeli-Palestinian conflict.

In a research project, undertaken during the 1990s, which used cognitive dissonance in order to analyze interviews with soldiers who served during the first Intifada, Liebes and Blum-Kulka (1994) found that soldiers were often confronted with having to reconcile two contradictory important values. On the one hand, they had willingly volunteered for the army, since serving their country was important to them. Furthermore, it was important for them to remain loyal to their unit. However, since, at times, soldiers were called upon to act in ways that violated Palestinians' rights, this conflicted with their values concerning moral behavior vis-à-vis a civilian population. In order to deal with this inconsistency, some soldiers reframed the situation in order to lessen their discomfort ("We're at war; therefore, we need to do what needs to be done"), while others engaged in "negotiations," for example, with their commanding officers, about tactics to be used when engaging with Palestinian citizens. In this way, the soldiers managed to hold on to both values, to some extent, without experiencing deep psychological pain.

Neuman and Tabak's study (2003) used cognitive dissonance to analyze former PM Netanyahu's inconsistent rhetoric, between his attitudes and behavior, when he signed agreements with the Palestinians that relinquished territory, while also declaring that his government would not withdraw from territory over the Green Line. The researchers found three different strategies that Netanyahu used to reconcile his contradictory stances with his good relations with his supporters, averring that Netanyahu's strategies did not derive from an intrapersonal sense of discomfort, but rather from Netanyahu's understanding that he needed to retain his support base. Therefore, he used strategies in which he shifted the blame to non-Likud predecessors, used positive reformulation of the negotiations, and whitewashed what he did, in order to "prove" to his constituents that he had managed to turn a bad situation into a good one.

In a later study (2016), Head connected the ability of Jewish-Israelis to be empathetic toward their Palestinian neighbors to cognitive dissonance. According to Head, when Jewish-Israelis are educated to be empathetic to the suffering of their neighbors, this can lead to recognition of the history of both Israelis and Palestinians. By engaging in empathy, the sides do not disregard their own suffering, but manage to acknowledge that neither side is a complete victim. According to Head (2016), empathy can help create cognitive dissonance, which can become "a constructive vehicle for social and political transformation" (p. 107). In this context, empathy becomes a motivating force to reduce the conflict through acknowledging the suffering of self and other.

To conclude, in order to understand the context of the lives of *Otef Aza* residents, it is important to consider the psycho-social aspects of their lives. These aspects impact the personal, interpersonal, and collective levels, and the ways in which residents understand their lives vis-à-vis themselves, their families, their neighbors, their community, their country, and the "enemy"—the Palestinians in the Gaza Strip. In Chap. 11, therefore, we will return to these psycho-social conceptualizations and present our theoretical model of how they intertwine with the four major themes we discerned in our analyses, as well as the ways in which *Otef Aza* residents perceive the Palestinians in Gaza, and the concepts of patriotism and Zionism in their lives.

We now present the themes that we found in the residents' stories and social media materials, beginning with the theme of routine emergency and war.

References

American Psychiatric Association. (2013). *Diagnostic and statistical manual of mental disorders*. American Psychiatric Association.

Aronson, E. (1997). Back to the future: Retrospective review of Leon Festinger's—A theory of cognitive dissonance. *The American Journal of Psychology, 110*(1), 127–137.

Avidor, S., Palgi, Y., & Solomon, Z. (2017). Lower subjective life expectancy in later life is a risk factor for posttraumatic stress symptoms among trauma survivors. *Psychological Trauma: Theory, Research, Practice, and Policy, 9*(2), 198–206. http://dx.doi.org.databases.sapir.ac.il/10.1037/tra0000182

Ballenger, J. C., Davidson, J. R., Lecrubier, Y., Nutt, D. J., Foa, E. B., Kessler, R. C., & Shalev, A. Y. (2000). Consensus statement on posttraumatic stress disorder from the International Consensus Group on Depression and Anxiety. *Journal of Clinical Psychology, 61*(Suppl 5), 60–66.

Bar-Tal, D. (1998). Societal beliefs in times of intractable conflict: The Israeli case. *The International Journal of Conflict Management, 9*(1), 22–50.

Bar-Tal, D. (2000). *Shared beliefs in a society: Social psychological analysis*. Sage Publications.

Bar-Tal, D. (2007). Sociopsychological foundations of intractable conflicts. *The American Behavioral Scientist, 50*(11), 1430–1453.

Bar-Tal, D. (2013). *Intractable conflicts: Socio-psychological foundations and dynamics*. Cambridge University Press.

Bar-Tal, D. (2017). Self-censorship as a socio-political-psychological phenomenon: Conception and research. *Political Psychology, 38*(S1), 37–65. https://doi.org/10.1111/pops.12391

Bar-Tal, D., Abutbul-Selinger, G., & Raviv, A. (2014). The culture of conflict and its routinization. In P. Nesbitt-Larking, C. Kinnvall, T. Capelos, & H. Dekker (Eds.), *The Palgrave handbook of global political psychology*. Palgrave Studies in Political Psychology Series. Palgrave Macmillan. https://doi.org/10.1007/978-1-137-29118-9_21

Bar-Tal, D., Sharvit, K., Halperin, E., & Zafran, A. (2012). Ethos of conflict: The concept and its measurement. *Peace and Conflict: Journal of Peace Psychology, 18*(1), 40–61.

Bayer-Topilsky, T., Itzhaky, H., Dekel, H., & Mamor, Y. (2013). Mental health and Posttraumatic Growth in civilians exposed to ongoing terror. *Journal of Loss and Trauma, 18*, 1–21. https://doi.org/10.1080/15325024.2012.687325

Besser, A., & Neria, Y. (2012). When home isn't a safe haven: Insecure attachment orientations, perceived social support, and PTSD symptoms among

Israeli evacuees under missile threat. *Psychological Trauma: Theory, Research, Practice, and Policy, 4*(1), 34–46. http://dx.doi.org.databases.sapir.ac.il/10.1037/a0017835

Besser, A., & Zeigler-Hill, V. (2014). Positive personality features and stress among first-year university students: Implications for psychological distress, functional impairment, and self-esteem. *Self and Identity, 13*, 24–44. https://doi.org/10.1080/15298868.2012.736690

Besser, A., Zeigler-Hill, V., Weinberg, M., Pincus, A. L., & Neria, Y. (2015). Intrapersonal resilience moderates the association between exposure-severity and PTSD symptoms among civilians exposed to the 2014 Israel–Gaza conflict. *Self and Identity, 14*(1), 1–15. https://doi.org/10.1080/15298868.2014.966143

Billig, M. (1987). *Arguing and thinking: A rhetorical approach to social psychology.* Cambridge University Press.

Boker, A. (2019, November 17). The Resilience Center in Otef Aza discovers: Every second resident suffers from continuous trauma. https://13news.co.il/item/news/politics/security/otef-gaza-research-939763/ (in Hebrew)

Braun-Lewensohn, O., & Rubin, M. M. (2014). Personal and communal resilience in communities exposed to missile attacks: Does intensity of exposure matter? *The Journal of Positive Psychology, 9*(2), 175–182. https://doi.org/10.1080/17439760.2013.873946

Calhoun, L. G., & Tedeschi, R. G. (2006). The foundations of posttraumatic growth: An expended framework. In L. G. Calhoun & R. G. Tedeschi (Eds.), *Handbook of posttraumatic growth: Research and practice* (pp. 3–22). Lawrence Erlbaum.

Chaitin, J., Sternberg, R., Arad, H., Barzili, L., Deray, N., & Shinhar, S. (2013). 'I may look 75, but I'm really a pioneer': Concept of self and resilience among Israeli elder adults living in a war zone. *Journal of Happiness Studies, 14*, 1601–1619.

Coleman, P. T. (2006). Intractable conflict. In M. Deutsch, P. T. Coleman, & E. C. Marcus (Eds.), *The handbook of conflict resolution: Theory and practice* (2nd ed., pp. 533–559). Jossey-Bass.

Dekel, R., & Nuttman-Shwartz, O. (2009). Posttraumatic stress and growth: The contribution of cognitive appraisal and sense of belonging to the country. *Health and Social Work, 34*(2), 89–96.

Diamond, G. M., Lipsitz, J. D., & Hoffman, Y. (2013). Nonpathological response to ongoing traumatic stress. *Peace and Conflict: Journal of Peace Psychology, 19*(2), 100–111. https://doi.org/10.1037/a0032486

Dickstein, B. D., Schorr, Y., Stein, N., Krantz, L. H., Solomon, Z., & Litz, B. T. (2012). Coping and mental health outcomes among Israelis living with the chronic threat of terrorism. *Psychological Trauma: Theory, Research, Practice, and Policy, 4*(4), 392–399. http://dx.doi.org.databases.sapir.ac.il/10.1037/a0024927

Eshel, Y., & Kimhi, S. (2016). Community resilience of civilians at war: A new perspective. *Community Mental Health Journal, 52*(1), 109–117. http://dx.doi.org.databases.sapir.ac.il/10.1007/s10597-015-9948-3

Festinger, L. (1957). *A theory of cognitive dissonance* (Vol. 2). Stanford University Press.

Friedman, M. J., Resick, P. A., & Keane, T. M. (2007). *PTSD: Twenty-five years of progress and challenges.* In M. J. Friedman, T. M. Keane, & P. A. Resick (Eds.), *Handbook of PTSD: Science and practice* (pp. 3–18). The Guilford Press.

Gelkopf, M., Berger, R., Bleich, A., & Cohen-Silver, R. (2012). Protective factors and predictors of vulnerability to chronic stress: A comparative study of 4 communities after 7 years of continuous rocket fire. *Social Science and Medicine, 74*(5), 757–766.

Gil, S., Weinberg, M., Shamai, M., Ron, P., Harel, H., & Or-Chen, K. (2016). Risk factors for DSM–5 posttraumatic stress symptoms (PTSS) among Israeli civilians during the 2014 Israel-Hamas war. *Psychological Trauma: Theory, Research, Practice, and Policy, 8*(1), 49–54.

Greene, T., Itzhaky, L., Bronstein, I., & Solomon, Z. (2018). Psychopathology, risk, and resilience under exposure to continuous traumatic stress: A systematic review of studies among adults living in southern Israel. *Traumatology, 24*(2), 83–103. https://doi.org/10.1037/trm0000136

Head, N. (2016). A politics of empathy: Encounters with empathy in Israel and Palestine. *Review of International Studies, 42*(1), 95–113.

Hirsch, T. L., & Lazar, A. (2012). Experiencing processes of growth: Coping and PTG among mothers who were exposed to rocket attacks. *Traumatology: An International Journal, 18*(2), 50–60. http://dx.doi.org.databases.sapir.ac.il/10.1177/1534765611426792

Hobfoll, S. E., & London, P. (1986). The relationship of self-concept and social support to emotional distress among women during war. *Journal of Social and Clinical Psychology, 4*, 189–203. https://doi.org/10.1521/jscp.1986.4.2.189

Hobfoll, S. E., Canetti-Nisim, D., & Johnson, R. J. (2006). Exposure to terrorist stress related mental health symptoms, and defensive coping among Jews and Arabs in Israel. *Journal of Consulting and Clinical Psychology, 74*, 207–218.

Johnson, J., Maxwell, A., & Galea, S. (2009). The epidemiology of posttraumatic stress disorder. *Psychiatric Annals, 39*(6), 326–334. https://doi.org/10.3928/00485713-20090514-01

Koppel, T. (2015, March 2). 'Silence! We're giving a speech.' *Yisrael Hayom.* https://www.israelhayom.co.il/opinion/262899 [in Hebrew]

Kriesberg, L. (1998). *Constructive conflicts. From escalation to resolution.* Rowman & Littlefield.

Liebes, T., & Blum-Kulka, S. (1994). Managing a moral dilemma: Israeli soldiers in the Intifada. *Armed Forces & Society, 21*(1), 45–68. https://doi.org/1 0.1177/0095327X9402100104

Litvak Hirsch, T., Braun-Lewensohn, O., & Lazar, A. (2015). Does home attachment contribute to strengthen sense of coherence in times of war? Perspectives of Jewish Israeli mothers. *Women & Health.* https://doi.org/1 0.1080/03630242.2015.1022688

Moghaddam, F. M. (2014). Editorial. *Peace and Conflict: Journal of Peace Psychology, 20*(1), 54–67.

Neuman, Y., & Tabak, I. (2003). Inconsistency as an interactional problem: A lesson from political rhetoric. *Journal of Psycholinguistic Research, 32*(3), 251–267.

Nuttman-Shwartz, O., & Dekel, R. (2009). Ways of coping and sense of belonging in the face of a continuous threat. *Journal of Traumatic Stress, 22*(6), 667–670.

Nuttman-Shwartz, O., Dekel, R., & Regev, I. (2015). Continuous exposure to life threats among different age groups in different types of communities. *Psychological Trauma, 7*(3), 269–276. https://doi.org/10.1037/a0038772

Nuttman-Shwartz, O., & Regev, I. (2018). Life in a continuous traumatic situation: Perspective of the older population. *Ageing and Society, 38*(5), 954–973.

Padan, C., & Elran, M. (2019, February). *Communities in the Gaza Envelope: Case study of social resilience in Israel (2006–2016).* The Institute for National Security Studies.

Regev, I., & Nuttman-Shwartz, O. (2016). Living in a continuous traumatic reality: Impact on elderly persons residing in urban and rural communities. *American Journal of Orthopsychiatry, 86*(6), 652–661.

Resilience Research Center. (n.d.). What is resilience? https://resilienceresearch. org/resilience/

Rosler, N., Hagage Baikovich, H., & Bar-Tal, D. (2020). Rhetorical expressions of ethos of conflict and policymaking in intractable conflict by leaders: A comparative study of two Israeli prime ministers. *Peace and Conflict: Journal of Peace Psychology..* http://dx.doi.org.databases.sapir.ac.il/10.1037/ pac0000491

Shahrabani, S., Rosenboim, M., Shavit, T., Benzion, U., & Arbiv, M. (2019). 'Should I stay or should I go?' Risk perceptions, emotions, and the decision to stay in an attacked area. *International Journal of Stress Management, 26*(1), 57–64. http://dx.doi.org.databases.sapir.ac.il/10.1037/str0000094

Somer, A., & Bleich, A. (Eds.). (2005). *Mental health in the shadow of terror: The Israeli experience*. Tel Aviv University.

Somer, E., & Ataria, Y. (2015). Adverse outcome of continuous traumatic stress: A qualitative inquiry. *International Journal of Stress Management, 22*(3), 287–305. https://doi.org/10.1037/a0038300

Stein, J. Y., Levin, Y., Gelkopf, M., Tangir, G., & Solomon, Z. (2018). Traumatization or habituation? A four-wave investigation of exposure to continuous traumatic stress in Israel. *International Journal of Stress Management, 25*, 137–153.

Stein, N. R., Schorr, Y., Krantz, L., Dickstein, B., Solomon, Z., Horesh, D., & Litz, B. (2013). The differential impact of terrorism on two Israeli communities. *American Journal of Orthopsychiatry, 83*(4), 528–535.

Tedeschi, R. G., & Calhoun, L. G. (2004). Posttraumatic growth: Conceptual foundations and empirical evidence. *Psychological Inquiry, 15*, 1–18.

Tzachor, Y. (2019). *Life in the shadow of the conflict*. Carmel. (in Hebrew).

Vogt, D. S., King, D. W., & King, L. A. (2007). Risk pathways for PTSD: Making sense of the literature. In M. J. Friedman, T. M. Keane, & P. A. Resick (Eds.), *Handbook of PTSD: Science and Practice* (pp. 99–115). The Guilford Press.

Waller, J. (2002). *Becoming evil: How ordinary people commit genocide and mass killing*. Oxford University Press.

4

Routine Emergency, Emergency Routine, and War

This chapter focuses on how the ongoing dangerous security situation permeates every aspect of *Otef Aza* residents' lives: their daily routines, mental health, sense of security, parenting, and their ability to work and/ or attend school. It is with them day and night, seven days a week, 365 days a year.

In our analyses, we found the theme was comprised of five main components. (a) As the security situation has worsened, residents see life as vacillating between "Heaven and Hell." In order to try to cope, they have created what we termed dynamic Danger Scales, which rank situations— and hence residents' cognitive, emotional, and behavioral responses— according to perceived level of danger, (e.g., quiet and normality, incendiary/explosive balloons, mortars, "drops of *Kassams*,"[1] massive attacks, tunnels, etc.). These responses are influenced by a combination of residents' personal experiences and the development of terror instruments, employed by militant groups in Gaza. At the same time, however, *because* the dangers have become more complex, the borders between the emergency routine, rounds, and wars have become blurred. Thus, at

---

[1] During "normal" routine emergency, broadcasters often refer to one or two rocket attacks a day as "drops"—a euphemism that upsets *Otef Aza* residents.

© The Author(s), under exclusive license to Springer Nature Switzerland AG 2022
J. Chaitin et al., *Routine Emergency*, https://doi.org/10.1007/978-3-030-95983-8_4

times, residents struggle with demarcating the different situations, which, in turn, leads to more stress, dread, and growing despair, as well as questioning their desire to remain in the region. In other words, the mechanisms that residents adopt to help them deal with the dangers end up complicating their lives. (b) The transitions from routine emergency to emergency routine to war have led residents to develop praxes for dealing with the dangers. Residents have created concrete actions to cope with the dangers and fears. (c) Since the situation in *Otef Aza* is so volatile and unpredictable, the residents have learned how to quickly and sharply change their behaviors. They often describe these transitions as being like a switch—that they are directed to turn on and off. While, on the one hand, being able to move quickly between dangerous and quiet situations can be a lifesaver, it also takes an emotional toll, wearing down residents' resilience. (d) Life in the *Otef* has influenced residents' parenting, and their thoughts and emotions concerning how staying in the area is impacting their children. A number of people question their decision to remain in the area, some wonder if staying is harming the children, others hope that they are managing to protect them, and a few believe that the experiences are strengthening them. (e) Finally, during the escalations, residents often become "refugees," leaving for safe places in the country. Sometimes they go for one or two nights, sometimes for a week or two, and during Protective Edge, many escaped for months. This was another topic presented by the residents.

We now present examples from the interviews, photographs, and social media materials that demonstrate these thematic elements, beginning with a YouTube video made by residents of the Eshkol Regional Council—*Routine Emergency.*

Routine Emergency: "Ha, Ha, Ha—Eshkol Regional Council—To the *Mamad*!

This 3:53-minute-long video (Janis Productions, 2018—see Fig. 4.1), created by and starring residents of all ages from the Eshkol Regional Council, is a take-off of Stephane Legar's music video *Comme Ci Comme*

Fig. 4.1   *Cherum Shigra* (Janis Productions, 2018)

ça (2018). It was produced a few months after the fires began in the region, and much of the video has stills and videos of the scorched land. In the beginning, a couple enjoying a romantic picnic, during the *Darom Adom* festival,[2] is interrupted by the male soloist, Tom Amsalem, who tells them: Go to the *mamad*![3] The video then tells the story of how the ongoing security situation disrupts everyday life, such as when to enter and exit bomb shelters, take in the laundry, fix the air conditioner in the *mamad*, brush one's teeth, go the bathroom, put out fires, and so on. The clip features, among others, members of the *tzachi* teams (Community Emergency Teams), the *ravshatsim* (the security coordinators in each

---

[2] The Red South Festival, which takes place annually during the month of February, celebrates the widespread blooming of the anemones. Hundreds of thousands of Israelis come to the area to enjoy numerous attractions in the communities, the flowers, hikes, and so on.

[3] An acronym for resident safe space—the safe room, made from reinforced concrete.

community), and the mental health professionals from the local Resilience Center. The words in the song include:

> Hey, a kite fell here!
> Routine emergency,
> my living room was burned,
> routine emergency,
> life here in Eshkol is ooh la la, ooh la la
> but the explosions!
>
> Routine emergency, emergency, emergency routine …
>
> a *Kassam* fell,
> my roof caved in,
> a government minister came,
> for a selfie in the area,
>
> routine emergency …
>
> the agriculture – routine emergency
> the income – routine emergency
> school – routine emergency …
> the vacations – routine emergency
> the nursery schools – routine emergency
> entire life – routine emergency.

This video conveys the myriad challenges faced by *Otef Aza* residents, the volunteer work of different teams and professionals, and the apathy/ignoring of the situation by governmental leaders, leaving the viewer laughing, while wiping away tears.

This Place Is Either Heaven or Hell—The Danger Scale

Our interviewees often talked about the changes that have developed in the western Negev, concerning the security situation. Over the years, the area even changed its name, becoming known as *Otef Aza*, due to the ongoing Israel-*Hamas* conflict.

Tamar, a 50-year-old politically center, secular woman, who moved from the center of the country to a *kibbutz*, after she got married, is a social worker. She began her interview with her first memories of the area:

> I came to live here, not in *"Otef Aza"*, but rather in the Eshkol Regional Council ... over 20 years ago ... I needed to find work, I was a social worker in Tel Aviv; I went to a job interview and on the way from the *kibbutz* to the interview, to my left and right were wheat fields ... I had come from the traffic jams of LaGuardia and Hashalom[4] and I said to myself, "It doesn't matter what job they offer me, I'm taking it, if this is the landscape that I'll see when driving back and forth" ... I'm talking about this because ... the beginning was life in a very peaceful and quiet agricultural place.

Later, when talking about her job as head of social services in her region, during Protective Edge, Tamar painted a very different picture. Years of living and working in the beautiful, yet deadly, region brought her face to face with hundreds of traumas. Here we do not hear about the Heaven of the region, but rather about the many events that required Tamar to find mechanisms that could cope with the extremely difficult and challenging times:

> Protective Edge was an event not only on the national level, but also on my personal level, it was very, very difficult, and demanding, I learned a lot ... but also paid many high prices ... there is a saying—when people deal with emergency and preparedness, "Get prepared for a long-term event, and where the last war finishes, the next war begins"; from my personal experience, that's very true ... I didn't understand how long Protective Edge

---

[4] Major highway intersections in Tel Aviv.

would be, I didn't understand that I was entering such a long campaign and I don't think that I managed my strength and resources well … you have to know if you're going on a 10-kilometre marathon or a one-kilometre marathon, because you prepare yourself in a different way, and I went out on a one-mile marathon, and it was 10, so imagine what happens to a person, like that … Protective Edge ended on a very jarring chord of the events of Kibbutz Nirim[5] and Daniel Tragerman.[6]

The next example comes from Tali, a 50-year-old secular, center-left *kibbutz* member, who grew up on the kibbutz, where she still resides. During one rocket attack, she miraculously escaped being killed, when a rocket hit her car. Tali talked about how, over time, it has become difficult for her to differentiate between levels of danger, sometimes misjudging a situation as being less dangerous than it objectively is. This had added to Tali's sense of insecurity: by trying to "normalize" abnormal situations, she, simultaneously, understands that she is "disconnecting" from the fear that she is experiencing:

> You so much want to give [the kids] independence, but there are periods when you say "Wait, you can't go by yourself now" … and when things begin to heat up … there's some kind of disconnection from the fact that you're in the most dangerous situation … once, a rocket fell near the children's houses … I said "Okay, there was a rocket and it wasn't during an operation … Okay, we're in the same situation that we were in before, so he can go by himself to the nursery school" and it was only later that you process it … when you're in the middle of it, you try so hard not to get close to your fears and you put up some kind of screen.

Yoni, a 36-year-old right-wing religious man from a village, also talked about the changing dangers, but presented a different perspective. He averred that, perhaps paradoxically, it is easier to cope with wars than with the routine-emergencies, since the latter leave people confused and anxious. He, thus, on one level, appears to be proposing that the government and army should not fear to go to war, since, in the end, this will

---

[5] When two *kibbutz* members were killed.
[6] A four-year-old boy from Nahal Oz, killed when hit by a mortar shell.

decrease ambiguity and, perhaps, bring some kind of closure to residents and the problem:

> I say that the day-to-day life of *Otef Aza* is much more complicated than the war, because in war there's a very clear order to the actions, psychologically, your head becomes very clear, I have friends in *kibbutzim* ... and they don't experience it every day, but it's in their head that they don't know when it will come, during the routine, they don't know where it will come from; during war, you say "Okay, now it's wartime, it'll be a mess here and I can make a rational decision here, to some extent—to go to grandma's in the north, to stay here, to send the kids and be careful." The routine is routine emergency, and it will always be routine emergency. Therefore, I think that the real innovation or challenge is during the day-to-day, the round of fighting is easy, in some way.

We now look at Sigal's words from her interview, focusing on her I-poem. Sigal is a 65-year-old pensioner who worked in the medical profession in a big hospital. She and her husband moved to a *kibbutz* very close to the border, 18 years ago. Sigal presented dissonance in her interview about her strong love of this Paradise that is paired with the many traumatic events she has faced over the years. This is not only because of where she lives, but also because she could get no respite, since she had to remain in the area, due to her job. Here are parts of her I-poem:

> I love to take photographs
> I would drive to work
> Because there was no choice
> I think that we have it really good here,
> I'm glad that we don't have to raise kids here
> ...
> I'm sure it's really hard
> I have people, my personal contacts
> I enjoy the freedom
> I don't have to get up in the morning and work
> It's so much fun
> ...
> I would see the rocket shootings from Gaza

Because of work, I had to travel
...
I remember that during a siren at the hospital
I remember that event
I saw the panic, the panic
I saw this discrepancy
...
I don't want the city
I tried the city
And I don't want it
I understood that's not what I want
I travel everyday
I saw the houses of Gaza
...
I don't want this
...
I'm happy
...
I had big hopes after the disengagement[7]
...
I've achieved everything I wanted
I know that everyone responds differently
I get into an elevator
I don't like the announcement in the elevator at all
...
When I hear some noise,
I jump.

From this I-poem, created completely from Sigal's words, there are many instances of dissonance. She talks about how "good" she and her husband have it, while living so close to the Gaza Strip, which is a warzone. While the nature in the region offers her great opportunities for photography, which she loves, the rockets and the panic, and her hypervigilance, are juxtaposed with "the fun." Sigal talks about how she desired country life, while simultaneously emphasizing that she is glad that she does not have to raise her children there, as it must be "very hard." In

---

[7] From *Gush Katif* in 2005.

sum, life is a mixture of Heaven and Hell that makes life an emotional and physical rollercoaster, which combines panic and fun.

Noa, a 36-year-old mother from Sderot, with left-center and secular views, also talked about how life has changed for the worse, in terms of the security situation. Noa says that the "rules of the game changed" during Protective Edge, leading her family to see the war dangers in a different light than they had before:

> During Protective Edge, within seven minutes, there were some 10 *Kassam* rockets, it was like, wow! Crazy! Today, in 20 minutes, we have 50. I remember well this experience of the first barrage, because up until then, there was *tzeva adom*; you hear that the shooting ends, you go outside and now, all of a sudden, it changed the rules of the games … you can't know what to expect … it really changed the reality here, also Iron Dome can't handle this and the moment that there's a barrage, you know there will be bombings.

Shalom, a 46-year-old politically center, secular man who lives on a *moshav*, noted that, due to his *moshav's* topographical location, it is usually out of heavy rocket range. However, for several years, he has worked at the nearby college, located in the middle of the danger zone. This has led him to construct a danger scale in which he differentiates between the potential dangers of the two locations, though he is actually always close to the Gaza border. Despite his efforts at ranking the dangers, making home life more "normal" than work life; his words suggest that the entire situation is one that defies the notion of "normal" (It is like "any citizen in a war zone"; "I'm still there."):

> In connection to my being a college employee, in actuality, the daily experiences during security periods of *tzivei adom*[8] become a bit standard, the balloon terrorism that was here a while ago and now it has calmed down a bit, with the hope that it won't return, the endless fires, the smell of the smoke, the feeling is as if you're living in an ongoing warzone … something is always happening … I really feel during these periods like someone who is in a warzone, like any citizen in a warzone … when I get [home], the

---

[8] The plural of *tzeva adom*.

intensity of the flame decreases a drop since … we live 200 meters further away, as a rule, we don't have so many rockets because [of the topography] … we can't really get hurt because they're low, and here it's high and all kind of things; when I come [home] it's a bit less intense, but when I hear *tzeva adom*, I completely identify with my friends from work, who are experiencing these moments, something traumatic that I'm not experiencing at that moment, I'm still there, I'm still there.

Hila, our next example, is a 40-year-old center-left woman from a *moshav*. For years she worked as a therapist in a Resilience Center. She described the routine emergency of 2017–2018, before her interview (undertaken in mid-2019), as mainly containing fires and loud, violent nightly demonstrations on the border (as opposed to rocket attacks). She described this as a situation that has worsened and has had negative impacts on the daily lives of the residents, including the children whom she treated. However, when taking a closer look, it is possible to see that she is not only talking about others, but also about herself, suggesting that the defense mechanisms used by residents are becoming less efficient to cover the anxiety:

I was a therapist for many years, but I think that something in the version of the last year, year and a half is showing its signs in the public, that is, when there is nightly noise [on the border] … the shutters rattle and that makes everyone jump, whoever says that it doesn't is either a big liar ((she chuckles)) or has hearing problems, it makes everyone jump because it's a crazy noise, but using rationalization, you contain it, but for the little children, this defense mechanism doesn't work good enough and it's very frightening.

In sum, residents often talked about the extremes that they have experienced in the *Otef*. The extremes move from Heaven—when life is fun, calm, pastoral—to Hell—when everyone "jumps," and there are "endless fires" and "barrages of rockets." This Heaven and Hell is the given of the *Otef*, with people knowing that just as life can be amazingly beautiful, it can turn to frightening and deadly, in a moment's time.

Praxes of Dealing with Dangers and Fears

Another finding that emerged from our analyses was that *Otef Aza* residents have developed praxes for coping with the security dangers. On the one hand, these praxes, with their psychological and/or physical functions, provide them with some sense of control during a war situation, which they do not control. However, on the other hand, while engaging in these behaviors, they often realize that the situation is "crazy," and that people who do not live in a warzone need to neither produce nor engage in such practices.

For example, Noa, from Sderot, talked about how she made their safe room into a fun place for her children and how she and her husband figured out the "safest" way to bring their son to and from his nursery school, during Protective Edge:

> I prepared a box for the safe room, it has toys and chocolate and that's the *tzeva adom* box, only when there's a *tzeva adom* are they permitted to open it up; it works like a charm, they run and open up the box, the entire world fades away, and they're busy with the chocolate and the games. It's crazy … Yoav was in the secured children's house and I said that since he is going to a safe children's house, I'm calm, on the way, we would go together, so that one holds him and the other would get out of the car, if there was a *tzeva adom*. Today it seems crazy to me, today I look at that and that looks completely crazy to me, but, at the time … the rockets flew over that *kibbutz* … it was relatively a place where you could go and feel [safer], that's it, it ended.

In a 2.5-minute video, made in February 2020 by the Israeli branch of the International Committee of the Red Cross (ICRC), Smadi Shmilovitch, the co-director of *Tzachi* at Netiv Ha'asara, a *moshav* adjacent to the northern border of the Gaza Strip, talks about praxes her family and community have devised for living with the security threats. However, these concrete actions, as Shmilovitch confesses, do not solve the root of the problem. As a result, she is discerning that her and other residents' resilience is beginning to crack:

In our trunks of our cars, there are bags arranged for our children, according to their names, a bag for Omer, a bag for Idan, a bag for Elad, because at any given moment we can find ourselves here under bombardment, the children leave here under a blanket of anxiety … that's why we have listed here ((she points to the wall in her office)) every grade, we try to send out every grade *together*, to a certain place that takes them in during the day, but at night we have to return to here, and there are parents who don't want to return. (0:54–1:27)

Another example of a praxis created by *Otef Aza* residents comes from a flyer, created by the coalition Unity with the South (published on Facebook, on August 12, 2019—see Fig. 4.2).

This flyer calls residents to come to a "celebration" to mark the 12th rocket attack round of the year, to be held on the next Friday at 16:00 at the Sderot junction. Here, members of this coalition use humor to express their anger, frustration, and stress. The caveat listed on the bottom left

Fig. 4.2   Escalation Celebration (color online)

announces that the event may be cancelled, depending on Ismael Haniya's (*Hamas'* political leader) actions, insinuating that it is the *Hamas* that controls what will or will not happen in *Otef Aza*.

The illustrations on the blue background contain regular balloons (for the "party"), exploding balloons, and explosives. The small blue crescents might also symbolize the crescent moon—the major symbol of Islam. The white sign, with the logo of the coalition, includes a heart—suggesting that it is the Israelis, who have love, as opposed to their *Hamas* neighbors. Thus, this flyer mixes light with dark, toys with explosives, love with hatred, all done in a tongue-in-cheek fashion, which gives them another way to cope with the dangers.

In sum, we see that three praxes employed by *Otef Aza* residents is the ability to turn a danger situation into a "party," getting prepared to leave at a moment's notice, when rocket attacks begin again, and the use of humor/satire to deal with the risks. These praxes have become part of everyday life—a life of routine emergency—and so the residents appear to be able to use these practices immediately when danger comes knocking.

Making Quick, Sharp Behavioral Changes— Turning the Switch On and Off

Some of the interviewees described the ability to make quick, sharp transitions between emergency and routine for coping with the dangers, and as a way of returning to "normal" life, as much/as soon as possible. On the one hand, this acquired ability helps residents live with the ongoing dangerous situation. However, the ability to make such transitions also comes with a price. That is, while the "switches" work in the short term or, sporadically, in the long term, the constant switching causes distress as attempts to overcome the fear do not always work.

Yael, a 21-year-old woman who was born and raised in Sderot, shared her thoughts about these quick transitions:

I think it's something that we got used to, and when you do this from a young age, you become good at it, when the brain moves from routine to emergency and from emergency to routine so quickly, it succeeds and you do it.

When talking about Protective Edge, Yael said, how even during and immediately after this very traumatic war, people made quick and sharp transitions, because there was no choice. Her message was, if you are going to remain in the area, this is an ability that you must possess:

I felt that this is another war, like all the others ... How is it more than Pillars of Defense? Something felt different ... my friend, who babysat for the boy that was killed by the mortar shell, like, it's crazy, it's crazy. But, in the end, you go back to routine like you did after each *tzeva adom*, after each war, you go back to routine, the routine continues.

Noa also talked about the ability to make quick transitions. She described her surprise at discovering, when new to the area, that such transitions are "normal":

The first time we experienced a *tzeva adom* ... was one night, before *Purim*[9]... there were three to four *tzivei adom* at night ... our house is designed like a train [with rooms, one after the other], so our room was here, Yoav's room was here, here another room and the safe room here, so we needed to get up, go get Yoav, run to another room and then run and we always heard the boom before we reached the third room, we didn't manage to get up, grab Yoav and reach [the safe room] ... in the morning, after we went through that night of battle ... the tradition here ... is that on the day you get dressed up in a costume, everyone assembles at seven in the morning for a community photo, with music; it's nice, and I got up in the morning and everything here is normal, everyone came out and no one said anything about what had happened, it was like nothing had happened and I was in a bit of shock ... I felt like I need to talk about it ... but people carried on as usual, kids went to school, as if nothing had happened.

---

[9] A Jewish holiday in which children get dressed up in costumes and there are parties.

However, Noa later recounts how she learned to quickly move between emergency and routine when rounds end, and even *during* rounds of escalation. By making transitions from a *tzeva adom*, when you must be in the *mamad*, to "normal, family" behaviors, when there is a lull in the violence, she stated that parents can help protect their own and their children's sanity and resilience. However, her words also demonstrate that she is not completely convinced that, at some point, these quick switches may reach a breaking point:

> During the first rounds, Yoav wouldn't agree to come out of the safe room, so we had dinners in the safe room and played in the safe room and I gave him three-second showers and today there can be a barrage of rockets, and 10 minutes after it ends, I make them come out to the living room and we continue playing there and make a cake, because I'm trying to make the situation normal, I tell them "Now it's emergency … we need to be careful and go into the safe room" … so they know that there is emergency time, but once it's over … we go right back to routine … once, after a bad night … we took Yoav to school, he didn't want to go … he said his stomach hurt, we brought him into the classroom, when I came to pick him up … he was happy and I said to him "Here, you overcame it, you coped with it and it wasn't as bad as you thought" … we learned how to live with this, but I also know that tomorrow morning a *Kassam* can find us during the wrong moment, and we'll have an experience that will show us that we can't live here any longer, so I know that what I now think is stable, and that I'm resilient, I also know that in one moment everything can change, and that's not an easy feeling to live with.

Avi, a 48-year-old religious man with right-center political beliefs from Sderot, also talked about how these transitions were often unfathomable. He said:

> The thought that you can go from emergency to routine in a second and a half, up until now, people simply haven't bounced back from that, how we went to sleep at midnight, when we were heading into a long war of attrition, and then in the morning, everything's okay and we're supposed to carry on.

A final example comes from Tali, who, as noted above, barely missed being killed by a rocket when driving home. Tali noted her desire to return to "normal" life after/during escalation of the violence, and her disillusionment with government/army officials who say the area is safe, when it often is not:

> When they said there's a "*hudna*",[10] during Protective Edge, that it's possible to come back, I remember that I returned and during the war went to the beach … I said "I believe them", because if they say that … there's peace, so I'm in my routine and I go to the beach, in spite of the fact that it's clear to me that perhaps it's dangerous there, or if there's routine and I need to return to work and my usual activities and it's as if the war ended, so I can also go to the beach and feel safe, and it's really frustrating and insulting, and mainly, the feeling that they're deceiving you and it's not easy dealing with this.

In summation of this sub-theme, we see that *Otef Aza* residents have become adept at "turning the switch of danger on and off" in order to function during hazardous times, while returning to "normalcy" when there is a lull in the fighting. While residents have learned to engage in this back and forth, it exacts a psychological price, eating away at their sense of trust in their ability to adequately gauge if there is a problem or not. Furthermore, they understand that while such movement is imperative, they also understand that it is not authentic, and imply that this "ability" may run its course soon.

Parenting—What Is This Situation Doing to My Children?

Another theme that we discerned connected to the residents' thoughts and feelings about their parenting and the effects the hostilities have on their children's psychological and physical health. There were parents who often asked themselves if they were doing the right thing by

---

[10] Ceasefire/truce, in Arabic.

Fig. 4.3 Ronit's Son and the Carrot Field (July 2020) (color online)

remaining in the area, some who talked about the measures they took for coping—such as sending their children for psychological therapy and some—who belonged to the religious stream—who saw the experiences as strengthening their children's Zionist ideologies and moral values, and empowering them.

Ronit, a 46-year-old center-left secular woman, moved to the area from the country's center when she and her husband were looking for a community with quality of life and economic benefits. They settled on a *kibbutz* directly across from the Gaza border. Ronit talked about the effects of the war on her children and shared a photograph (see Fig. 4.3) that reflects her internal conflicts about exposing her children to the warzone and remaining where they are. She mainly focuses on the "good" with only hinting at the "not so good." Ronit said:

> My love for this place was for this wonderful village life, being close to the earth, it was magical for me, to pick the carrot from the earth, when you

live in the center, you go on a trip to do this … here the kids experience it … my son in the nursery school goes for a walk in nature every day … this is one reason I came and wanted to live this *kibbutz* dream, the education here … is worth the price. This photograph is from the day that we went to pick carrots and I saw the carrot and it completely amazed me … I had never seen a carrot in the ground … if I felt that I'm living in a dangerous place … without any benefits … then I don't think I would fight so hard to stay here, but there are so many advantages to this place … my kids are so close to nature and there is really amazing education, I often say: "Where else will I find this?" … sometimes this place, when it's quiet, is so good that it covers up all of the things that aren't good, not always, but on the quiet days, it's so good that you can't think about something else.

In our opinion, due to the angle of this photo, the photograph emphasizes the "dream" and "magic" of which Ronit speaks. The fields and the carrots look huge, in comparison to her small son. It appears as if she chose this photo, and her explanation, to express how the vastness and abundance of nature might somehow protect them. If she were to move away, perhaps the magic would disappear, leaving the children with a hole where this beauty and marvel once were. However, this fantasy portrayal also has a few cracks—both visually and in her words. Visually, the photo shows the very uneven land and the (small) abyss, perhaps symbolizing that her children are on rocky ground and can fall at any moment. Furthermore, in her explanation of the photo, she notes that the quiet fails to completely cover up the "bad." In other words, while everyone loves an idyllic world, it is not reality. The reality is, that on the bad days, the children cannot roam freely in the fields and pick carrots, but rather are enclosed in their reinforced concrete rooms, which is the only objective measure that can keep them safe from rockets.

Sa'ar, a 47-year-old politically center, secular *kibbutznik*, also talked about the effects of the situation on his youngest son. On the one hand, he talks about the regressive behavior of bedwetting, while simultaneously averring that "it doesn't affect their lives." He contradicts himself, and perhaps he does so as a coping mechanism that helps him feel that he is not endangering his children by remaining in the *Otef*.

My youngest son, during the last period, had symptoms of bedwetting at night, but on a daily basis, the children were born into this reality, they know, better than us, what to do when there's a *tzeva adom*, without any hysterics, really without anything, *tzeva adom*, they drop everything and run to the *mamad*, wait a minute or two and go back to their routine; it doesn't affect their lives.

Adva, a 43-year-old self-defined "light" left-wing mother of three boys who lives in Netivot, also talked about this topic. She and her husband moved to the area several years ago, first to a *moshav* and then to the city. While Adva said that she is "not a hysterical woman," most of her interview reflected her deep anxiety about her children's wellbeing, because of the constant dangers of war. Her words express decision-making that does not objectively make sense. Furthermore, her laughter, when she hears herself describe choices she has made, demonstrates that she, too, understands, that she may not be as rational as she thinks she is. This is compounded by the fact that her boys, now in their late teens, no longer agree to sleep in the *mamad* and are flippant about the dangers:

When we moved to the *moshav*, the kids were little, and then began more rounds of fighting, that was already harder because it's very frightening when the kids are little, once there was a siren and one of the boys was outside and I couldn't find him, I became hysterical and began yelling, and I said: "Okay, I'm not going into the *mamad*, in good conscience ((she laughs))," I put the other two in and I began looking for him, in the end, he went into some house under construction, there was a bomb shelter there and he took very good precautions; I was the hysterical one outside … [once] we had a siren at night and I couldn't wake up one of my boys, so I laid down on top of him, I took one of the boys [to the *mamad*] and I said: "Okay, whatever will be, will be," but I really couldn't wake him up, since then, each time there would be a round, they'd stay in the *mamad*, but today, they're not willing [to do this], they're already big ((she laughs)), [they say] "They can lob their *Kassams*".

Hila, the therapist, also talked about the effects of the war on her children. This text almost seems to have been delivered by two people. Most of it focuses on her daughter's traumas, developmental delays and regression, and the inability to have a normal childhood life, while the last part talks about how living in a war zone is good for children, as it ultimately strengthens them. It appears that Hila is unsure about what she should do, as a parent. On the one hand, she is painfully aware of all the problems, while, on the other, she avers that, in the end, she is not causing her children harm:

I assume that there are other areas in the country … that produce scars, if a child who is developing normally is supposed to be dry by age two, two-and-a-half … my little one is dry, but every time there's a round of fighting, or if she hears a plane, and, from her perspective, that means that there's war now, there is wetting at night, so you see how it influences them, we can be sitting in the garden and playing, and a plane flies over, which is background noise in our routine, or helicopters … from their perspective, when there's a helicopter, the mess is starting; you can see her drop every-thing, run inside to her bed, because her room is the *mamad*, and that's it … she doesn't come out, so the heart is seared … you see her sitting there and shutting her ears ((Hila shuts her ears)) and say: "Mommy, how can I eat this way?" and that's after you persuaded her to come out of the *mamad*, so there are some developmental delays or nightmares … Yaron and I begin the night [in bed] and we can end it with three or four in the bed ((she chuckles)), depending on how many join us during the night and what the level of anxiety was during the night … but I think that over time, it's making them stronger, I see the progress that my big daughter made, she also had many fears and she underwent a significant process and today, she's not the same girl, I'm sure that it has an impact on her, but she has come through it stronger.

Yonatan Kanaskevitch's film (August 2020) *Leaving Home* follows Maya Simchi-Atar, a young woman who was born and raised on Kibbutz Nir Am, and some of her family members, including her sister, Amit. In the film (minutes 10:31–11:48—see Fig. 4.4), Amit talks about the effects the situation is having on her parenting and on her children's psy-chological states:

When it really touches your kids, it touches your soul … it's very, very strong … for the 20 years that I have experienced this, the first time that I

Fig. 4.4 *Leaving Home* (Yonatan Kanaskevitch, August 2020)

experienced it as something difficult was how long ago? Two months? Three months? The last time there were [rockets], we were here, me, Shai, Itai and Shira, with my mother and we were playing Hide 'n Go Seek and there was a *tzeva adom* and everyone had just gone to hide, and Itai had hidden behind a bush here, behind one of the houses, and *tzeva adom* and he's hiding behind one of the bushes and we can't find him for the first few seconds, everyone ran to the *mamad* and … I'm screaming like a lunatic, and I see where he is and I run, the boom had already happened, from that moment on, the boy changed, and then I ask myself "What am I doing to my kids?" … then, I say: "Okay, it's quiet." I never succeed in bringing myself to say: "Am I screwing up my kids?" or "Am I making them stronger?"

The last example comes from Avi. When talking about the impacts that the "endless" war situation has had on his children, he presents them as strong, patriotic children who are willing to sacrifice themselves for their country (see Fig. 4.5). He connects their values and principles to his and his wife's Zionist ideology. Avi says:

We've already been in the situation for 18 years … and despite how difficult it is … my oldest was born into this reality, my son is 20 and a combat soldier … I note this because, in spite of the real difficulty of life here, thank God, my family is strong … we teach our children … to continue to

Fig. 4.5   Avi's Son with Two Friends (May 2019) (Avi concealed their faces to protect the soldiers' identities)

be kind with themselves and with the country and to remain here and, in the end, this is part of our ideology … ((Avi shows a photograph)) here is my son the soldier … with two of his good friends … there is some special pride of young guys saying: "Here, I am with my weapon and I'm ready to defend my country' … this is my eldest son … my son had every reason to be spoiled and not enlist in the army … but he feels the need to go and fight … he says "This is my life's mission, we want to sacrifice ourselves … We'll continue to fight in spite of the difficulties, that's the right path" … a child is the education he got from his parents … throughout his adolescent years, he never broke …the opposite is true … I was a paratrooper and throughout his teen years, he said … "I'm like my dad; I'm going to be in the paratroopers' and then he said he would be in the elite paratroopers' unit and then he said "I'm checking out the commando unit" … he wanted to go to the best, "I want to defend this country" … there's a war going on over our heads … he could have chosen mediocrity, but he chose to go the extreme, in the good sense.

In summation of this sub-theme, it is clear that parents think a great deal about the effects that the dangers of the region are having on their children, often wondering if they are making the right choices about deciding to remain. On the one hand, some of them talk about how the situation is strengthening them, making them able to face challenges and/or reinforce their ideology and values; while on the other, they cannot help but note the negative effects, such as developmental problems and regression. Therefore, the parents in the *Otef* often reflect on their parenting: they often vacillate between loving the Heaven while hating the Hell of their children's childhood experiences, not really being able to find peace concerning their parental decisions.

Becoming a Refugee

Many residents—especially the mothers and children—immediately leave the area when there is a sharp escalation in the violence and some of our interviewees also discussed this topic. Noa talked about her experiences being an internal refugee—on the block on which she lived—because when was in her final months of pregnancy, she could not make it in time to her safe room, which was on another floor. As a result, she stayed in different community members' homes, who had left Sderot for safer ground. She said:

> I went through the entire operation in my eighth and ninth months … and one night at 2 a.m., after a few times that there was a *tzeva adom* … one neighbour … called and said: "Come sleep in our house; you can't sleep upstairs anymore". We took the things and moved to her house … we weren't in our home for two months … we'd sleep one night here, one night there, we asked on the community WhatsApp who was leaving Sderot … some people went for three days to the north, we slept in Alon's house for weeks because they left for longer … on the weekends we would leave on Thursday and come back on Sunday.

The film *Leaving Home* (presented above) features Maya, who has been traumatized by the wars and routine emergency. Maya continuously vacillates between remaining at Nir Am—her home—and leaving for Tel-Aviv—a place that provides her with safety. In recent years, due to the rocket attacks and fires, and the frightening uncertainty of what the next day will bring, Mays has found herself in a semi-refugee status. In one scene, after Maya and Ofer (her husband) were in the *mamad*, escaping a rocket attack, Maya is shot sitting on the floor, looking very distraught (minutes 4:40–4:57):

> Ofer and I just had an argument in the *mamad* … I told him how badly I want to get out of here, from the *kibbutz*, and that is something that right now isn't appropriate for him, for all kinds of reasons, and he thinks that it's a mistake right now to go back to Tel Aviv.

This scene is immediately followed by a shot of rockets and Iron Dome explosions in the sky, with a man's voice saying: "It's so crazy." Together, these scenes express how difficult it is for residents to decide whether to stay or go, and the personal and family crises they face, when trying to make the "right" decision for them.

Later, in the film (minutes 13:01–13:32), the filmmaker accompanies Maya to the Sderot railroad station, where she is catching a train to Tel Aviv, to escape the region. During the train ride, Maya says:

> It is lucky that there is Tel Aviv. It is **lucky**[11] that there is Tel-Aviv. Really. In Israel. Nothing can ensure me [that there won't be rockets there], but right now I am in the biggest danger, which has turned life in *Otef Aza* to routine. A war routine. And, I don't want this routine. I want breaks.

The final example comes from Rami, a 61-year-old left-wing kibbutz member, who said that he suffers from post-trauma. Rami lives on the *kibbutz*, where he was born and raised. In the past, he worked with the army to help organize the region during the escalations in violence. However, he underwent a complete change in perspective over the years, which was a result of traumatic war experiences and, since then, says that he can no longer tolerate rounds of violence and war:

> The situation becomes chaotic … on the personal level, during all these wars, during this crazy decade, it entered my soul and I become completely crazy, I go nuts! I escape from Israel, during … Protective Edge, I disappear

---

[11] In all the quotes, the emphases we present in the book were in the original.

from here … I leave, I'm incapable of holding it, and then, all of a sudden, everything comes up, the Gazan children, and the Gazan mothers and the Gazan teenagers, and our teenagers, and it all gets jumbled in my brain, and from that moment I'm upset … I'm furious, I'm furious *with us* and I leave the area, I *leave* the *kibbutz*, I leave Zionism, that's it, I abandon everything! I abandon it, I'm incapable, I don't have love anymore, I have *loathing*, it all comes up, the whole Zionist story and my father's settling [the *kibbutz*] and my father's stories about how he came to the area … I leave.

Chapter Summary

As can be seen from the above, life of constant war, or potential war, is ever-evolving, complex, multi-level, and emotionally draining for *Otef Aza* residents. Residents are always primed "for the other shoe to drop" and can never be sure what the next day—even the same day—will bring, and how/if they will be able to successfully cope. This is because the dangers have become more varied and dangerous over the years.

In order to deal with this life of emergency, residents have created and adopted ways to help them deal with the ever-present dangers. Their repertoire of praxes and humor, their worry about their children, and their ability to leave the area, when life becomes too much for them, have become intrinsic parts of their routines and habits. On the one hand, they exhibit creativity that helps turn the abnormal and toxic situation into "normal." On the other hand, they express awareness that these praxes and abilities are not part of what one should/could consider a normal life, as evidenced by their constant deliberation if they are living the kinds of lives they want for themselves and their children. Being caught between routine and emergency, with the emergency of the terror attacks and wars becoming more and more of their routine, extracts a high psychological price that demands continual adaptation to a life full of frightening uncertainties.

In short, the routine and emergency are always on *Otef Aza* residents' minds, and, thus, comprise one of the most meaningful lenses through which they understand their lives.

5

I Am My Others' Keeper: Mutual Concern, Belonging, Volunteerism, and Creation in the *Otef*

One verse from Genesis, in the *Tanach*,[1] states:

> Now Cain said to his brother Abel, "Let's go out to the field." While they were in the field, Cain attacked his brother Abel and killed him. Then the LORD said to Cain, "Where is your brother Abel?" "I don't know," he replied. "Am I my brother's keeper?" (Genesis 4: 8–9)

While this verse is often widely cited in the world, in our interviews, we found numerous references of the opposite—residents who felt deeply connected to their brothers and sisters, in general, and in *Otef Aza*, in specific. They talked about many acts of volunteerism, creation, and development, and about their strong sense of belonging to and concern for others in their own communities and in the region. The residents' engagement was expressed in diverse cultural, political, social, and community formats, and, at times, even endangered their lives. The interviewees, moreover, presented these behaviors and feelings as comprising much of their personal and collective lives.

---

[1] The Old Testament—the Jewish Bible.

© The Author(s), under exclusive license to Springer Nature Switzerland AG 2022
J. Chaitin et al., *Routine Emergency*, https://doi.org/10.1007/978-3-030-95983-8_5

How does this theme—of being there for others—connect to the meaning of life for residents of the region? In our analyses of the interviews, photographs, and social media materials, we found that many residents from all the different sectors (i.e., different ethnic backgrounds, younger and older, secular people, and religious people, from different political orientations and from different kinds of communities) emphasized mutuality, community togetherness, solidarity, volunteering, and the ability to see what the other/s needed. Therefore, for most of our sample, daily life was characterized as offering opportunities to give of oneself, even/especially in times of escalation of the violence. It was further noted that such behaviors were one way for the residents to cope with the stress and traumas related to the ongoing political violence. We also discerned that many people also talked about giving of themselves in connection to soldiers—a result that did not surprise us—given the centrality of the army and soldiers in Jewish-Israeli life.

While Israeli culture is characterized as a culture that values mutual aid and concern for the group (Birenbaum-Carmeli, 2001), the importance of caring for one's communal/regional brothers and sisters did not only appear to reflect this general culture, but rather the *Otef Aza* region, in specific. We found extensive expression of this mutual concern and support that tied specifically to the area, perhaps because of the dangers that the residents experience.

We now present examples from the different materials and analyses that reflect this theme, beginning with community solidarity.

Community Solidarity in the *Otef*

Noa, a 36-year-old mother of two, is from an urban *kibbutz*[2] in Sderot that she joined about seven years ago. Noa talked at length about the solidarity and the importance this community has for her and her family:

---

[2] Since the late 1980s, there has been a movement to establish *kibbutzim* in urban areas. In 1987, an urban *kibbutz* was established in Sderot.

[T]he *kibbutz* is not detached from society; it doesn't live in a bubble … they first … rented apartments and afterward, about 10 years, they moved to this street … they jointly purchased land on this street, which was empty … together they built this building (the community house) and they took joint mortgages … today there are 20 families that live on the same street and there's a very strong feeling of community. Every Friday we have a *kabbalat Shabbat*[3] and we eat dinner together … we celebrate holidays together … On Pesach we go camping together for four days … and the entire community is together … here there is very strong solidarity, one family … one of my neighbors had an operation that had complications; he was at death's door … and the entire community was harnessed, there was really amazing solidarity … a small, intimate community that's for us, it's much more meaningful, the connection that we have with the people here is very deep, it's a bit like an extended family … I feel that I have a deeper connection with most of the people here than I have with my extended family, and the kids grow up with kids of different ages and the big kids play with the little ones. It's a kind of paradise.

Rami, who was born and raised on the *kibbutz*, where he still lives, also spoke at length about the importance of solidarity and mutual concern in the *Otef*. In his interview, he emphasizes the change that he sees in his *kibbutz* concerning the focus on the individual's need, which he perceives as eating away at the solidarity and mutual concern that he finds so important. From his perspective, the growing bureaucracy and management have lost sight of "the person," and it is the person and the people that are important to him. This can explain his strong emotions when he talked about this topic:

I define myself as a person who **believes** in community, life in solidarity, support, the topic of mutual aid, I am very **socialistic** in my approach, and I believe in this value that is called mutual aid … I want **to see the other**, and I want to share things with him, and I want to know that the other sees me and what he needs, so yes! So, my grandparents' and my parents' very, very basic sentence "each one according to his needs and his ability and each one receives what he needs and gives what he can", **at the end of the day**, I completely agree with this! This doesn't match **whatsoever** how my

---

[3] A weekly (religious) ceremony on Friday evenings when Shabbat begins. Kabbalah = welcoming.

kibbutz is acting, from my perspective, because here there are many systems that organize … and regulate, but they don't see the person! … **I** believe in the person … I love the people here **very much, very much** … this disconnect hurts me … **the people interest me!**

Volunteering and Commitment to Life in the *Otef*

Volunteering: Helping Out in Many Ways

In the interviews, we found many instances of people who either volunteered in different ways in their communities and in the region, in general, or talked about how others engage in such volunteer work. For example, Ziona talked about the "grandmothers," who make hundreds of sandwiches every day, to give to soldiers traveling to and from their bases; Avi talked about the volunteering that many people do in Sderot in educational frameworks; Orna talked about a number of her volunteer activities, for example, with the Ethiopian immigrants, who live in the area; and Adva talked about how her sons have worked with youth, on the autism spectrum, in their town.

Adele, a 65-year-old secular, center-left woman from *kibbutz*, talked about volunteering undertaken in her community during the different wars. In addition, she spoke about her acts of volunteerism, which included mapping the fires in the region, working as a medical clown in the nearby hospital, and fighting for the rights of the residents, especially on campaigns to pressure the Israeli government to "see" the "invisible" residents, who have lived through years of war and terrorism. We begin with her words about the community organization and then present an example of her personal work:

> We began receiving *Kassams* then, and in 2006, they built the security rooms around the children's houses[4] … this is really the most organized community—throughout all of the operations, after Protective Edge, they

---

[4] *Kibbutzim* have children's houses—day care for children from infants through high school.

came to learn from us and talk to people here … because we really did organize well, and furthermore, the State didn't declare that this was a war and then there was the possibility that people would stay because it wasn't a closed army zone, so the people who were 80 said—it's frightening, it's really scary when they walk around here with their walkers and you know that there's no chance that they'll reach the *mamad*, and that's without mentioning that every morning we opened up the clubhouse, which is in a shelter, and they would come to the clubhouse and we'd bring all kinds of activities for them, but to think that when they were on the way to the clubhouse in their motorized carts, there could be a *tzeve adom* … there's nothing to be done … *Tzachi* always had a list of who was here, so they would know who was here and we would organize in our neighbourhoods and eat dinner together, people were really happy. On the morning of the 26th of August, when my home was hit, people came over and sat with me and helped me decide what to do.

When talking about the map of fires that she has created, so that people, in Israel and abroad, will understand what the fires are doing to the area, Adele said:

I see that there are many opportunities where we could have lost lives and I see people working here 24/7. You know, there were a few days when there were 20 fires and I'm mapping them and mapping them, and I said to myself: "Whoa—I'm so tired of this!!" and all of a sudden I thought, what am I complaining about? There are people here who are running from place to place in order to put out these fires and that's our people … some of them … that's their work, but most of them … there's a group of volunteers and each community has its group of volunteers, who do it 24/7.

Arieh, a 55-year-old center-left man from Sderot, also shared many instances of volunteering and helping others, because, in his words, "that's me." For over 25 years, Arieh worked in a local NGO and created and developed the program for helping disabled people in the community live independent lives. In addition, Arieh says that whenever anyone—in his family, in his circle of friends/colleagues, or in his town—needs help, they turn to him, a phenomenon that he finds very rewarding. In his interview, he also speaks about how people from Sderot are people who love to help others:

> I really, really love this place … **I grew** up here … I really love it here, really … **I really love this place**! I really love this place, the people, it's really important to me … my niece had a stroke! And here, I saw the community; **it's amazing!** You don't understand … this is daily support … daily, it's to come and do shifts … And you see them … if I show you the WhatsApp group, you simply won't believe it … I always say there are good people, there are good people … it's amazing! It's like, **loving to give**, it's people and it's traveling and it's money and it's time and it's a cross-section of her friends, it's young people with little children … they go on Friday and Saturday, it's holidays, and it's at night and in the day, and it's driving and everyone is **from here** … and to the hospital in Tel Aviv and it's gas and also parking and it's **also** time and work days … I can meet somebody from Sderot at Rosh Hanikra,[5] it doesn't matter where, immediately he offers you help, or in the army, I get to a base, and everybody, it's a small place! So, everyone, it's not that I'm his friend, I may never have even talked to him, the moment he knows that you're from Sderot, if he's in charge of equipment, so he gives you **extra equipment**, if he's in charge of the food, you get the best food, that's the way it is … I really love this place, I love it … I also **raised** my children **to really give** more than they get, that's the most … that's the part of **giving** … anyone who knows me, knows that I **really**, I really enjoy helping people … the moment that I hear that somebody has a problem, I **show up**! It's not a question if I will come or not or help or not, and I see this in my children … I see this with my kids, **always, always, always**, my kids know that it doesn't matter, if it's two o'clock in the morning, six in the morning, it doesn't matter when, I come to get them and it doesn't matter from where! … the children have always, always gotten used to the fact that we are always there to help them, to support them … my son chose to go to *Golani*,[6] it's not something to be taken for granted, today people don't only not volunteer for *Golani*, **they don't enlist at all!** … when I see what I did [with my kids], I see that I didn't do a bad job! In terms of their education, giving … this is a home

---

[5] A *kibbutz* in the north of Israel, near Lebanon.
[6] The *Golani* Brigade is under the command of the IDF's Northern Command. It is comprised of four battalions, and stationed throughout the West Bank and on each of Israel's borders. (See *Golani* Brigade—https://www.idf.il/en/minisites/golani-brigade/)

that is always, every child, every group, all his friends, it's here! … We'll do it! We will! We'll do it! … **it makes me feel good** to see that they don't only think about themselves! … it's automatic, every time that somebody needs something, it's me! … the help and the support and the caring … it's important that you know that really in a situation, it also gives a sense of security … I can't not help … I will invent the wheel, I will go out of my way, the moment that **someone** asks me for something, I must help … that's me.

Orna, a 50-year-old center-left, secular woman from a *moshav*, also presented many stories that connected to volunteering, in several frameworks. For example, she talked about the satisfaction she felt when hosting soldiers during Protective Edge. There is almost something humorous in Orna's words: she expresses great concern about taking care of soldiers during Protective Edge, when it was the soldiers who were supposed to be protecting the residents. This example demonstrates how connected Israeli civilians feel toward Israeli soldiers and how volunteering to help them appeared to Orna to be a very natural behavior:

I'll tell you an example that we had in the community … One of the soldiers in the *Golani* brigade is a resident here, and at the time, I was the head of the *moshav* committee. He called me and said that [the *Hamas*] was firing grad rockets and hitting ranges where the soldiers were and they didn't have any shelter and soldiers died as a result of this and he asked if our community, could take in [soldiers] and of course, without any hesitation, I said yes, but how will you take in 500 soldiers ((she chuckles)). So, I said "**Yes, come**!" And where will you put up 500 soldiers? How will you feed 500 soldiers? How will you worry about protecting them … so we recruited the school and they slept in the school. Look, this was enlistment of the community, the public pool … belongs to me and my husband, we've had the franchise for many years, and we donated it for their benefit. They would arrive in the morning and stay till the evening and they would have meetings and meals there … the residents, the moment they heard, I messaged them in the community group, "Guys … such and such a battalion is coming and everyone should help however they can" and you don't understand what happened. It was an evening in the middle of the week, the residents came … with food and things that they brought to the pool and the soldiers, they were welcomed with applause, and they simply took care of them … it makes you feel good and there was an atmosphere of being together in the community for the benefit of this thing and they were with us for about a week and then later on it was also to tell the residents that the officers were always telling me: "We want to watch over them because later we'll have to go back and we don't want them to get too spoiled because it will be hard for us to get them back to the routine of fighting … so stop loading them up, stop bringing them things" and to tell the residents "stop" and have them listen to you because the guys after-wards need to return to the front … there was cooperation between the army and the residents and the educational system, to sleep in the schools isn't something to be taken for granted … and then the parents [of the soldiers] also became arriving and it was during the period when soldiers from this brigade were killed, it was an awful period and all of a sudden parents knew that they were in good hands … people remember our com-munity as a place that was good to their children that took them out of the inferno … when you help one another, the soldiers protect us in this really significant period and we can help … we do what we can and everything is with mutuality … it was amazing.

Daniel, a 68-year-old religious left-wing man from a *kibbutz*, also touched on the topic of supporting soldiers, even though, in his inter-view, he strongly criticized idealization of the military in Israeli society. Therefore, his criticism of militarism and idealization of "generals," on the one hand, and expressing solidarity for Gilad Shalit—a soldier who was kidnapped by the *Hamas* and held in captivity in the Gaza Strip for five years—on the other, reflected how entrenched the importance of soldiers and the army are for Jewish-Israelis, in general, and for Jewish-Israelis who live near the Gaza border, in specific, and how criticism does not cancel out his worry about the soldiers. Daniel said:

I've lived through several wars, I was in the army and my children were in the army … but I'm a bit uneasy about sanctifying the army the way it is sanctified today … and the fact that every general is at the very least a Minister, if not the Prime Minister, is something that I am definitely uneasy about, I think it's excessive … there's a certain trend in the Israeli public to sanctify the army and everything connected to it, and not to be critical and accept every word as holy … I don't think that it's forbidden that an officer will become a politician, but the fact that it has become automatic, I think that we've suffered a lot and the country was burned by army people … because they were generals, they could go to the top of the political pyramid and it wasn't justified … [showing one of his photographs that he chose to share for the study] this was a performance that was part of the [events] working for the liberation of Gilad Shalit, here at Eshkol Park,[7] I think that Shlomo Artzi[8] also performed, and there were really diverse people and all kinds who came there … it's just a photograph of a lot of people, some of whom I knew, but most I didn't, who were here together … this is *Am Yisrael*,[9] for me patriotism is more about the people and the values that it holds and the multi-culturalism, which is found in the people.

Daniel shared his photograph (see Fig. 5.1) of an event that took place in the heart of *Otef Aza*, which was attended mainly by *Otef Aza* residents. To begin with, it is interesting that he said very little about the context of the photograph—the event for freeing Gilad Shalit—a soldier who had been kidnapped and was held in captivity by the Hamas in Gaza for five years—but rather concentrated on the diversity that he perceived in the audience. We also see the photo as reflecting his solidarity with and support of the soldiers. It is interesting that he took a shot which showcased women, as opposed to men (who more stereotypically connect to soldiers, even though women in Israel are also conscripted into the army). Furthermore, in the center, there is an empty blanket, which is pink (a color usually associated with girls and women). Perhaps this is symbolic of the missing soldier, who he perceived as being somewhat weak (given that he was in captivity) and the central, soft place that the attendees were holding for him. This blanket, located in the front center of the photograph, can also represent the central status that soldiers have in Jewish-Israeli society.

By sharing this photograph, Daniel might also be saying that, for him, alongside his "unease" with idealization of the army, he like many others

---

[7] On July 5, 2010, the Israeli Philharmonic Orchestra gave a concert to call for the release of Gilad Shalit, who, at the time, had been held by the Hamas for four years.
[8] A popular Israeli singer-songwriter.
[9] The People of Israel, Jews.

Fig. 5.1   Daniel—Happening for the Release of Gilad Shalit (July 5, 2010)

in the *Otef*, keep the soldiers in their minds and hearts. Therefore, when they are taken from them, in this specific conflict region, people from the region, from all backgrounds, come together to give of themselves and demonstrate their commitment to bringing the soldiers back.

Volunteering and Working: Even When Potentially Endangering Oneself

The idea of continuing to work, and specifically, volunteering, even when it puts the resident in danger, was a topic that came up in several interviews. One of the foci of this theme was the fires that had been caused by incendiary balloons and kites since 2018.

Tali, the *kibbutz* member, who was wounded in a *Kassam* rocket attack, was one of the interviewees who talked about the importance of giving of one's time for one's community and region, even if it is potentially dangerous. She talked about her brother's and nephews' volunteerism in helping put out the fires that, at the time, had destroyed much of the forest and agricultural land around their community and in *Otef Aza*:

> My brother … would go with his kids to help put out the fires, it was an afternoon activity. They would take the car and check where the fire began and would begin putting it out and actually this year, the fires are continuing, but last year, the situation was completely different, the situation was much more dangerous every day. Here, there was smoke and to go put out the fires, there was always a kind of solidarity like that, between all of the farmers. It doesn't matter if it was in the fields of the neighboring *kibbutz* or in ours. The famers organized, they tried every afternoon to put out the fires and that's dangerous, for the person and that was the attempt to save the fields and to prevent the fire from reaching the roads.

Hila, a 40-year-old center-left woman from a moshav, who described herself as spiritual, also talked about the fires and about the people in the *Otef Aza* region, who risk their lives to work their fields, even when facing the dangers of the fires. One of her photos (Fig. 5.2) reflected the significance of such commitment, in her opinion. Hila said this about the photo:

> We see a tractor and in the background there's a fire and he's working in the fields and I love this area so much because in each season, the landscape has a different color and different smells, there's something really beautiful about this area … from the moment they began with incendiary balloons, the landscape changed its color and became completely black and that sucks … most of the area is a rural area and tractors go out to plow, it doesn't matter what's happening, in my opinion, that is the epitome of our strength and power, facing the fire, the Israeli flag arrives and it's waving and I think that the strength of *Am Yisrael* is also in our ability to survive … and our challenge … is to stand strong against this and be strong enough to say we are a bit weak, but still very proud of this place.

The next example (see Fig. 5.3) of this aspect of volunteerism comes from the interview with Ziona—a 71-year-old center-right, secular woman from a *moshav*. Ziona stressed the camaraderie created among the

Fig. 5.2 Hila—Tractor Working in a Burning Field (2019)

people who volunteer. She, too, shared a photo of volunteering to fight the fires:

> These are the guys who go and put out the fires that the Gazans send with their balloons or their kites, in addition to their work, they also took it upon themselves to protect the home of the people, of what exists and that connects to Israeli patriotism because as I told you, we are like ants. They are doing that with the fire … everyone creates the circle of friends and becomes solidified.

These two photographs are typical photographs of *Otef Aza*: photos such as these are often found on social media, and four of our interviewees chose pictures that focused on the topic of the fires and firefighting. In Hila's photograph, we see a tractor with an Israeli flag that is centered between the orange fire and a dry field. It is impossible to see the driver of the tractor. Therefore, one interpretation of this photo is that Hila wanted to convey that the particular person is unimportant, but rather that this is the context of all/most of the farmers in the *Otef,* and that,

Fig. 5.3 Ziona—Putting out a Fire (January 2019)

furthermore, this is not only a local battle, but rather an Israeli battle. This is like Ziona's photo—here we also only see the back of the firefighter, which, again, emphasizes that the particular firefighter is unimportant, but rather one of many. Furthermore, the tractor and the firefighter are in the center of the photos—they are major actors in the burning fields of *Otef Aza*. In both photos, furthermore, it is impossible to know what time of day it is, conveying the message that the fires can occur throughout the day or night and, thus, are a constant danger. In sum, the photos, along with the interviewees' words, highlight the sacrifice and camaraderie seen by *Otef Aza* residents as characteristic of the region in which they have chosen to live.

Ofra, a 58-year-old secular, center-left woman from a *moshav*, talked about another topic that connected to volunteerism for the good of others—the work of *Tzachi*—that was noted by interviewees in our study and in the social media. Among other volunteer acts, Ofra headed *Tzachi* for many years. In her I-poem, Ofra presents the heavy responsibility on her shoulders, and her choice to put herself in danger. In her words, "I don't understand how to live without this":

Ofra's I-poem
I'm the one who puts the people into the *mamad*
I'm the one who makes the announcements
I'm the one who takes control
I have people
…
I'm busy day and night
I have no family
I have no work
Why do I do this?
And I think
When I'm busy
When I have a role
I don't have the time
Because I'm the one responsible
And I need to function
I don't have the privilege of being afraid
…
I will cope
I don't run away
I can choose
I say that I won't run away
I've had situations in my life
I have a story of One Thousand and One Nights
…
It's not a question if I'll leave the house or not
Of course, I'll leave the house
I'm aware
That I could die
I'll leave the house
I'll put on the vest and helmet and go
I'm always aware of the danger
I'm aware that there are bad people
I'm aware that there are terrorists
I'm also aware that there's another side

I'll save a small child
I think we came to this universe
In order to give and help
I don't understand how to live without this

Avi, a 48-year-old right-center religious man from Sderot, talked at length in his interview about the importance of education and socialization toward values that make his children, and other young people in Sderot, "special." He talked about the economic sacrifices that he has made: for years he worked in high-tech, making a high salary, but decided to make a change, go into education, and live in Sderot, instead of in the center of the country, where life would be safer and more comfortable. One of the photographs that he chose (see Fig. 5.4) focused on the topic

Fig. 5.4 Avi—Young Leadership in Sderot (2019)

of young leadership in Sderot that volunteers, even during times of imminent danger. This is what he said about his photograph:

> This is a picture that I took … a month before Protective Edge, I was given responsibility for the youth here in Sderot, and then Protective Edge began. I didn't know that it would happen, and we discovered amazing youth here, youth that could have been … broken and destroyed, 200, 300 teenagers who really challenged us, in a good way, that is, alongside many youth who are destroyed … that's very logical in this reality, Protective Edge was in 2014, that is, 2013 was already a year of attrition … the youth who were 15 to 18, youth who grew up in this reality … here there are mainly teens from the religious youth movement … who wanted to come everywhere and help. They went to the hospitals, to funerals … they went to people and cleaned their houses, they went out with groups in the street to make people happy, we brought them special shirts, and then the war of attrition began in Be'er Sheva and Ashdod, there were … a lot of rockets in these areas … and they said that they're going now, some of their parents called me and said "Listen, it's dangerous" and I told them that they should decide; I'm not forcing anyone … "I'll be there myself with them." We were 76 people … after they sat there for a few days and prepared kits for working with the children, we went to one of the neighbourhoods in Be'er Sheva, they took kids from 10 buildings; they went house by house so the parents could shower, parents who hadn't showered for a few days. It's crazy, they cleaned the bomb shelters—**something nuts**—you need to understand that the youth of Sderot, who had every reason to be devastated, became the leader and that's amazing, they also had every reason to get themselves out of there and go to stay in a free *zimmer*,[10] we were offered a lot of these, and in the picture we see a few kids who are running an activity for other children and someone is standing with her back to us and we see the writing on the shirts that they made for them.

As in the photographs from Hila and Ziona, in Avi's photo, as well, we do not see the faces of the teenage girls who ran the activity, nor the faces of most of the children. Perhaps Avi wanted to safeguard the anonymity of the teens and children. However, as in the previous photos, perhaps the message is that the particular people are less important than the overall idea—young people in Sderot are giving of themselves to help

---

[10] A 'room' (from the German/Yiddish—adopted in Hebrew slang)—a rustic bed-and-breakfast type of vacation venue.

children, even during rocket attacks. Here, as opposed to the other two photos, we have young women (as opposed to adult men), who are undertaking this serious task—keeping children occupied and happy, when facing danger on a daily basis. The words on the shirt—which is in white and blue, hence reminiscent of the Israeli flag—say: Sderot Youth. Leadership. Initiative. Responsibility.

Our last example from this sub-theme comes from the umbrella group of activist groups in the *Otef Aza* region, called Unity with the South (established in 2019). This organization's main goal is to make the residents of the region less "invisible" to the government leaders and has concentrated mainly on calling for leaders to take action that would bring quiet to the region.

In this post (see Fig. 5.5), from December 22, 2019, however, the group turned to an international figure, Fatou Bensouda, the chief prosecutor of the International Criminal Court. They invited her to come to *Otef Aza* and see the violation of the residents' human rights and the war crimes being carried out by the *Hamas* against Israeli citizens with her own eyes. They called upon her to open an investigation into these crimes that, at the time, had been going on for 19 years, instead of considering prosecution of the IDF, whom they perceive as solely protecting residents of the border region.

The post included a poster. On the top of the poster are the logos of the regional councils and Sderot. The poster is red, with sketchings of buildings faintly in the background, and includes a white font that appears to be full of bullet holes. The red can be seen as representing blood, and the letters in white as disintegrating from the rocket attacks. This appears to be an analogy of a war-torn area that is being decimated and wounded. The big buildings suggest that a large civilian population is being attacked. The poster and post contain strong metaphors often used by *Otef* residents, when talking/writing about the *Hamas* and/or splinter militant groups: war crimes, violation of human rights, rocket attacks, trauma, and the IDF. The language, furthermore, is concise and strong.

The message that the post and the poster convey is that Hamas and the splinter groups are committing war crimes against innocent people in the *Otef* and, as a result, the chief prosecutor is mistaken about who is the aggressor—it is the *Hamas* that has been carrying out a very bloody war against innocent citizens, which the IDF and regional leaders are trying

Fig. 5.5 Unity with the South—"Firing at Israeli Citizens Is a War Crime" (December 2019)

to protect. In sum, then, the poster/post conveys the message that the chief prosecutor of the ICC is ignoring the real perpetrator, and it needs to change this mistaken behavior and prosecute the real war criminals.

In sum, volunteering and helping others, who are being bombed and whose land is being destroyed by fires, was a theme that appeared to be central for several interviewees. This theme was found across the sample, reflecting the words of men and women, of different ages, from all kinds of communities, and religious and political orientations in the *Otef*.

Such work and volunteerism appear to be an important source of meaning for residents. It appears to us that volunteering, especially the kind that often places people in danger, is a way for residents to promote and express their sense of agency. While not having the ability to end the intractable war, through their volunteerism, they express the notion that they are far from passive victims of the Israeli-*Hamas* conflict. Instead, by talking about and engaging in this work, they convey that they are both willing and able to contribute, in order to make their region a desirable place to live.

Creation and Development in the *Otef*

Another topic noted in the interviews was the creation and development of projects that aimed to make residents' lives better, more interesting, and more meaningful, in the *kibbutzim*, *moshavim*, villages and towns. The interviewees discussed initiatives that they had undertaken to make the area a place where residents would want to continue to live, despite the dangers from the ongoing war. That is, people did not only speak about creating and/or developing institutions, services and communities for their personal gain, but rather for communal benefit.

For example, Zohar, a 65-year-old man who has lived in Sderot since he was an infant, has been developing initiatives for the town since he was in his teens. As a teenager, together with other youth, they published a newspaper about and for youth. As a young man, he helped establish the Sapir College and has been working there ever since, developing the pre-academic track for people from diverse backgrounds, and later headed the Diversity in Academia program, which is part of the national *Tikva Yisraelit* program.[11] Furthermore, he was one of the founders of the Sderot Cinematheque—which he sees as an institution that enriches the lives of the Sderot residents, as well as the neighboring rural communities.

A second example comes from Ronen, a secular man from a *kibbutz*, who defined himself as left-wing. Much of Ronen's interview focused on his deep desire to develop himself and others in his community and in

---

[11] *Tikvah Yisraelit*—Israeli Hope in Academia—was launched in 2016, as an initiative of President Rivlin. The program aims for enhanced diversity, representation, and cultural competence within academic institutions, so that graduates will embody values of diversity, equality, and justice as citizens and in their future employment.

Israeli society. For example, during his military service, Ronen worked with young soldiers who had dropped out of school and/or grew up in neglected neighborhoods. In addition to his volunteering, his professional life is in the field of mental health. As a young adult, Ronen wanted very much to live in a *kibbutz*, a place which he thought had "potential," a place in which he could contribute. While he considered moving to a young kibbutz, Ronen chose to move to an older *kibbutz*, since it offered him the opportunity to move things forward, from the "crossroads," in which the community was situated. As he notes, such a move gave meaning to his life:

I was looking for a *kibbutz* where I could have influence from the beginning, a younger *kibbutz* ... the *kibbutz* where I live ... it's a different culture ... I love distant and backwater places, places where nobody wants to be, but what I did find in my *kibbutz* is exactly the opposite, the visionary side in me, the initiative side in me. I saw this *kibbutz* as being at a crossroads. Then, there wasn't a freeway in both directions ... there was a narrow road, there were between four to five busses a day ... there wasn't a train, it really sounds to me like a pioneering story now ... I came to a place like this where I see a lot, a lot of potential ... I see the crossroads, I see that here, things will be developed, I knew that there would be an educational center ... I saw the potential of the regional school ... I said "It won't be bad here. Worst case scenario, if we don't manage with the *kibbutz*, we'll manage with the area", and Sderot, I was never afraid of development towns ... I knew that I wanted to be in a region that is diverse and interesting ... I'm a person who's always creating and searching ... searching for meaning ... I decided to take it upon myself to connect the *kibbutz's* cultural activities and the community center in the town nearby, to be the go-between ... to transmit information between the two and, from time to time, to initiate mutual invitations ... that connection led to my participation in regional activities ... and that's how I found myself being like I imagined myself, as a very active person, a multifarious person, which is very fulfilling ... all of the creative powers are found in people, we have a beautiful area here ... there are strips of beautiful sea here, there could be bustling tourism ... [there's] an integration of diverse cultures here, great diversity, suddenly there's room for the Karaites[12] and there's room for the different streams of Islam … place for different streams of Jews, there are *Charedim* and … *Mizrahim* and then all this diversity can produce here folklore … each person can develop himself, there can be a blossoming of education, everything can blossom here … clean industry, less traffic jams … more gardens … there can really be something fantastic in this area, because of the amazing diversity we have here.

Another example of initiative and development comes from Asher, a 73-year-old center, secular man from a *moshav*. Asher has been a farmer most of his life. In the 1970s, he and his wife helped found a *moshav* in the Sinai desert that was eventually returned to Egypt, as part of the 1978 Camp David Accords. When they understood that they were to be evacuated, he and others in his group looked for a new place to create a *moshav*, and they settled in the Eshkol region.

Here is Asher's We-poem, which focuses on the creation of the new *moshav* and the central place that creating a *moshav* "from scratch" and developing it into a big, thriving community has had in his life. In his interview, Asher almost always used the pronoun "we," as opposed to "I." That is, it appears as if Asher tends to think in collective terms, emphasizing how important being part of a group is for him and that he understands creation and development as possible when people work together on a valued collective initiative that enhances the area:

Asher's We-poem

We were a group from the *garin*[13]
We joined the first *garin*
We settled in Sadot
We were farmers
We had to evacuate in April 82
We travelled throughout the country
We looked for possibilities
We found a slot

---

[12] The Karaites belong to a non-mainstream group in Judaism that sees the written Torah as the sole authority for *halakha*—Jewish law.

[13] Literally, a core or a seed, used to denote a group of people who establish a new communal kind of community

We established a new community
We are a very big community
...
We are in *Otef Aza*
...
Here there's a climate and land
That we know
The only one we could immediately settle
...
We collected
Ran around
And planned it by ourselves
We collected members
We determined for ourselves
That we are making the infrastructure
...
We took guarantees from people
We said that we're not going to act recklessly
As soon as we reached 65
We began to make progress
We jumped up to 155
...
We did
What we thought about doing
We planned the shape of the community
...
We did all
That we thought was right
We upheld the agreements
We did everything
That we committed to
Everything that we committed to doing
...
Since then, we've done other projects
We completed the project
The best that we could
...

The final example comes from the interview with Ovadia, a 78-year-old secular, center man from a *moshav*, right on the border with the Gaza Strip. Ovadia was born in Egypt and lived there until he was 16, when the Egyptians expelled the Jews around the time of the 1956 war between Israel and Egypt. Ovadia eventually became an agronomist and a specialist in crops and irrigation that interested Egyptian farmers. His family, like Asher's, also lived in a *moshav* in the Sinai desert, which was evacuated when the Sinai was returned to the Egyptians as part of the 1978 Camp David Accords. Because he was born in Egypt, and hence, fluent in Arabic, Ovadia was asked by the Israeli Ministry of Foreign Affairs and the Ministry of Agriculture to be an emissary in Egypt and work with the government and farmers to develop their agriculture. As a result, Ovadia and his wife and their five children lived in Egypt for five years. After their return to the new *moshav*, now within Israel's recognized borders, Ovadia worked with a local NGO and led numerous training courses that brought Egyptian and Gaza farmers into Israel in order to get advanced agricultural training. Ovadia said:

> In 82 we left our community in Sinai, and we knew we would come to the present-day *moshav* because of a few aspects. (a) The euphoria of the peace was very high, and we wanted to contribute to the cooperation between us and our neighbors … we thought it might happen, and in the beginning it did, but later on, with the increase in terror, the roads from Gaza to Israel were closed and we were left in the *moshav*, separated completely from Gaza … when we settled here, it was very hard … but we decided to settle here close to the border and not somewhere else where we could have enjoyed relative quiet, for we hoped that our relations with the Palestinians would come to fruition and we could do joint activities for peace, that was the vision … my wife today works for peace and I respect this, I like this and I help her as much as I can … when we returned to Israel [after living in Egypt], I continued my work in training programs for thousands of Egyptian academics who settled on new land in the western part of the desert and they came to this house. The group would come here: 50 people would come here to me. I host them, *ahalan wa'sahalan*,[14] I greet them and take them to the training courses … and we set up centers, one in Bror

---

[14] "Welcome" in Arabic.

Hayil[15] ... we hosted more than 3500 people ... and we expanded the activities to trainings for Palestinians and Jordanians and there was partnership for this activity ... we called it a Regional Project ... this was a special experience to see this cooperation, the wish to be in touch with one another and to study and we were happy to do this work and it succeeded beautifully ... we live in a community that's very special. It accepts differences and the relations between the members, you can say, are excellent—mutual help, support, joint concern for the seniors, for the young adults, for the youth ... the opinions differ and you can understand this, but there is no hate because of the different opinions ... we respect one another and love one another ... we'll continue to hold on even during the hard times and, in my opinion, this is our contribution to the country that needs secure borders.

In summation of this sub-theme, we see that another way that *Otef Aza* residents give of themselves for others is through creation and development in their communities and in the region. Residents find it important to create communities and institutions "from scratch," as this gives meaning to their personal and communal lives. They express pride in their initiatives, emphasizing the high-quality joint work with others, and the contributions that it brings to the area, on the social-cultural levels. While some of this work is mainly internal—such as the creation of a *moshav* for Israelis and building connections between a *kibbutz* and a development town—other work also has an external component—such as Ovadia's peace work with Egyptians and Gazans.

Chapter Summary

As noted above, many of our interviewees appeared to see caring for their communities' brothers and sisters as having great significance for their personal and collective lives. They expressed concern not only for their families, which of course would be expected, but also for their communities, the entire *Otef Aza* region, and, also, at times, the greater *Otef Aza*-Gaza region. This care, solidarity, giving, and creation and development

---

[15] One of the *kibbutzim* in the *Otef.*

did not take place in a safe, quiet environment, but rather in a context of ongoing war and terrorism. We found it interesting—and inspirational—to hear so many stories of giving without asking for anything in return, especially when people put themselves in physical danger to safeguard others.

We could have expected that since the residents live in such a dangerous environment, they would concentrate on their and their families' survival, with little energy and resources to think and help others. However, we found the opposite. The interviewees emphasized their love of the area and the people, and their deep sense of belonging. We understood their stories of giving as reflecting this love and sense of belonging, as well as the need to engage in "doing." We further propose that residents' choice to engage in so much "doing" helps them cope with the ongoing stress and traumas that they face.

We now turn to the next theme that we found in our analyses—the State of the Western Negev versus the State of Israel.

Reference

Birenbaum-Carmeli, D. (2001). Between individualism and collectivism: The case of a middle class neighborhood in Israel. *The International Journal of Sociology and Social Policy, 21*(11), 1–25.

6

The State of the Western Negev Versus the State of Israel

Look, first of all, that war [Protective Edge] was on the second of July; everyone counts the 50 days, from the beginning of the invasion etc. etc. We were hit here for 10 days without any response, nothing, people didn't understand. People lived here, they were bombing us and no one did anything. The army is completely quiet: there are no clear instructions concerning what it should be doing, it doesn't even shoot back, doesn't respond, nothing. That is, we count 60 days, but during those first 10 days, the residents were beseeching me: "Why don't you give an interview?" The media doesn't want us, like, it's uninteresting; we're not interesting, like, we don't exist.

(Haim, former head of the Eshkol Regional Council, a 62-year-old secular man from a *kibbutz*)

In this chapter, we focus on *Otef Aza* residents' emotions and thoughts regarding what they perceive as the Israeli governments' and media's abandonment of them, as well as the "cold shoulder" that some of them feel come from Jewish-Israelis from other parts of the country. This topic, which appeared in a number of the interviews and was very prominent in the social media materials created by residents, reflected the strong sense of disappointment, frustration, and anger of residents toward the

J. Chaitin et al., *Routine Emergency*, https://doi.org/10.1007/978-3-030-95983-8_6

country's leaders, journalists, and citizens, who residents saw as not seeing them. In Adele's words, *Otef Aza* residents are "invisible."

In this chapter, we present examples that reflect this disappointment, frustration, and anger, and the different ways in which the residents express their criticism, as well as the ways in which residents experience governmental policy, or, as most of them say, the lack of policy. We found that people used different strategies to express their sense that the Western Negev was actually a "State" of its own, separate from the State of Israel, since they felt that they were ignored, and only remembered when there was a war or severe escalation in rocket attacks.

One strategy that residents used was humor and satire, often expressed in the social media materials. Another strategy was to produce films, which often included women and children, documenting demonstrations or videos made especially for the social media. These video clips focused on the message that the government had the responsibility to find a solution to the terror attacks and end the suffering of innocent victims. In addition to these strategies, our interviewees also talked about these feelings concerning the ways in which the government not only ignored their suffering, but also related to them as pawns in a game.

As we demonstrate below, the aspects of this theme contain emotions of despair, frustration, anger, and disappointment, mainly toward the government, then toward residents from other regions in the country, and mainstream media. These emotions were expressed in different ways, such as satire, protests, and voices that arose from our interviewees.

We begin with the aspect of being invisible to the government.

"Please Shoot a Missile at Tel Aviv": Frustration, Anger, and Disappointment with the Israeli Government

Gal is a 35-year-old politically center, secular woman who lives in Ashkelon. In her interview, she talks about how the Israeli government's policies and actions change, according to the targets of the rockets, with what she perceives as clear discrimination against *Otef Aza* residents.

When reflecting on this issue, her frustration overcomes her and she "longs" for an attack on a major city in Israel, like Tel Aviv, because then she believes the government would change its usual pattern of ignoring the pain of the *Otef* residents, and take serious actions against the attackers:

> You say "I'm not worth anything anymore", if it used to be "Ho! Now they're shooting at a city of one hundred and fifty thousand people,"[1] then today those one hundred and fifty thousand people are not worth being treated seriously, unless they will start to shoot northward. It has often been so frustrating that we would laugh here … the escalations started … and we'd say "Come on, come on, please shoot a missile at Tel Aviv, a missile at Tel Aviv", just so the government would do something about it … we would actually say "please shoot at Tel-Aviv" and then we would know that they would do something about it. It's a terrible feeling, that the country is abandoning you, that you're being told you're less important … There's also this thing that they constantly say "*Otef Aza*", and in the end, you feel like you are "*Otef Yisrael*", because you're the layer that protects Israel, Tel Aviv and such from Gaza, you envelop Israel so that it won't be attacked.

The next example comes from Avi, a 48-year-old religious man, with right-center political views, who lives in Sderot. Avi, as opposed to Gal, demonstrates how the residents' emotions of abandonment and solitude have led, in some cases, to the creation of strength and empowerment in the local communities. Avi's We-poem, presented below, expresses the journey he perceives was made by *Otef Aza* residents, who began as victims, but have become activists, working for a normal life, since they see the Israeli government as failing to offer a sustainable solution. In addition, Avi claims that the government does not see the area as economically viable. Therefore, he avers—six times in his interview—that the region needs to be transformed into a viable economic region. From Avi's perspective, only then will the political echelon begin to take *Otef Aza* residents seriously.

The We-poem also expresses a process of awakening. At first, Avi uses words that symbolize weakness and helplessness, perhaps in order to

---

[1] Referring to Ashkelon.

convey the feelings that arise due to their dire situation, for example, "we felt," "sufferers," and "we're in an ongoing trauma." The next stage includes words that indicate activism, mixed with anger, and even rage, for example, "threatening," "block," "we'll just stop," and "get out of there." At the end of the poem, Avi presents his understanding of the results of this struggle: the residents exhibit resilience and are strong. They demonstrate that "we move on," "we are one hundred percent enlisted here," and "we'll continue to fight."

Avi's We-poem

…
We felt that stress
We are now 18 years
…
If we won't be here, everyone will leave
…
We're here in Sderot
We explain to the whole world
That we're in ongoing trauma
…
We were twenty-four thousand inhabitants
And we went down to eighteen thousand
We have a mission
We had to get to Tel Aviv
…
We're the great sufferers
We'll pay for it
We're just moving away
[we didn't] say that we got used to it
…
We felt 18 years on our shoulders,
we went to bed at twelve at night
Knowing we're headed for a long [war of] attrition
…
We're in a period
We're in "go-no go"
We're not economically viable
We're threatening the government

And we'll block the country,
We'll go to Ayalon[2] today
...
We'll stop our vehicles
We'll take out the keys
And we'll get out of there
Then we'll become economically viable,
So we are economically viable
Then we'll be economically viable
And we move on
We're one hundred percent enlisted
In life, we have to sacrifice
We will continue to fight

As we can see, Avi notes at the end of his poem the necessity that the collective "we" sacrifices themselves, in order to change the current situation.

Our next interviewee, Yoni, a 36-year-old religious man who lives in a village, also referred to this willingness of his. He addressed the lack of governmental policy regarding what he sees as the only solution for this conflict—a military one. Furthermore, he states that he is even willing to risk his own life, if necessary:

Until the State of Israel decides that we're going to solve the problem of Gaza ... even if we will have five hundred dead, five hundred dead soldiers, that's what they say we'll need to solve Gaza's problem. Until then, it's just another round and another round. In the end, someone will have to make this decision that we end this story and the more we postpone it, the greater the price will be ... If in the next five years there is leadership here that decides it's going to finish this story, then it's great, and secondly I believe I'm willing to pay this price, if it needs to be me, then I have no problem paying this price for it to end ... It's a disgrace that a country allows such a reality, just a disgrace, you understand. [They're] afraid of the price ... if the price is five hundred killed and that's what will end this story, so I'm ready to be a part of this. It's not my personal question; if the country asks me to pay this price, then I'll happily pay it, I have no problem paying it ...

---

[2] The main expressway through Tel Aviv.

I strongly believe that you should always look at the long-term in anything, the more you look at the long-term … it's reassuring and it is also creates certainty.

Magia Lanu: We Deserve It (?) (!)

Our next example comes from Ronit, a 46-year-old secular woman who lives in a *kibbutz*. In a photo that she shared (see Fig. 6.1), Ronit is writing graffiti on a bomb shelter on a road near her *kibbutz* with the words *Magia Lanu*—we deserve it. This slogan represents an initiative of local activists, who wanted to call attention to the plight of the State of the Negev, and here it has a double meaning.

First, it can be addressed to the decision-makers, by confronting them with the reality of terror attacks, asking if *Otef Aza* residents deserve to continue living in such a dangerous reality. In this case, the sentence would end with a question mark (Do we deserve it?). Secondly, it can be

Fig. 6.1   Ronit—*Magia Lanu* (We Deserve It) (2020)

interpreted as an act for raising awareness among area residents, by calling upon them to take responsibility for their own future—since the government obviously has not. In that case, if the residents do not act, the slogan could end with an exclamation mark—reflecting the notion that they deserve what they are getting, for not putting constant pressure on the government to solve the conflict (We deserve it!). Furthermore, the slogan is written in red, as a message of danger, and as a symbol of the *tzeve adom* often heard in the area.

By writing graffiti on a shelter, with this question mark-exclamation mark, Ronit expresses her frustration at being part of a sector that has withstood war for 20 years, with no end in sight. In addition to frustration, it also reflects a mixture of emotions: helplessness (?), anger (! ?), a plea for help (?) and a call for action (!).

The next example comes from the video clip produced by "Israeli Movement," a grassroots organization that wants to symbolically return to 1948 and create a state that has a political system that works for all of its citizens—Jews and Arabs. The clip is titled *Tzeva Adom* (August 2019).

This 48-second video (Fig. 6.2) presents a girl, who has spent her life, running for her life. It shows her at ages 3, 10, 14, and 18, and the last frame contains a sound of a missile exploding with the words on the screen: "18 years of *tzeva adom*, 3 prime ministers, 7 defense ministers, 3 wars, 0 solutions. Do you think we're moving in the right direction?" The girl is symbolically wearing a red dress and a white shirt, reflective of the *tzeva adom* (red color) and innocence (white). The soundtrack of the video clip is the siren and the girl's breathing.

This powerful short video can first be understood as a call to the Israeli government, as it shows that during these 18 years of attacks, decision-makers have not worked to find a true solution. Secondly, the video can also be seen as turning to the Israeli public, in an attempt to raise awareness regarding the fact that children, who were born into this life-threatening reality, have never known a peaceful reality. In short, this film sends the message that by continuing to ignore the dangerous reality of the region, an entire generation has been harmed, and may even harm the next one.

The grassroots group Unity with the South produced a number of short video clips that aimed to raise awareness in the larger public

Fig. 6.2 *Tzeve Adom* (Israeli Movement)

concerning the years of suffering of *Otef Aza* residents, and to hold the Israeli government responsible for not solving the crisis. Here, we present one of these clips (Fig. 6.3).

In the clip, the presenter is filmed in such a way that her image looks pale, almost transparent. Here, she expresses the residents' emotions of being invisible and unimportant to the government and, perhaps, to other Jewish-Israelis throughout the country. She turns to the viewers and asks, "Are you there?" "Do you see me?" The women then explains that her—that is, *Otef Aza's*—feelings of solitude derive from the fact that people, from all sides of the political map, accuse the *Otef Aza* residents for voting for the "other camp," and even claim that they deserve to live with the dangers. Then, she complains of being the "bulletproof vest" of the country, while also "getting punched" (by the *Hamas*, the Israeli government, and Jewish-Israelis from outside the region). The clip finishes with the appeal to *see* her and the residents of the region, to see their suffering, hear their demand for a normal life, and to join and support *Otef Aza* residents in their struggle.

Fig. 6.3   Invisible—Unity with the South (2019)

The next initiative, aimed at getting government officials to take action, tied into the idea of *Magia Lanu*, and was called *Tnu Ligdol b'Sheket.*[3] On November 4, 2018, over 100 high school students from *Otef Aza* embarked on a protest march, from the Eshkol region to Jerusalem, which was supported by the teens' parents and teachers. Since the initiators were adolescents, we did not interview them (our study focused on adults). However, since this initiative was posted on many social media sites by adults from the region and noted by a few interviewees, we present it here.

Roi Rahaf, from Kibbutz Mefalsim, one of the initiators of the march, explained the reasons for the action, which created media interest in the serious dangers faced by the area's youth:

---

[3] Literally—Let us grow up in quiet. See: Matan Tzuri (November 8, 2018). Gaza vicinity youth march reaches Jerusalem. *Ynet.* https://www.ynetnews.com/articles/0,7340,L-5392985,00.html provides a newspaper report in English.

After the last weekend we spent at home, which was really difficult, and, in general, everything we've gone through for years, we decided to organize this march to Jerusalem. Our goal is to emphasize that a solution can be found, that we're not transparent, that we deserve a normal regular childhood, like that of any other child in this country.

This march created solidarity among students in the rest of the country: they uploaded pictures of themselves to different social media with signs containing messages of support and solidarity. Some of these teens even joined the march. Another organizer of the march, Alon Levy, explained his motives for creating this protest:

> This isn't a political campaign; we want the citizens of Israel to know about our situation, we want to live like everyone else. We have a Facebook page and Instagram of the trip, and we invite teenagers from all over the country to join us.

Another similar voice of criticism, against the government, came from Tamara, a 73-year-old secular woman from Sderot who defined herself as being politically in the center. Tamara criticized the Israeli government for not taking any actions to solve the ongoing crisis. Furthermore, she described how there is apathy about the *Otef Aza* reality, that she has, sadly, even identified among residents of the area. Tamara feels that residents of the region have given up trying to change their situation, perhaps due to their unsuccessful attempts to do so in the past. In addition, and as we showed earlier regarding the area's youth protest, Tamara said that living in such an emergency routine has a significant influence on children, for example, when they develop anxiety symptoms. Moreover, she notes that despite the difficulties residents experience in their daily lives, the population in Sderot is growing. In sum, based on her experiences, Tamara puts little faith in the government, and sees the region's residents as being the only ones who can bring about a change. However, she simultaneously feels that residents have lapsed into a helplessness that keeps them trapped in an intractable conflict:

I don't know if it's possible to get used to such a situation, because we heard from prime ministers and others. Every time a rocket fell, then someone came and assured us that it is the last *Kassam* that will fall in Sderot, and that it's outrageous, because we have a problem with the children. It's quite scary. They are hurt and I saw it. I saw the bed wetting … and also the children's outbursts of rage that couldn't be explained. There's no reason for it, and aggression that we had to deal with. Children who would throw chairs at friends; it's not something a three-year-old should be doing … friends I met say that it's still hard, because when the mother is pregnant, the fetus also absorbs everything … I don't like to say it, but I just don't believe in the government. Either they don't want to or they cannot [change the situation]. I think they have ability; I think they have it, but not so much desire, and we're just being abandoned. In Sderot, the population is abandoned because we've been hit the hardest, we and the region. Now, I talked to someone who lives in Ashkelon and he says that now they suffer and often [the media] does not inform them at all about what is happening. I don't know why it's like that. Maybe it's because … we're silent … I used to go to demonstrations, and we would close the roads and burn tires and David Buskila (Sderot's mayor at that time) handcuffed himself at the Knesset and we set up a tent there. Now, I don't know if people are tired, but I still don't agree with it. I'm not comfortable with it personally, because I keep asking why if we go 40 miles from here there is a different life out there. Don't you feel it? You never felt it? That Tel Aviv and Rishon Letzion is neither Sderot nor Ashkelon, or even Ashdod? So, I don't know. A lot of people have left, and when Alon Davidi (the current mayor) arrived, then they started coming back. So now you know, if they hit Sderot, they hurt a large population … when we arrived there were 7000 residents here in Sderot and now it is 34 [thousand].

The next example comes from the interview with Micha, a 55-year-old traditional, center-left man who lives in a *moshav*. He describes the chain of events that led him to ask himself questions regarding Israel's leadership and how committed it is for his safety:

Questions like: "Is this area important to anyone?" We felt very disconnected, as if this is our problem, and then the concept of *Otef Aza* was born, because, at first, only Sderot was mostly hit, and then it [the rockets] had longer range, and [hit] more settlements and then … you feel the damage to morale, security and economics. And also mainly, you have this feeling that you are not being counted. I mean promises, promises, all kinds of politicians would come and threaten the other side, "If and if and if they continue to shoot" … until the first operation that was Cast Lead, and after that we thought it would solve the matter, but it really didn't solve the issue. On the contrary, it only increased and increased the circles of hatred … We saw no solution on the horizon and more than that, we lost confidence in the army and the government and politicians.

As noted above, when trying to get the government to notice the *Otef* residents and to solve the conflict, residents have often expressed their emotions and thoughts in creative ways, using humor and satire to convey their message. Many of the posts and video clips on Facebook and YouTube are highly creative, with one main message to the Israeli leaders: *We are here. You are responsible and doing nothing. What are you going to do?* Here are some examples.

In February 2020, the right-hand "map" presented in Fig. 6.4 appeared on Facebook. This "map" was a spoof of the official IDF Homefront map—presented on the left. The original map defines each area, according to distance from the Gaza Strip, and the number of seconds that people have to find shelter during rocket attacks.

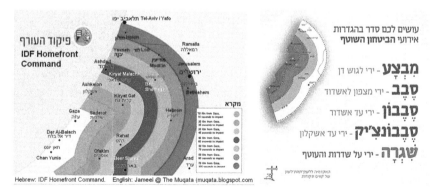

Fig. 6.4 Maps of rocket attacks and their definitions

The satire shows the map of distances concerning rocket attacks, with a new legend, as perceived by *Otef Aza* residents. The poster "clarifies the definitions of ongoing security events for you." *Operation* = rocket attacks on *Gush Dan*,[4] *Round* = rocket attacks on Ashdod and north of the city, *A Little Round* = rocket fire on Ashdod, *a Teeny-weeny Round* = rocket attacks on Ashkelon, and, finally, *Routine* = rocket attacks on Sderot and the *Otef*.

Routine and the names of Sderot and *Otef Aza* appear in red, to emphasize the ongoing fighting in the region, as opposed to the temporality expressed by words, such as *operation, a little round,* and *a teeny-weeny round*. Furthermore, we can assume that because the residents are "accustomed" to rocket attacks, no special definition is needed to describe this situation: it is "routine." Moreover, when rockets hit outside *Otef Aza*, it calls for a military operation, because no one expects people from the center to have to put up with rocket and mortar fire, while it is reasonable to assume that such a reality is acceptable for *Otef Aza*. The main message of this poster, therefore, is that *Otef Aza* residents are unimportant, so the government does not need to take care of them, unlike cities and regions, which are closer to the important center of Israel.

The next example comes from a post written by Julia on Facebook on Other Voice's Facebook[5] page in May 2019. Other Voice—a grassroots organization of residents from the *Otef Aza* region—was established in January 2008 and calls for a non-violent/non-military solution to the Israel-Gaza conflict. This post was titled "This is what is really important—THE EUROVISION!!!"

I AM YOUR TOY

Look at me—I'm a pawn in your war games
You don't care if our lives are worth nothing
Our leaders—they throw us away
(Pam pa hoo, turram pam pa hoo)
Hey—they think that we've got no brains
As our lives go down the drains
we don't matter to them at all—hey, hey, hey, hey

---

[4] Tel Aviv and the major cities in the center of Israel.
[5] As noted in the Preface, Julia is a peace activist and very active in *Kol Acher*/Other Voice.

Well take all your bombs and go home
Your *Kassams*, mortars, and booms
but leave us the red alert app on the smartphone
Wonder Bibi don't you ever forget
Hamas and *Jihad*—you're all the best
You're a bucka-mhm-buckbuckbuck-mhm boy
Bucka-mhm-buckbuckbuck
We're your bucka-mhm-buck-mhm-buck-mhm
We ARE your toys!
We ARE your toys!
You stupid boys!
You stupid boys!
You'll take us down
And make us frown
But—hey—that's life
Oh, sorry—meant death
WE ARE YOUR TOYS
WE ARE YOUR TOYS
YOU STUPID BOYS
YOU STUPID BOYS
WE ARE YOUR TOYS, WE ARE YOUR TOYS, WE ARE YOUR TOYS

Does that win us 12 points?

This song is a parody of the Israeli song "Toy" (music and lyrics—Doron Medley and Stav Berger, performed by Netta Barzilai)—which won the Eurovision Song Contest in 2018. The last comment—"Does that win us 12 points?"—refers to the highest score a singer can achieve in the contest.

In the introduction to the poem, Julia writes that the Eurovision song contest, which was being held in Israel—since "Toy" had won the contest the year before—is so important that "it doesn't need to be interrupted by a few rockets" that were hitting *Otef Aza* during the final preparations for the song contest. Choosing to write a parody of what was probably the most famous Israeli song of the time, is contrasted to the lack of awareness of the Israeli public, concerning *Otef Aza* reality. Moreover, the question about scoring the most points, at the end, has no answer, suggesting that this song will not change anything regarding the situation.

The request to leave residents the red alert (*tzeva adom*) app expresses the feeling that since the Israeli government is doing (less than) the minimum to care for their security, the least it can do is provide residents with the app, so they will know when to take cover.

The song contains expression of despair, sadness, danger, and anger concerning a situation that can lead to death, since the Israeli government is not working to end the conflict. Julia uses capital letters to emphasize the message that the area's residents are toys in a political game, controlled by the Israeli government. Furthermore, the post attacks the leaders twice, first by calling them "STUPID" and then by calling them "BOYS." That is, they are not adults handling this crisis in a serious manner. Moreover, Julia uses the words "our," "we," and "us" to show that the emotions and criticism are shared by all *Otef* residents.

Another creative example comes from a YouTube video, "Best Regards to the Government: The Alphabet Song—The *Otef Aza* Children's Version"[6] (August 2019). At the time of this writing (October 2021), this video (see Fig. 6.5) had over 108,000 views on YouTube. It was a joint project by Israeli Victory, which "guides American and Israeli policies to support Israel's victory over the Palestinians in order to resolve the Israeli-Arab conflict,"[7] and Unity with the South. The clip contains the original melody of children's "The Alphabet Song," but with a different vocabulary, based on the daily reality of *Otef Aza* children. For example, it contains the words: fire, big fence, tunnel, *Hamas*, stabbing, and so on.

Additionally, the song emphasizes the contrast between healthy surroundings for children and the chilling reality children experience, which includes terror attacks and *tzeve adom*. In terms of choreography, the children are seen running for cover, lying down on the ground, and covering their heads, with rockets continually flying overhead. Moreover, the transitions between the verses contain balloons in different colors, with explosives tied to them, showing the contrast between colorful innocent balloons—for children outside of the *Otef*—and the incendiary balloons—for *Otef* children—which burn the fields surrounding their homes.

---

[6] The original version of the song, written by the late Naomi Shemer (a famous Israeli songwriter), can be seen in the clip from the Israeli children's television channel Hop! (https://youtu.be/gCAznfygWTY).

[7] See https://www.meforum.org/israel-victory-project/ for information on the project.

Fig. 6.5 "The Alphabet Song" (2019)

Toward the end of the song, the children sing "Best regards to the government; we'll meet again during the next operation." The message here is that the Israeli government only sees and cares about the residents during the wars, ignoring them the rest of the time. In addition, when a person sends "regards" to someone, this usually means that you do not see this person too often, just like the residents feel regarding Israeli leaders.

The song ends with the chorus, with the words: "There is no dove and no olive branch," referring to the lack of hope for a peace process.

The next example is a parody (see Fig. 6.6), made by members of Nachal Oz, a *kibbutz* directly across from the Gaza Strip, of the popular Israeli pop song "Yasu," "Enough of this boom boom, taka boom boom!"

The performers, all *kibbutz* residents, sing about the rocket attacks and the incendiary balloons. The song tells the story of the explosions that occur, usually at night, around and in this *kibbutz*. The male soloist begins with: "In a small *kibbutz* in the Negev, the northern Negev, with a

כמה רע זה עושה לי

Fig. 6.6   "Yasu!—In a Small Kibbutz in the Negev"

cup of coffee looking at the sunset … let's throw a mattress on the floor"—describing what people are forced to do, when the entire family needs to sleep in the *mamad*. One of the male singers is a rapper, with rockets flying over his head with the name of each war. Another male singer is dressed in a military vest and has a rifle, representing the community's security force. The women sing: "What a night awaits me! It's so hurtful, so, enough of this boom boom, taka, boom boom."

In the middle of the clip, the singers run over a little bridge, carrying a hat made from a balloon, in the shape of a rocket, a mattress, the rifle, a chair—props signifying the rocket and incendiary balloon attacks. The women singers also sing about the trauma they still have from Protective Edge, and that three seconds after the alert sounds, the rocket falls. At the end of the song, the rapper says, *tzeva adom*, and the performers/*kibbutz* members jump up from the bench and run away, followed immediately by a boom.

The four men and women are wearing black, which symbolizes danger and the burned fields. The song's message is that the lives of the residents in the area are constantly in danger from balloons and rockets, followed by explosions and sleepless nights while the singers ask the question—"Bibi—do you love me?" The implied answer is "no."

"Two Worlds": Feeling Abandoned by Jewish-Israelis from Other Parts of Israel

So far, we presented a variety of ways in which *Otef Aza* residents express their negative emotions and thoughts regarding the Israeli governments' policy regarding their safety and the ongoing war. The message they convey is that they are neither seen, nor heard by their national leaders.

We now turn to what the residents think and feel when they encounter Jewish-Israelis, from outside the region. We found in the interviews that *Otef Aza* residents often feel abandoned by their fellow countrywomen and men—even by some family members. Residents discussed their frustration and, at times, even anger at the other Jewish-Israelis, since they perceived these others as apathetic to their plight. Our interviewees expressed that while they were struggling to create some kind of normal life for themselves and their families, the encounters with other citizens left them with the feeling that there are two detached worlds within the small country. While they—the *Otef* residents—must deal with ongoing terror attacks, which turn their lives upside down on a regular basis—Jewish-Israelis from other parts of Israel not only are living a normal and good life, but often seem unconcerned or uninterested in the pain experienced by people who live near the Gaza border.

For example, Arieh addressed this in his interview, when he spoke about taking a break from the rocket attacks in Sderot—his hometown—when he went to stay with family in a city in the center of the country:

> I wanted to see something, so I said I was going out to a pub. I wanted to chat with people. People didn't know what I was talking about! They didn't understand what I was talking about! I say these people live in this country… what's going on in China, what's going on in the United States,

what's going on in Europe, whether it's heavy rains or [something else], but if it's terrorism, people don't know what we're going through here. Not that they need to do something! But they don't know what you're talking about? Seriously? Are you for real?! ... People who don't live here, don't understand what we're talking about! They really don't understand.

Sigal also addressed this issue, when she emphasized how her colleagues from Be'er Sheva responded to a rocket attack—an event that she faces often, but was extremely surprising and stressful for them. Sigal uses the metaphors of the "world of here" and the "world of there"—even though, in geographical terms, the distance is 43 kilometers (29 miles). When Sigal talks about this interaction, she expresses that although she has known these colleagues for years, they have no idea what her life is like on a daily/nightly basis. Furthermore, she stated that these colleagues make comments about the Gazans which anger and frustrate her. Work, as a result, does not provide a safe space for Sigal as perhaps she would like:

The world of here and the world of there. You walk around the hospital and you realize they live a normal routine, and we didn't sleep at night because all night long there were booms and shooting and a mess. So, it's as if there are parallel realities in life. You live a life that they don't understand at all what you're talking about ... I was in the intensive care unit and they started debating whether to run with the beds or not to run with the beds, because it's not at all protected. I told them that it's best of all to stay put, and I saw the panic, the trepidation, and these are people who have been trained. At some point, you just ... say that for me it's a life routine; for them it's once in a while, once a year, once every two years, once in three years, but for me it's all the time. And you sometimes come after a night of not sleeping, and everything is as usual, everything is normal, no problem. And they also deal with things that you say to yourself that an average family here in our area deals with other things, completely other questions, starting with existential questions, like what is the message we're teaching our children? ... I saw this gap here, between people around me, who cursed the Gazans, but also people who said, "Let's do things differently ..." But, at the hospital, I saw so many extremist views ... "crush them ... kill them, until they get down on their knees, they don't know what's good for them". Sorry, who are you?? And it was always during the difficult times, when they would shoot at Be'er Sheva specifically. So, you learn that this is your reality. You live in one place and they are on their planet.

Yoram, a 51-year-old man from a kibbutz, also expressed his anger as a result of what he perceives as disparagement from residents of the rest of the country concerning the emergency routine *Otef Aza* residents experience in their daily lives. Like Sigal, he also uses the metaphor of "two worlds." As an example, he says that some of the local farmers risk their lives when they go out to work and, thus, carry guns for protection. Afterward, Yoram compared this daily routine to a daily routine of a bank clerk, in order to emphasize what he sees as the unbearable gap between the lives of residents in the region and those in the rest of the country:

> It's so annoying to me that in the center and north [of Israel] they're saying "Oh, okay. One or two missiles fell here". You must have heard on the news at recent events that people said, "Okay so they were hit by some missiles, nothing happened"… And they [the *Hamas*] can shoot at any area in the country. This basically means that people in the center know now after going through Operation Protective Edge and all the other wars what we are going through. They do not live life as we live it there. There are farmers in *kibbutzim* who are plowing fields with armored tractors and personal weapons inside the cabin. These are more serious guys in my eyes than someone sitting in the bank branch and entering data into the computer how much money a person owes the bank, and all sorts of things like that. I call it "two worlds" because people don't know what we're going through here.

In summation of this sub-theme, when *Otef Aza* residents meet with ordinary citizens living in other parts of the country, they are frustrated, dismayed and angry to learn that, often, these others have no idea—and, perhaps, even worse, no interest—in understanding what they are living through. These encounters give residents the feeling that they are on their own in the intractable war. Not only does the government ignore them, but often their fellow citizens as well.

The Absence of the Media: "No Injuries, No Damage (Not)"

The last aspect of this theme relates to residents' perceptions that Israeli mainstream media is ignoring their plight or only engaging in partial—and thus distorting—reporting. For example, journalists and news broadcasters report that when a rocket falls, and there was no physical damage: "There were no injuries; there was no damage." As perhaps could be expected, many *Otef Aza* residents find this characterization extremely disturbing, since it does not acknowledge the psychological damage that residents experience after living through years of *tzeve adom*—regardless if the rocket fell in an open field or was even a false alarm.

Almog Boker, a journalist and a television reporter who is also a *kibbutz* resident in the *Otef*, decided to put an end to this phenomenon. Therefore, while reporting the *tzeve adom* and different terror attacks on the area, he stresses that while "there was no physical damage to people or property, there was psychological damage."

Another important aspect expressed by the residents regarded the lack of reporting or inaccurate reporting of their situation. Some interviewees expressed anger that mainstream media often ignored terror attacks in the *Otef* or downplayed the negative effects events were having on residents. Moreover, some of them insinuated that the media is a tool that the government and the army use for their own purposes. Therefore, residents feel that the media, which is supposed to report news, is not doing its job by ignoring what is happening in the *Otef*. As a result, they are also being harmed by the absent media.

Here is what Tali, a 50-year-old center, secular woman from a *kibbutz*, said:

> There's a feeling of a lack of transparency … in what is in the news and what really happens. There is no direct overlap between them and, in fact, when you know it [the rocket] fell and you are told it didn't and vice versa, that you know it is quiet and suddenly you hear in the news that it's not, it's hard to contain it … we feel that they're deceiving us, as if we are invisible, that other things are more important and that we're being used.

Avi (cited above in his We-poem) also addressed this issue by saying: "In the *Otef*, we were taught that the real war does not start on the day we feel it, but on the day it really starts to affect [the country] and reach headlines that last longer than three minutes on Ynet." And here is how Adele expressed her emotions regarding the apathy of the media, when talking about trucks that bring materials into the Gaza Strip, while they are attacking Israel and building tunnels:

> It annoys me that we let this supply go in, despite the balloons and that there is a conscious concealment of what is happening. They are not informing [the public] about all the balloons and all the fires and there are many fires that I know are caused from balloons and the media is not informing [the public] about it … I think this is what I can do for my country, to represent the situation not only to people abroad, but also to people in Israel who do not understand what is happening here and even my son, who lives in Tel Aviv and he completely knows what it's like to live here, is not always aware that there were missiles. He's not fully aware of the situation here with the fires.

Chapter Summary

In this chapter, we focused on the harsh and, at times, unbearable feelings of solitude and disregard that area residents often feel concerning the way the government, Jewish-Israelis in different parts of the country, and the media relate to them and their plight. These emotions and thoughts were mainly targeted toward the Israeli government and the decision-makers, for not making a real effort to actually end the conflict. We brought the voices of some of our interviewees, as well as other residents of the area, via their social media posts, who expressed their opinions and feelings in a very touching way, but also with humor and satire. We saw that they have different opinions regarding the desirable solution to this conflict, but all of them agree that active steps need to be taken.

It was clear from the residents' words that they expected to receive support and solidarity from people from other parts of the country, concrete help from the government and coverage from the media. Therefore, when they found this support, help, and coverage lacking, this increased their feelings of being "invisible," and as one of them said, "second-class citizens." As one way to try to combat this disappointment, people created and adopted different initiatives.

We now turn to our last major theme discerned in our study, which, while being an independent theme, also ties together the previous three: Life in the *Otef*: It's Complicated, Conflictual, Paradoxical.

7

Life in the *Otef*: It's Complicated, Conflictual, Paradoxical

The last major theme that we discerned in the interviews and social media materials was the complexity of life in *Otef Aza* that also exposed paradoxes and inner conflicts held by residents. In many instances, we found that residents would say one thing and then later (sometimes immediately) in the interview contradict themselves, sometimes appearing aware of these contradictions and sometimes not. These contradictions, as well as their detailed descriptions of all the complexities they face in the *Otef*, demonstrated—once again—just how dynamic life in this area is, how many dilemmas it raises for residents, and how much they reflect on these issues, most seeing life as anything but a dichotomy between "we are/life is good and they are/life is bad."

While this chapter presents a look at a theme not discussed earlier, it also ties into the three previously discussed themes, since these three themes have complexity at their basis. Therefore, this chapter focuses on the complexities, conflicts, and paradoxes that we discerned in the interviews, photographs, and social media materials, while tying them, at times, to the other themes discussed earlier.

In Chap. 3, we presented the different understandings of the concept *cognitive dissonance*. We noted that this concept can reflect an internal

J. Chaitin et al., *Routine Emergency*, https://doi.org/10.1007/978-3-030-95983-8_7

discrepancy between a person's contradictory feelings/cognitions/beliefs (e.g., Festinger, 1957) and/or interpersonal criticism of inconsistency (Billig, 1987), in which the cognitive dissonance occurs in dialogue, rhetoric, and argumentation. That is, whereas Festinger conceptualized cognitive dissonance as an *intrapersonal* phenomenon, Billig saw it as an *interpersonal* phenomenon. In the materials that we collected, we found both kinds of dissonance. There were people who expressed two contradictory ideas/feelings/beliefs and appeared to be struggling with reconciliation of the two, and there were people (sometimes the same) who appeared to be reacting to interaction with others, such as family or friends, that raised complexities and paradoxes, which led them to reflect on their lives in the region and to express their struggles with how to resolve these conflicts. In our understandings, the residents often expressed dissonance that had both internal and external sources that nourished one another.

Overall, we found two complexities/paradoxes that concerned most residents: (1) being stressed/traumatized by the situation versus feeling that "life is good" and that they were usually in control, and (2) reflections on remaining in the region versus the desire to leave.

Furthermore, we found a third issue that reflected complexity among the residents who defined themselves as peace activists. These activists are, simultaneously, victims of the terror attacks and wars—as are all residents of *Otef Aza*—while also extremely concerned with the humanitarian crisis in Gaza, and the violation of the Gazans' human rights. These residents often publicly call for measures perceived as highly unpopular (to put it mildly) by many of the other *Otef Aza* residents, as well as Jewish-Israelis from other regions. These include calls to end the blockade on the Gaza Strip, to negotiate with the *Hamas* government in Gaza, and to hold the Israeli government responsible for its part in the humanitarian crisis in the Gaza Strip. These stances have often led to extremely tense relations with other *Otef* residents, who, at times, respond with verbal and physical violence toward the peace activists when they pass by their demonstrations and/or read their posts/see their videos on Facebook.

We begin with the complexity of stress/trauma versus the feeling that life is good and under control.

"Life Quickly Turns Upside Down: It Stresses Me/It Has Little Effect"

Ofra, a 58-year-old woman from a *moshav* who led *Tzachi* for many years, alongside her work with the elderly and her art studio, talked about the frequent, quick changes that add complexity to a life that shifts between "still waters" and "life being turned upside down." We discerned that she vacillates between having a sense of control over the situation when she says that she does not think that it "stresses me out" and simultaneously emphasizing how everything that is normal can change in a moment, depriving her of the calm. Here, we see a reconciliation of two opposite feelings—the calm of the clubhouse and art gallery, and the boom of the rockets. While we cannot know if Ofra is indeed dealing calmly with this complex situation as she states, or is (also) in denial over the toll that the security situation is having on her, there is no doubt that such a life reflects a paradox. This complexity, thus, requires her to continually try to reconcile the two:

I manage a clubhouse for independent pensioners; it's very important, this is my work. In addition, I'm an artist and I have a gallery that gives private drawing lessons, because I'm also an art teacher. I've done many things in my life, including heading *Tzachi*. My life is a kind of still waters until something happens. When something happens, everything gets turned upside down and then, in the end, it works itself out, there's some kind of solution to the situation and my life returns to still waters and then again it can happen, on *Shabbat*, in the middle of the night … boom, something happens and I forget everything and it turns the place upside down … in a second my life turns upside down, but later on, in a moment, it returns [to normal] and I've learned to live with this, I don't think that it will stress me out, but I know that it can happen any moment and when it happens, I deal with it.

The next example comes from Yoram, a 50-year-old secular, center *kibbutz* member who moved from the center of the country to the kibbutz a few years before Cast Lead. He, too, described a reality that is comprised of emergencies and dangers alongside a reality characterized by a strong sense of belonging to his community:

> We moved to the *kibbutz* ... the lifestyle was rural, calmer ... a cow barn, a garage, joint holidays, all of these things, wow, I liked it, you get away from the whole thing of the city, of the craziness and the malls and all of this and you also mature, so you don't connect to it so much and you say "Wow! I like it here". You open the window and you see the field across from you ... it's in front of your eyes ... you begin to appreciate what's a field, what's a tree, what are dunams that are planted there, and you have all the crops, if it's potatoes, carrots, all of these things, so you begin to appreciate the place more and more ... the place where you're raising your children ... we didn't imagine that we would go through ... three wars ... it wasn't easy because the house where we lived, they're old houses, so they don't have a *mamad*. There was only a public bomb shelter in each neighborhood and you would run, when rockets were flying, may the same thing not happen to us, but, over time, we also added a *mamad* to the house, so the kids are also calmer ... so let's say that, overall, my wife and I aren't sorry about this move that we made, because you discover new friends ... friendships are made and connections are made ... it only became better and improved with time and I am very very happy about this step that I took ... it's true, there are security situations, there are bad moments, but you live it, it's already engraved in you, you're used to the situation, you know how to deal with this situation, so, for me, it's like "Okay"—it happened to me, you carry on, that's it, in general.

As in the case of Ofra, we cannot unequivocally assert that Yoram is trying to convince himself that he does not feel an inner contradiction when he actually does, between the quiet that he now loves so much and the "bad moments" that are "already engraved in you." However, since he brings up the two opposite feelings, one next to the other, it appears that Yoram understands that some explanation is needed why he does not feel stress or traumatized and why he feels in control. It is interesting that he only hints at the issue of stress, when he mentions that his children feel calmer, since they built their *mamad*. Therefore, they no longer need to run to the public bomb shelter "when rockets are flying"—which is a polar opposite of having the fields spread out "in front of your eyes" and being "very very happy" about living in the *Otef*. However, he gives no detail of specific experiences, and he only implies that his children felt stress, not him.

The next example comes from the interview and photographs chosen by Eli, a 65-year-old left-wing, secular man from a *kibbutz*. Eli chose two photographs that reflect the complexity/paradox of the *Otef Aza* region—the Heaven and Hell. Furthermore, when he explains why he chose these photos, Eli expresses contradictory feelings and perceptions concerning his Gazan neighbors:

> I have two photos … Otef would be **happy** if I had [chosen] other pictures, I could have chosen **flowers** and things like that, and **nonetheless** in order to emphasize the point, this is a picture from yesterday, this is a carrot field, with a present for kids, **especially** for kids … I chose it because it is **nastiness**, this is the **worst thing** that you can do … to send an explosive that looks like it's a present for children, **adults** can deal with it, they **know** how to deal with it, but this is the pinnacle of the despicableness among many pinnacles, this is **one** of the pinnacles of despicableness … this shows how **angry** I am with the neighbors, with some of the neighbors … ((showing the next photo)) **it's** across from our house, it's a fire across from our house, that's what it looks like, flames two meters high, and it was **here**, 20 meters from our house … my other photos have birds, all kinds of nice things … this is about our life **here**, this **too** is our life because on a daily basis our life is comfortable, really **nice, pleasant**, outside, good air, good weather, usually it's **good here**, but these are two of my photographs … I stood there with a hose from my neighbour's **house**, they weren't there, so I stood there with the **irrigation** hose, in case a spark would reach the house, so it wouldn't cause harm, and by the way, the person who **helped** here, that also needs to be said … when there was a fire in the field, they work here with tractors to make a small ditch … the guy who did this is an **Arab worker**[1] who works here on the *kibbutz*, he drove with his tractor into the fire, **physically**, into the fire, the wheels were **actually in the fire!** … he tried to make sure that it wouldn't reach the row of bushes … I think they are good people. I have no problem with Arabs, I think they are my brothers, I really think they're my brothers.

---

[1] In another place in the interview, Eli emphasizes that this man is from Gaza.

Eli's photographs (see Fig. 7.1) reflect how sinister life can be for children (and adults) in a place that often epitomizes the good life. In the first photograph, there are balloons, which turn out to be a deadly "present," intended to attract children and then harm then. In the second photograph, there is a child on a bicycle, while behind him, a fire rages. The juxtaposition of the Heaven and the Hell reflected in the photos, noted by so many residents (including Eli) is clear: lush fields of vegetables and a child on a bicycle often meet fires and explosives.

However, the paradoxes are evident not only in the photos, but in Eli's words as well. First, he talks about his anger toward the Gazans, remarking later that the Arabs are "good people," drawing special attention to the worker from Gaza who risks his own life to fight these fires. While we could hypothesize that Eli was differentiating between terrorists and ordinary, innocent people, he does not use these terms. Therefore, it appears as if he is torn about his feelings/perceptions toward the Palestinians in Gaza. On the one hand, he sees them as reaching "the pinnacle of despicableness," while, on the other, he sees them as "my brothers"—two statements that he repeated twice. We see this emphasis, therefore, as reflecting just how torn he is when it comes to his emotions and cognitions concerning the Palestinians in Gaza.

Fig. 7.1 Eli—Balloons and a "Present," a Child, and a Fire (2019)

The next example comes from Sigal—Eli's wife.[2] Sigal is a 65-year-old who defined herself as being secular, with center political views. She talked at length about the terror that *Otef Aza* region residents face and about her anger/disappointment with the ways in which Israeli society and its leaders have developed over the years.

In terms of complexity/paradoxes, we saw expressions of very different sides of Sigal's experience in the *Otef.* On the one hand, the dangers that residents face appear to deeply concern her on the personal, family, and community level, and on the other hand, the area's natural resources bring her a sense of peace and wellbeing. As a result, a dissonance appears in her interview—rockets and trauma in her interview versus the sunset and kingfisher in her photograph. However, in the photographs we also see paradoxes—the beautiful sunset against the barbed wire fence and the kingfisher, shot in the center of the barbed wire fence. It as if Sigal is saying with her photographs—we have amazing natural phenomena here, but we can't freely appreciate them, since we/they (the sunsets, the birds) are (also) trapped by the dangers around us. There is also another element that she notes connected to the outside—outside there are not only natural wonders, but also tear gas, rockets, and fires, that connect the outside to dangerous experiences.

Another aspect of complexity comes to light when Sigal compares taking shelter in the public shelters versus taking shelter in the home *mamad.* While having a *mamad* in one's house is better than having to run to an outside shelter, and then spending nights away from your home, being in a *mamad* can lead to loneliness, because people do not have community members to help support them through the rocket attacks, since each one is alone in his/her *mamad,* sometimes for long periods of time. Furthermore, she notes that having a *mamad,* often does not help, since it is impossible to reach it in time. Thus, her experience of the *mamad* is also a paradoxical one.

Finally, it is interesting to note that Eli, her husband, chose photographs of the terror tactics, while Sigal chose to present the nature of the region (see Fig. 7.2). Perhaps, when they discussed their upcoming

---

[2] Each person in our study was interviewed separately, and the interviews were conducted one on one.

Fig. 7.2   Sigal—A Sunset, a Kingfisher, and Barbed Wire × 2 (2020)

interviews, they purposely decided to present different aspects of their lives in their photographs. However, whether they made such a joint decision or not, both, through their words and photographs, present the paradoxes of life on the border.

Sigal said:

> In the routine in the *Otef*, you do what you want and exactly at the same moment … each moment, you know that it can end. The run to the *mamad*, it's a bit funny here, because there's no time to run to the *mamad*. We often hear the booms before the *tzeva adom*, but the routine … it's important for us to maintain the routine … because that's the sanity. But we know, we know that really, really, in a few moments, it ends. I worry about the people who come to visit us, the grandchildren, the kids who come on Friday … and all of the demonstrations on the fence, with tear gas, and you go outside and there's the smell, and you get a WhatsApp— "Stay inside the houses because there's tear gas outside." All kinds of things like this, so you, you need to take the little kids from the house to the car. After dinner, you go outside, and you need to put them in the car. There's a very strong smell outside, it's very problematic, and your eyes are burning … but that's the routine, that's more or less the routine which changes, every few months, the routine here becomes something a bit different.

Later in the interview, Sigal also compared the experience of sitting together with people from the community in the public shelter—as they did during the 1967 war—and sitting in the private *mamad*, by yourself or with family members, when there are rocket attacks:

> I remember the Six Day War; we were in the bomb shelters because there were *fedayeen* … we slept in the shelter … I remember people around me … but here, it's really more a family [experience], because you have a *mamad*, so you run to the *mamad*. Divide and conquer. It's not that we're together in a shelter. Each one is in his room and this is a bit problematic when you're alone. You know that everyone is in the same situation, but it's not. The experience is one of being alone, you're alone with your anxieties, with your fears, yes, and it doesn't get better over time, you don't get used to it, there's no such thing, there's no such animal, it's frightening, it's more frightening than it was in the beginning.

The next example comes from Tamar, a 50-year-old secular, politically center woman from a *kibbutz* who, for years, oversaw the social services in one of the regional councils in the *Otef*. Tamar decided to leave this central position because of her experiences during Protective Edge. She felt that she had not managed this emergency as well as she could, not understanding, at the beginning of the war, that she was handling a "marathon" and, thus, should have allocated resources differently than she did during the war. Of course, this is hindsight; there is no way that Tamar could have known ahead of time that the 2014 war would last 51 days—as opposed to the 23 days of Cast Lead and the 12 days of Pillars of Defense. She shared her thoughts about how she dealt with the challenges she faced during this war and reflects on how she might have better handled her responsibilities during this very tense time.

We hear how Tamar's feelings and thoughts about her work and her sense of belonging have led to internal conflicts. She expresses, simultaneously, paradoxical feelings and thoughts. Tamar reflects on her dedication to and love of her former position—a position that placed her at the center of the stress and trauma, but was also the helm of control. In her interview, we hear about her hours of reflecting on how she had handled her job during Protective Edge. This reflection led her to the desire to make a new path for herself. In this new path, she became a "baby"—as opposed to the responsible adult she had been—for a number of months.

She was looking to reinvent herself, while also noting the loss of meaning that this change has brought with it. Tamar said:

What happened was that Protective Edge was an event beyond the national level. It was also on the personal level; it was a very, very difficult event, demanding … and I don't think that I managed my strength and resources well … I continued to head the department, but in 2016, something began to "prickle" me and I want something else, but I don't know what, and I went through a process of a lot of thinking and checking and what am I and where am I going, where do I want to be … looking for a vision and in 2017 I decided that I want to end my job. That was a very difficult decision to make. First of all, for me with myself, because this is a place I love, it had become a home … it had become part of my identity, it's a place I love, it's actually leaving part of yourself and leaving something of you in another place and moving on, so I went through a very long process … to leave the job, from my point of view, was like you telling me to jump off a roof of a tower, when it's clear that I'm going to crash and slowly, slowly, it became something that was possible, that is, the tower became shorter and shorter. It's possible to jump off it. In the end of 2017, I asked to finish … I received a lot of support, which was good, because it was to leave without knowing where I'm going … I wanted a vacation … I said "I want maternity leave without the baby", that was my image, that I'm the baby … I took vacation and finished the job with another good escalation [in violence] before, a "goodbye kiss" … I was on vacation for several months and it was really good … it became clear to me that I was going to be independent and now I'm independent and do all kinds of things, I try to mainly do what I like, but I'm really at the beginning of defining myself … I discovered something very, very meaningful for me and this is that I really enjoy my independence, the independence, the independence … I discovered that there are two things that are missing for me today, one is to belong, because I had a very, very strong sense of belonging … I think that to live in *Otef Aza* and, for sure, to work in the *Otef* and, for sure, to work in the essence of the *Otef*, this is an experience of strong belonging … and I lost the feeling of clear belonging, when you don't need to ask yourself "Where do I fit it?" … and the second thing that I lost, that I'm trying to slowly rebuild, is the feeling of meaning that you don't have to search for [meaning], because there, in essence, was the clear meaning for why I'm there, and in the new things that I do, there's a different kind of meaning, which is a meaning for someone else. For example, if I give someone advice about his life, it's not mine, it's his business, If I give a lecture … and then leave, they remain with the knowledge and what they need to develop. Do you understand? So, I lost the thing that's mine, the sense of meaning that others depend on me, I was there with a lot, a lot of responsibility that I loved and that's it, I'm very glad to be where I am today, taking my first steps.

The next example comes from Gal, a 35-year-old politically center, secular mother of three who lives in Ashkelon and works in one of the local colleges. Gal was originally from the north and moved to the south when she attended school and met her husband. After completion of their degrees, the couple remained in the region, eventually having children and settling in an apartment.

Gal's interview is full of dissonance and paradoxes—both the internal and interpersonal kinds. For example, officially, they live 30 seconds away from rocket fire. However, in reality, they have less time to take cover. Living in an apartment, especially during the COVID-19 pandemic, coupled with the need, often to remain close to a *mamad* during rocket attacks, has led them to the idea of buying a house in one of the *kibbutzim* so that her family will have more space and outdoor opportunities. Therefore, she talks about "upgrading" their housing situation by moving to a kibbutz, which is *closer* to the Gaza Strip (within an immediate to 15-second time frame for taking cover). So, simultaneously, Gal talks about "upgrading" to a residence that places them closer to the danger, while laughing about her use of the term, understanding how illogical this must sound to people outside of the *Otef*.

Furthermore, in her interview, as well as in two of her photos (shown below), Gal focuses on the paradoxes that the region offers—camaraderie, quality of life, physical and psychological danger for children, and despair. Therefore, while she is "crazy about the area," she admits that her children are scarred and scared, and that while she and her husband will not consider moving away, they are deeply frustrated and in despair:

> We're crazy about the area and now we're more experienced with living in this area. We're even looking to upgrade. I say "upgrade" and that's funny,

but to upgrade ourselves, to one of the *kibbutzim* nearby … If someone in Tel Aviv will hear that I want to upgrade, he'll laugh in my face, but we're looking for this place, a house, *kibbutz* education. I think that based on what we have already lived through and know, and from our friends, there's a huge difference and when this security situation … heats up as opposed to when everything is calm, we say "It's the difference between Heaven and Hell", that is, when there's no security situation and everything is quiet, to live here, is Heaven and when there is, it becomes a serious Hell, but I think that the advantages of this place highly outweigh these disadvantages and I'm taking into account that my children are already scarred. I see this and I'm taking it into account, that is, this is one of our considerations about moving closer and we'll take 15 seconds off the time we have from the 30, that could influence us … it's one of our considerations versus the space that you promise them in the *kibbutz* and the education. So, we're checking out things, while asking ourselves the questions … we're trying to decide what's right for us … we begin to think if this is what we wish for them, and then the reflection, they are actually, "Who are we fooling? Ashkelon is already 15 seconds, not 30 seconds, we're already *Otef Aza*". It's not that we now live someplace quiet and they'll discover this world. We're already living this thing. We're in Ashkelon, they know what a siren is … they're already scarred from it, so at least we're saying, "let's give them the best life we can when there isn't [escalation], the most amount of freedom" … so I say, okay, I'm not bringing them to some rosy place; Ashkelon is already inside. It's completely *Otef Aza*, we get hit the same amount, so perhaps it doesn't matter … I think this area is one of the most amazing regions in the country and this is my home … I have no plans on moving away because of the security situation … I don't see myself leaving and I also think that it's not right to leave, because … as the range of the fires grows, where will we go? … the solution isn't to get up and leave … It's our country and I live here … and that's also one of our considerations, we don't see ourselves leaving, so you say if "I don't see myself leaving the place and my kids are already scarred, so at least we'll give them the best life that I can when there isn't escalation".

When asked to show her photographs, Gal presented two that reflect the paradoxes of life connected to the college where she works and her home (see Fig. 7.3). Furthermore, the photos echo the complexity she feels when she notes that the message she wants to convey is that she

Fig. 7.3 Gal—Holiday Greetings on Campus and Let Them Grow Up in Quiet (2020)

(and, according to her, others) is against harming Gaza and Gazans. However, she/they need a solution to their frustration and despair:

> You see here a gathering of the department at the campus. It was for a holiday, in which we wished everyone a happy holiday and … here we see students … who spoke one after the other … I chose this picture because I thought that if you would photoshop it and erase the horrible *mamadim*[3] behind them, this could be a beautiful, pastoral picture, but they exist, the *mamadim* … they are one second away … and I think that in spite of the fact that they are decorated very nicely … they are *mamadim* and I took this photo because at one moment, in one second everything can change … the smiles, in one second, it can change and if it was a picture of one second after *tzeva adom*, the focus of the picture would be the … *mamadim* and not this … here, the main message is that … we all live in the area, we all experience this and we all work here. The topic is not "Black South," it was also "Black South" because of the fires, but the topic is … more "*Tnu Ligdol b'Sheket*" … it represents everyone's frustration … we all came to be photographed because of the deep frustration … of despair that they [politicians] aren't doing anything and there's no solution at all, and it's not a matter of "Hit them hard! Attack them! Go to war!" **No**, that's not what people here want, that's really not what people here want. The fact that at times they find someone who yells that in the news, it's only because it's catchy … I think many people here want an arrangement, if it's to transfer

---

[3] Plural of *mamad*.

money to Gaza … so it will be quiet here. For sure, we don't want to erase Gaza … it was a picture of despair, so I chose it.

The next example comes from Channa, a 32-year-old religious, right-wing woman who lives in a village. In her interview, she contradicts herself in a number of places, but explains these contradictions through her religious beliefs: "perhaps we feel the suffering, but we believe we're part of something larger." On the one hand, she stresses how she and her husband wanted to ensure that their children were not traumatized and scarred, as they were, from the evacuation of *Gush Katif* and the terror attacks in the West Bank settlement, where they once lived. On the other hand, they brought their children to *Otef Aza*, an area characterized by trauma and scarring. On the one hand, Channa talks about the tension during the wars and rounds, while, on the other, she describes how they make these traumatic events into "celebrations," with "barbeques."

One way to understand Channa's contradictions and explanations is that she employs cognitive dissonance: she needs to explain to herself why she remains in an area, when seeing the negative effects it is having on her children (and herself as well), but continues to see the area as wonderful, because of her deep belief that "God will save us." Channa said:

> We heard that people wanted to establish a new community … and it sounded interesting. We were searching for our place … my husband loved the open space and the landscape. He grew up in *Gush Katif* and he connected to it, it reminded him of where he grew up, except for the lack of sea, and we connected to the idea of settling the Negev, to establish a new place … we were looking for a place not only to live, but a place where we would feel that we were meaningful, a meaningful place …we thought it more relevant for us that we would raise our children in a village, a *moshav*, that we need the quiet and the open spaces … so we came here, we also wanted to distance ourselves from the Hebron mountains, from the area called Judea and Samaria because we were always afraid there, the Arabs were always around us and there were terror attacks and you drive on the roads and every day they can throw rocks and we said we want to live somewhere without this fear, that our kids won't experience this fear, so we came here and we also said we wanted a village that there's a chance that they won't evacuate, like *Gush Katif*. From all the trauma that we experienced,

we didn't want our children to experience such a scar, so we came here …
I said I didn't want my kids to experience the same fear of waiting to hitch
a ride because there's no dependable public transportation and this fear
that an Arab car will stop by you … we sat together, my brothers and my
parents and we said that we're scarred from the terror attacks and my
mother said, "What?! But this is our home," they didn't understand …
then we came here … but from my point of view, it wasn't like seeing this
fear every day of the daily travel and in the supermarket … in the end, I say
to myself that there really isn't any place in Israel that you can say is the
most sterile and the safest, because we are Jews and there's this tension
about the very existence of the Jews and you can experience it on a bus or
in Tel Aviv, when you're sitting in a café, it doesn't really matter where …
what keeps me here, in the end, are the people, the community, the friends
that are here, the resilience that's here … there is cohesiveness here, a lot of
"*Yalla*, let's be together," and do happy things, that make you feel good …
and since there has been here … a day of escalation, here a round, you feel
as if they are taking you to the extreme of what you can stand, but we have
the patience to experience it … yes, it's something that makes you tense
when every time there's a round like that, but we say "*Yalla*, take a deep
breath, we're okay and we'll make these days fun. We're here at home. We'll
have a barbeque and *yalla*, celebrations". And then when it's over, all of a
sudden … it takes away all of your spirit and patience that you had, you
don't understand. What happened? … we took my daughter to the
Resilience Center after a few rounds when we saw that it wasn't good for
her … she needed something that would help her, she began peeing in her
pants … at school, she wasn't functioning and it really helped her … my
role now is to make sure that my children will have it good and that they'll
live through it in the best way possible … we believe all of the historical
moves, they always wanted to destroy us and … God saves us from their
hands … period after period they came and wanted to harm us and God
saves us … this is highly connected to our life here, including the fact that
we live here on the firing line and sometimes in life, we live the threat, but
it's also something that God helps us and He saves us, even if we don't see
it, perhaps we'll feel the suffering, but we're part of something bigger.

In summation of this aspect of the theme of complexities and paradoxes, we see that life in the *Otef* raises numerous complexities that affect
the personal, family and community levels. People are torn between

different belief systems—be they political, ideological or religious. Their experiences are very difficult, but they strongly believe in living in the area, because, among other things, they deeply love the area, seeing it as a place that provides a strong sense of home. However, when the dangers come knocking on their doors, which they often do, they feel worry, despair, and troubled as they try to reconcile their contradictory feelings, thoughts, and actions and find ways to navigate their lives through this complex life.

Should I Stay or Should I Go? Heaven Versus Hell

As noted above, residents often mentioned the duality of the region—mostly Heaven, but, at times, complete Hell. During times of Heaven, they aver that there is no place else they would rather live. However, during times of Hell, life is unbearable, and it exposes their deepest fears and anxieties. As also noted in Chap. 4, many residents speak about the quick switch that they make from Heaven to Hell back to Heaven, and how such a "ping-pong" life takes a psychological toll. Therefore, we found residents who often vacillate between remaining in the region and leaving, especially for those with children.

Tali describes herself as being "post-traumatic," after narrowly escaping death, when her car was hit by a Kassam. She also talks about these rapid shifts from Heaven to Hell, and notes that it is "expected" (by whom? government officials? Jewish-Israelis in other parts of the country?) that *Otef Aza* residents will continue to live life in emergency, and that this expectation does not match the reality. Tali describes the great difficulty she has during the escalations in violence and the reasons why she decided, at least meanwhile, despite these difficulties, to remain: the feeling of mutual concern and of belonging to the community. As a result, her life contains trauma from the rockets, coupled with love from/of the community—a combination that makes it hard for her to decide if she should stay or go:

It impacts me, the way I act in my daily life: ... if the blind to the *mamad* is closed or not, it's in everything, when I travel ... this security situation is always here ((pointing to the back of her head)). It's dangerous now. It's not dangerous now. I'm going to work today. I'm not going to work, it's dynamic, in a second ... it affected me even in situations that weren't emergencies, if it was to travel, to come back in the car, I took five days of vacation and it affects me on regular days, to begin driving ... in the beginning, I always drove in the lane [next to the shoulder] ((she chuckles)) ... during the military operations, the difficulties ... hearing the booms every day, terrible, strong booms and understanding that it can fall on you ... I always lived in fear, during the first operation ... it was really complicated, because we had little kids ... we tried to be here as little as possible, because of the difficulty in hearing it ... there's also a dissonance in terms of the instructions, you need to be either in the *mamad* for a number of hours, that makes no sense, or be 15 seconds away from a *mamad*, and, as if, to have a normal life. It's a request that doesn't match reality. If you need to have a normal life and go to work, you can't be at a 15-second distance from the safe space. I began working in Ashkelon during Protective Edge ... the drive was really difficult ... When I was with the kids, I tried to be with them away from the *kibbutz*, I was mainly afraid to drive with them ... I think about leaving. If I could leave, and I think, yes. I have some desire to live in a safer place, but it's complicated ... A person who lives on a *kibbutz*, to change all of that and to move somewhere that isn't, also the thing of raising children in a safe place, so the question is: Is there actually any place in the country that is safe? Because there was a period that busses exploded in Jerusalem, and then you say, that everywhere, there's the place that isn't safe and here there really aren't higher numbers of people being killed than in Tel Aviv. On the other hand, you really feel the daily threat, which is a different kind of threat than traffic accidents, because it's the injury of someone who wants to kill you and of someone who doesn't watch over you, so it's a double injury, in terms of the state, you feel they're not protecting me enough.

Tali's photographs (see Fig. 7.4) also reflect this complexity and internal contradictions—saying one thing, immediately followed by an opposite thought. One photo shows the reality of the dangers, the fires from the incendiary balloons that encroach upon the *kibbutz*, and the other

Fig. 7.4 Tali—Matti Caspi and the Fires (2019)

reflects the solidarity and care when a popular Israeli singer, Matti Caspi, came to perform in the *kibbutz* during a war, in order to bolster morale.

Tamara, who provides the next example, is a 73-year-old politically center, secular woman from Sderot who originally came from Ukraine and settled in Sderot in 1990. Tamara was a nursery schoolteacher who directly witnessed many instances of adults and children being injured and killed by *Kassam* rockets, and she barely escaped death a number of times—experiences which left her, in her words, "post-traumatic." In spite of these frightening experiences, Tamara expressed her deep love and attachment to the town, even though she was often torn between her love of Sderot and her deep fear of living in such a dangerous place, which has taken a toll on her physical and psychological health. She dedicated part of her interview to talking about the short move they moved out of the region, and how Tamara never felt at home there, eventually convincing her husband to return to Sderot.

Perhaps to an outsider, this decision sounds irrational. However, it appears that for Tamara, the emotional attachment trumped the rational cognition. This example, then, demonstrates how inner struggles between emotions and cognitions, even in the case of post-trauma, can convince people that the heart wants what the heart wants, thus defying what many would consider "sense." Tamara said:

I'm very connected to the area … a few years ago my husband retired and said, "That's it. I'm tired of it. I want to leave Sderot." Then our daughters were very happy and said, "*Yalla, yalla,* come live near Netanya," because my oldest daughter lived near Netanya. So we sold our house … we moved and bought a house there, not in Netanya, but close by, and you know, I entered the house and I felt that it wasn't mine. I didn't have air. There are a lot of people that I don't know; when I walked down the street [in Sderot], I knew everyone, the children that I raised in the nursery schools, the parents that I still meet, but there, everything was alien to me. In short, we got there in 2016 and in 2018 we returned to Sderot, and that's it. In spite of the fact that this isn't my house, like it used to be, I felt that I am home … we didn't take the security situation into account at all; we took into account that we have many friends here, everyone knows us and I have two sisters who live here and my niece lives here and my husband didn't want to [come back], but I felt we needed to return. Because, first of all, there, he had a problem with work. I could have volunteered anywhere, in the nursery school, and he couldn't … he only worked for five months and I see that he's down, so I talked with a psychologist and she told me that we have to return to Sderot, "That's your home, if it's bad or good", so we returned … I think we needed to return. We shouldn't have left at all beforehand. I'm very, very sorry about those two years that we left … even though we had a house there with two stories and a huge garden and everything.

While most of our interviewees did not raise the question of leaving or staying in the region, it was clear that those who did talk about this topic were very torn over this issue. Their connection to the area is very strong, despite of and/or due to the intractable conflict that characterizes the region and the personal traumas they have experienced. From their voices, we hear that regardless of the decision these residents make—or have made so far—concerning remaining or leaving for good, this is not a closed matter. The dilemma remains, causing an ongoing inner conflict.

Working for Peace While Being Bombed and Burned

As noted above, peace activists from the region expressed a third kind of complexity in their interviews, postings, and videos on the social media. The first example comes from the interview with Roni, a 75-year-old left-wing secular woman from a moshav, which is the closest community to the border with the Gaza Strip. Roni's house was bombed and one of her farm workers from Thailand was killed by a rocket, as was her daughter's best friend. Roni belongs to different peace groups and spends much of her day, every day, working for peace with the Gazans, being in touch with them, and helping them with medical and financial matters, as well as obtaining exit permits.[4]

From her I-poem, we see expression of her complexity—she works for peace, even though she "shakes with fear." She is clear about her love for Israel, while telling the Gazans that she is their "mother." Roni's complexity, which combines a strong sense of Zionist ideology with a strong sense that the Palestinians need all their rights, which are being denied, is expressed throughout her interview. Here are parts of her I-poem:

Roni's I-poem
I was actually born in England
And I made *aliyah* from England
…
I feel completely Israeli
I met my husband, who is from Egypt
…
I met a people
That I didn't know
And I'm not only talking about the Egyptians
I don't understand

---

[4] Due to the blockade, it is nearly impossible for Gazans to receive exit permits to either enter Israel for a designated time/reason or leave via Israel to travel abroad. For information on this, see Gisha—Procedures and Protocols—https://gisha.org/en/procedures-and-protocols/

Where am I in this story?
I'm not 100% pure
I begin to understand
That it's not exactly like this
I must emphasize, this is my country
I feel that this is my place
I must also consider the other
I tried studying the Palestinian people
I read
I asked questions
And I'm not saying
That I have to get up and leave
I say—come sit next to me
And I said
What am I doing?
I came to Israel
...
I understood the power of dialogue
And I so deeply believe in this
I don't stop
...
I'll demand that they'll listen to me
And I do it here
And I do it abroad
And I try to reach people
And I create ties with people in Gaza
And I try to help them
I try to help them understand
That I am their Israeli mother
I emphasize this in every lecture
That I give in Israel and abroad
What I do
And all I say definitely comes
From love of Israel
I believe
I say
...
I'm afraid like everyone

I'm not looking at it from the outside
I know what it is
I live it
And I'm afraid
I go with groups to the look-out
I know
...
And I shake with fear
Until I finish giving my talk
I think
What can I tell them?

Our final example comes from Other Voice, one of the strongest voices in this context. As noted in Chap. 6, Other Voice is a grassroots movement of Jewish-Israelis from communities near the Gaza Strip (and some Palestinians from the Gaza Strip), working for a non-violent/non-military solution to the *Hamas*-Israel hostilities. Furthermore, this group, which has held weekly demonstrations, conferences, and seminars; written petitions; and spoken and appeared in international and national media, is often the brunt of anger and verbal and physical violence from Jewish-Israelis, since many in the region, and the country, see their messages as being on a scale that ranges from naiveté to traitorous.

The following Facebook post and photograph appeared on April 22, 2018. In this post, Other Voice reacted to the violence they encountered the week before, when they held a demonstration, at the Yad Mordechai junction (a major junction located close to the border with the Gaza Strip), calling for an end to the humanitarian crisis in Gaza and the reaching of a political solution:

When violent bullies can't stand that there are other voices—they call us traitors, because we have signs that say, "People in Gaza need water and electricity", and "Hope for people on both sides of the border". In the picture below, you see one of the results of the violence used against us during the last protest at Yad Mordechai. We will be there on Friday, between 12:00–14:00. Come stand with us.

In this photo (see Fig. 7.5), we see broken signs and a crumpled Israeli flag (in the top left-hand corner)—on the ground. The sign in the front says, "Try living with 3 hours of electricity every day"—referring to the severe lack of electricity in the Gaza Strip at the time. In the back, by the Israeli flag, the sign says: "Water and electricity are basic rights."

Fig. 7.5 Other Voice—Destroyed Signs (2018)

Furthermore, in the middle back—on one of the torn posters—the words "Life and hope" can still be read. However, most of the other signs cannot be read and/or are turned over. The colors of the photo are mainly browns/ monotones and it is mainly the blue of the Israeli flag that adds color. The photo also captured the wooden poles that held up the signs that now appear to be holding them down—perhaps creating the message that the messages of Other Voice are being trampled and stifled. Therefore, this photo and post convey the message that hope, peace, life, and concern for the Gazans' rights are in serious trouble in *Otef Aza*.

On the one hand, the photo could reflect the broken spirit of the activists, residents of the region, who face the dangers that all residents face, and because other Jewish-Israelis are keeping them from publicly sharing their messages of peace, hope, and concern for their Gazan neighbors in the public sphere. The crumpled Israeli flag, which was thrown on the ground, could also symbolize the lack of unity between the Jewish-Israelis and, perhaps, the message that, in the eyes of Jewish-Israelis who do not agree with Other Voice's stance, the demonstrators have no right to hold the flag.

However, we can also interpret the monochromic and depressing photograph, together with the defiant post, in a different way. The signs are on the ground, held down by the wooden poles, but the post says: "Come stand with us." That is, while these regional activists may be depressed by the ongoing war, and its horrific consequences on them and on their Gaza neighbors, they are determined to continue to rise up, not be deterred by the "violent bullies" and continue on the path of peace and human rights.

In summation of this sub-theme, when taking each interpretation both separately and together, given the diversity of people, it is clear that Other Voice members face much complexity in their lives, as they need to cope not only with the terror attacks from the Hamas and the Gaza splinter groups, but with Jewish-Israelis, from their area and from throughout the country, who are trying to silence their voices.

Chapter Summary

This chapter showed that life in the *Otef* is characterized by complexity, internal-personal and external-interpersonal/intergroup conflicts, and paradoxes. The interviewees and activists highlighted the dilemmas with which they deal, often on a daily basis. The analyses of the materials led us to the understanding that life in this region requires residents to engage in a great deal of deep reflection, thinking, and re-thinking about their life experiences. Furthermore, life in the *Otef* leads to a plethora of emotions—on the one hand, fear, anger, despair, and helplessness—while on the other hand, commitment, solidarity, love, and attachment to the area—and, at times, even empathy and care for the "enemy"—the Gazans. Moreover, these thoughts and emotions are not static, but evolve over time, depending on the state of the hostilities.

In short, life in the *Otef* is anything but a dichotomy.

Chapter Epilogue

If life was not complicated enough in *Otef Aza*, when the COVID-19 pandemic hit Israel, the Israeli Ministry of Health issued recommendations concerning what to do when there is a *tzeva adom* and a person (or more) is in quarantine (see the letter in Fig. 7.6). According to the letter, from Prof. Itamar Grotto—who, at the time, was the Associate Director-General of the Israeli Ministry of Health—in such a situation, the person/s in isolation should enter a safe space/*mamad*, which is different from the safe space available to the rest of the family. If there is not another safe space/*mamad* in the home, the isolated individual/s should stay as far away as possible from others, with a mask, with her/his face turned away. The person in isolation should also have a plastic chair that can be wiped clean with bleach.

And all of this is to be accomplished in 0–30 seconds.

www.health.gov.il

משנה למנהל הכללי
Associate Director General

משרד
הבריאות
להיים בריאים יותר

ג' בניסן, התש"פ
28 מרץ 2020
אסמכתא: 169674120

הנדון: <u>המלצות מיגון צבע אדום</u>

בעת אזעקת צבע אדום, אנשים הנמצאים בבידוד בית, יכנסו למרחב המוגן הקרוב ביותר. אם
ניתן להקצות מרחב מוגן נפרד משאר בני הבית עדיף, אחרת מבודד הבית יחבוש מסכה,
ישהה בנקודה הרחוקה ביותר משאר בני הבית, יקפיד כי פניו אינם מופנים אליהם, וימנע
ממגע פיזי ישיר איתם.
אם במרחב המוגן יש כסאות, יש להקצות למבודד הבית כסא פלסטיק שניתן לחיטוי אחרי על
ידי תמיסת אקונומיקה לאחר תום האירוע.

בכבוד רב,

פרופ' איתמר גרוטו
המשנה למנהל הכללי

העתק:
חמל אגף שע"ח

Associate Director General
Ministry of Health
P.O.B 1176 Jerusalem 91010
mmancal@moh.health.gov.il
081207 Fax: 02-5655983

לשכת משנה למנהל הכללי
משרד הבריאות
ת.ד. 1176 ירושלים 91010
mmancal@moh.health.gov.il
טל: 02-5081207 פקס: 02-5655983

Fig. **7.6** Recommendation for Taking Cover During COVID-19
Pandemic (2020)

References

Billig, M. (1987). *Arguing and thinking: A rhetorical approach to social psychology*. Cambridge University Press.

Festinger, L. (1957). *A theory of cognitive dissonance* (Vol. 2). Stanford University Press.

Part III

Patriotism, Zionism, and Interviewees' Perceptions of Self and Gazan Other

In this Part, we focus on the concepts of patriotism and Zionism, in order to learn how *Otef Aza* residents perceive these ideologies. However, before presenting the theoretical perspectives discussed in the academic literature and our empirical findings, which, at times, mirrored the academic literature and, at others, expanded and contradicted stereotypical perceptions, we will explain why we chose to explore this question in our work.

To begin with, we raised this question since there is often a widespread belief among Jewish-Israelis and others (i.e., Arabs, Palestinians, people from abroad) that Israeli citizens, who live near the Gaza Strip, *must* be diehard patriots and Zionists, understood in the most one-dimensional and stereotypical way. Otherwise, why would they continue to endanger themselves and their families by living in an area that is entangled in a very dangerous intractable war? Furthermore, in our review of the academic literature, we did not come across a psycho-social study that asked this question of the population we studied. Therefore, while there appears to be a myth that *Otef Aza* residents are "typical patriot/Zionists" (whatever that means), no one has ever investigated if this is true or what these residents even think about these labels placed on them.

Our second reason is that, as noted in the beginning to this book, Zionism—in its many forms—has been one of the backbones of the Jewish state, and was the reason for the first *aliyah* in the late nineteenth century (The First Aliyah—1882–1903, November 23, 2020), which eventually led to many other waves of *aliyot*[1] throughout the years. As we shall discuss in Chap. 8—the first chapter in this Part—for most Jewish-Israelis, and certainly for those who immigrated to Israel—Zionism is one, solid core of Jewish-Israeli society, even for those who do not accept it. And, as we shall demonstrate in Chap. 9—in which we present our analyses of how our interviewees viewed these concepts—Zionism continues to play an important part in Jewish-Israeli culture, even among those residents who either did not relate to the term or opposed it. In short, since discussions and perceptions of Zionism often pervade Israeli discourse, on manifest and latent levels, we believed it important to see what *Otef Aza* residents actually think and feel about this ideology.

We cannot leave this point, however, without acknowledging that for many—some in Israel and many in Palestine and in the world—the term Zionism is a red flag, as they perceive it as one kind of racist colonialism that has evolved into apartheid (e.g., Badran, 2009; Said, 1979). Therefore, we understand that this is far from a neutral term, and that there may be readers who find such a focus as an indication that we—the Jewish-Israeli authors of this book—explored this topic, in order to (perhaps) try to persuade readers that Zionism is a desirable ideology. Therefore, in order to be clear, our intent here was/is neither to promote nor to denigrate Zionism (and/or patriotism), but rather to systematically learn how *Otef Aza* residents perceive these ideologies, given that they are deeply embedded in Israeli social-political life.

The final chapter in this Part, Chap. 10, moves to the next major topic that we explored in our study, by turning the lens outward, to residents' perspectives of the Gazan others. We found that, almost overwhelmingly, our interviewees did not see the ordinary Gazans as their enemy, but rather as extremely unfortunate people who are caught between a rock (Israel) and a hard place (the *Hamas*) and are lacking resources and opportunities that make life good. Most expressed empathy and sympathy with the Gazans, clearly differentiating between them—who they often termed

---

[1] Plural of *aliyah*.

neighbors and brothers—and the unmistakable "enemy"—the *Hamas*—who the residents saw as responsible for the violence from Gaza.

When taken together, these three chapters offer a kind of holistic system, within the context of life in an intractable conflict. Residents' perspectives on (internal) Israeli issues of patriotism and Zionism are inherently connected to their perspectives on the external, Palestinian Gazans. These perspectives, thus, add another layer to our understandings concerning the meaning of life for Jewish-Israelis from the *Otef.*

8

Patriotism and Zionism: A Review of the Literature

For many years, scholars from philosophy, political science, social/political psychology, and conflict resolution have researched the concepts of patriotism and Zionism. This research has led to different definitions, different categories of patriotism and Zionism, and debates on whether they are ultimately "good" or "bad." Since there is extensive literature on these issues, it is beyond the scope of this book to present an in-depth discussion of patriotism and Zionism. As a result, we provide a basic overview of the topics. Furthermore, the sub-topics presented in this review were chosen since they captured what our interviewees told us, in addition to the new aspects that we discerned in our analyses, presented in the following chapter.

Even though there are many categories and definitions of patriotism, all forms have a common core: they all relate to patriotism as reflecting love of and attachment to one's country, and to the belief that that there is an entity larger than the individual that should be nurtured. While we tend to think of patriotism on the nation-state level, Cafaro (2009) reminds us that older understandings of "patriot," "patriotism," and "country" were more flexible, allowing for patriotic connection and devotion to different localities, on smaller scales. This perspective is relevant

© The Author(s), under exclusive license to Springer Nature Switzerland AG 2022
J. Chaitin et al., *Routine Emergency*, https://doi.org/10.1007/978-3-030-95983-8_8

for our discussion of patriotism among *Otef Aza* residents, as will be seen below.

Despite the vast literature on the topic, Ariely (2018) drew our attention to the fact that there has been little research on how people and diverse groups perceive patriotism. This is also what we found, when we searched for academic literature that examined *Otef Aza* residents' perspectives on patriotism: we did not find any studies that specifically explored the issue on this population. Furthermore, as noted in the introduction of Part III of this book, instead of assuming that *Otef Aza* residents have one perspective on patriotism and Zionism, we decided to hear what they had to say on the matter. As will be demonstrated in Chap. 9, the exploration of residents' understandings of these concepts uncovered a rich field of perspectives.

We begin with definitions of patriotism and research findings on the topic, starting with a general overview of patriotism. We then take a short detour to cosmopolitanism—which can be conceived as a negation of a more conventional approach to patriotism. From there, we consider the Israeli case. After these sections, we present and discuss the no-less-complex topic of Zionism.

Patriotism

Conventional/genuine patriotism is defined as love of one's country and a benevolent form of attachment to the nation (Adorno et al., 1950; Kelman, 1997; 2017; Schatz & Staub, 1997). While generally viewed positively (Ariely, 2017), patriotism has also been perceived as "obedience at the expense of democratic controversy" (Parker, 2002, p. 410). Patriotism reflects a number of aspects: (1) special affection for and pride in one's country (Kosterman & Feshbach, 1989; Nathanson, 1993; Primoratz, 2017), which can also reflect *symbolic patriotism*—love of the country's flag, anthem, and so on (Parker, 2009); (2) personal identification with and attachment to the country (Adorno et al., 1950; Nathanson, 1993; Schatz et al., 1999); (3) special concern for the wellbeing of and loyalty to the country (Kelman, 1997; Nathanson, 1993); and (4) a willingness to sacrifice oneself for the nation (Druckman, 1994; Godwin, 2016; Nathanson, 1993).

Blind/pseudo/authoritarian patriotism is described as an uncritical idealization of and submission to the nation. This type includes negative attitudes about outgroups that can have tragic results, such as persecution of minorities, bigotry, and chauvinism (e.g., Adorno et al., 1950; Davidov, 2010; Grammes, 2011; Kateb, 2008; LaMothe, 2009; Parker, 2009; Roccas et al., 2008; Zavala et al., 2009). Blind patriotism has been connected to *glorification* of the national group: glorifiers view their national in-group as superior to others. They emphasize respect of group symbols and feel insulted when group members do not demonstrate respect for these symbols (Roccas et al., 2008).

Constructive/democratic patriotism, an opposite form, reflects attachment to the country while questioning and criticizing practices seen as negative, in order to help improve the nation (Ariely, 2016; Deats, 2002; Grammes, 2011; Parker, 2002). Constructive patriots work for the rights of all, fashioning activists into *critical loyalists* (Staub, 2003). As Morris (1982) noted 30 years ago, "being critically engaged with one's country constitutes the highest form of love" (p. 210). National identification with the environment is also a form of constructive patriotism. However, while such a patriotism focuses on environmental causes, it is also a global concept, one that exhibits pride of place, but not fear of others (Siegel & Morris, 2010).

Thus, constructive patriotism is seen as reflecting good citizenship, associated with democratic values, tolerance, and benevolent intergroup attitudes (Roccas et al., 2006, 2008; Schatz & Staub, 1997; Schatz et al., 1999; Zavala et al., 2009).

Research that compared constructive and blind patriotism found that the two are negatively correlated concerning their relationships with authoritarianism, intergroup conflict, racism, xenophobia, a willingness to criticize the nation, civic participation, and a sense of foreign threat (Gomberg, 2002; Nussbaum, 2002; Richey, 2011; Sahar, 2008; Schatz & Staub, 1997; Schatz et al., 1999).

Constitutional patriotism (Habermas, 1996), another type of patriotism, has often been used in reference to the European context, as it conceptualizes a new kind of bond between European citizens and the

EU (Menent, 2016; Muller, 2007a). This brand of patriotism reflects citizens' attachment to superordinate liberal and democratic values and principles, rather than to national identities. As such, it is perceived as a way to create a sense of belonging that neither imitates nor competes with historically rooted specific national traditions (Canihac, 2017).

Since constitutional patriotism connects to the idea of a "post-national" identity (Lacroix, 2002), it is identified as having the potential to promote coexistence and cooperation among different peoples from different countries. This is because it is grounded in the belief that belonging to a particular cultural and historical community is not a sufficient base for citizenship (Ferry & Thibaud, 1992). One objective of constitutional patriotism is to foster a shared political culture. In the European case, it promotes creation of a social bond in the EU's liberal-democratic states, based on legal, moral, and political aspects, rather than historical, cultural, and geographical ones (Ferry & Thibaud, 1992).

While constitutional patriotism does not deny the importance of local, national, and regional identities, Habermas (1996) sees the overriding motives of constitutional patriotism as linked to universal principles of human rights and democracy, which serve as a guide for actions and policies. Furthermore, this kind of patriotism requires that states, and their citizens, critically look at themselves and recognize crimes they may have committed against others (Ferry, 2000). When countries and citizens adopt constitutional patriotism, they distance themselves from ethnocentricity (Joppke, 2005). As Parekh (2000, p. 204) stated: "We cannot incorporate 'them' so long as 'we' remain 'we'; 'we must be loosed up to create a new common space in which 'they' can be accommodated and become part of a new reconstituted 'we.'"

Environmental patriotism is another form of patriotism discussed in the literature. According to Todd (2013), who studied the American context, love of country usually links to a region's/country's national landscape. Therefore, patriotism is fundamentally an environmental concept. Patriotism establishes a connection to place, based on a commitment to community and obligation to the land. According to Todd (2013, p. 6), "environmental patriotism is the belief that a country's environment defines its greatness." This reflects Eckersley's (2004) notion that patriotism entails a deep and intimate knowledge of and attachment to particular places and Cafaro's (2009, p. 192) straightforward statement that "environmentalism … *is* patriotism."

As Todd further notes, such a patriotism also evokes an aesthetic and ethical connection to a place. It is aesthetic, because the patriotism is motivated by an appreciation for the beauty of the regional and national scenery and it is ethical because it relies on citizens' responsibility to protect natural resources that helps ensure democratic values.

Todd also avers that people's personal experiences create an attachment to their place that influences their perceptions of self and collective, in a broad ecological and cultural context. She presents three types of environmental patriotic action: "*conservation*—the wise use of natural resources; *stewardship*—an appreciation of beauty and respect for bounty of national landscape; and *democracy*—participatory engagement in environmental issues" (p. 105). Furthermore, environmental patriotism represents "patriotism without borders" (p. 104), since it avers that *all* peoples have the right to live in a healthy, peaceful, and sustainable environment. Thus, "environmental patriotism offers an expanded sense of homeland in order to promote global consciousness: to be patriotic beyond the nation, to be a patriot of the planet" (p. 104).

In sum, we can identify at least five types of patriotism discussed in the literature—on one extreme, we have blind patriotism/glorification—which is ethnocentric and nation-specific—and on the other, environmental patriotism—which extends to all people in the world. It is important to note that, to the best of our knowledge, no previous research on Israeli patriotism has explored the two types of constitutional and environmental patriotism.

Before leaving our short discussion of patriotism, however, we will briefly present the idea of cosmopolitanism—which can be seen as a negation of a conventional understanding of patriotism. Our reason for including this concept here is because it appeared in some forms in some of our interviewees' words, and also because we see this concept as not only relevant for the global times in which we live, but also for thinking differently about Israeli-Palestinian relations in the *Otef Aza*-Gaza region.

Cosmopolitanism

According to the *Stanford Encyclopedia of Philosophy* (Cosmopolitanism, October 17, 2019, para. 1), cosmopolitan—a word derived from the Greek *kosmopolitēs* (citizen of the world)—reflects numerous views in moral and socio-political philosophy. The core shared idea is that *all* people are (or can/should be) citizens in a single community. Different versions of cosmopolitanism envision this community in different ways: some focus on political institutions, others on moral norms or relationships, while others emphasize shared markets or cultural expression. For the most part, while the universal community of world citizens is perceived as a positive ideal to be attained, few forms perceive cosmopolitanism primarily as grounds for elimination of special obligations to local forms of political organizations. Versions of the notion also vary depending on whether thinkers relate to "world citizenship" in a literal or metaphorical manner.

Gusacov (2019), an Israeli educational academic, perceives cosmopolitanism as reflective of a moral idea, which is interwoven in a human fraternity, based on the obligation to work for the good of all. Nations that adopt cosmopolitanism would work toward the advancement of humanity, overall—whoever and wherever they may be. Cosmopolitanism may propose establishing a world government for the management of human affairs with equality, which would be supported by international law, an international parliament, and an educational system compatible with cosmopolitan values (Archibugi, 2012; Beck, 2011).

Warburg (2006) adds another interesting layer to cosmopolitanism by differentiating between the *cosmolocal—cosmopolitans* who are also committed to their local community—and "hard" cosmopolitans, who seek attainment of a lifestyle which transcends the "local," focuses on global aspirations, and respects the "others" in their "otherness."

According to Beck (2011), global risks are a significant catalyst for creating what he calls "imagined cosmopolitan risk communities," that is, communities with cosmopolitan tendencies that are being generated by nuclear, ecological, technological, and economical risks. In today's world, which contains vast globalization, transnational mobility, and mass media development, linking together people dealing with the same global risks is perceived as inevitable.

In terms of adoption of cosmopolitanism in Israel, Gusacov (2019) and Nussbaum (2002) aver that while this approach is comprised of positive and beneficial values, it would not replace local patriotic education in Israeli society. They propose integrating cosmopolitan values and viewpoints into patriotic education through strengthening communalities that exist between people in the world, but not beyond that (Gusacov, 2019; Nussbaum, 2002).

We now turn to patriotism in Israel.

Patriotism in Israel

Israeli patriotism cannot be understood without acknowledging its Zionist roots. Since the era of the *Yishuv*,[1] Zionist ideology has usually been a given for Jewish-Israeli patriotism. Zionism, like patriotism, is a complex concept that has been defined and related to differently by many scholars throughout the years. (Below, we present an overview of the ideology.) However, in order to understand the basis of Jewish-Israeli patriotism, we must begin by noting that, in its broadest sense, Zionist ideology emphasizes the deep connection of all Jews to their biblical homeland, which became the State of Israel in 1948. Shapira (2004) cited Berl Katznelson—a twentieth-century Labor Zionist leader—who asserted that Jewish patriotism predated the state, carrying the love of the homeland for generations, and was, therefore, patriotism connected to the Bible. While there are numerous variations of Zionism (Tyler, 2011), regardless of these variations, Zionism has been the cornerstone of Jewish-Israeli sense of belonging.

Another way that Zionism connects to patriotism, as Naveh (2018) noted, is that the Zionist collective narrative emphasizes the millennia-old persecution of the Jewish people, after its exile from the ancient Land of Israel. Furthermore, Zionist reactions against "anti-Jewish menacing forces of evil" (Naveh, 2018, p. 77) are presented as redemptive

---

[1] The pre-State Jewish community in Palestine.

processes. This Zionist narrative is disseminated to Israelis through holiday ceremonies, which emphasize how Jewish victims, who have been persecuted by evil enemies—in the distant past and in the present—have overcome these dangers. Politicians use this rhetoric in their speeches, and the Zionist message is found in media and artistic performances, in historical museums and monuments, and in the school history curriculum. Indeed, patriotism and Zionism are often conflated:

> Even prior to their encounter with the school history curriculum, young Israelis were exposed to patriotic time and space throughout the Hebrew calendar and the topography of country. This patriotic time was integrated into a patriotic space of the land, which served as location for journeys and visits, archeological discoveries, and historical reconstructions. The power of the Zionist historical narrative lay in the idea that history could be controlled, molded, and changed by the formation of an active, task-oriented Israeli reality. (Naveh, 2018, p. 78)

Therefore, the basis of Jewish-Israeli patriotism is often tied to Zionist ideology and narrative, and even though times have brought changes, this is the context within which Jewish-Israeli patriotism is generally framed. Furthermore, since many interviewees also conflated the two conceptualizations, we saw the importance of tying the issues together in this review.

And now to a brief presentation of research on Jewish-Israeli patriotism.

Arad and Alon's research (2006) of Israeli patriotism found that nearly 90% of their Jewish-Israeli sample expressed a strong willingness to fight for and remain living in the country; respondents expressed deep attachment to a country perceived as being under constant threat. Jewish-Israeli patriotism was stronger among the right-wing, the religious, the more affluent, older citizens and among people with less formal education than among the left-wing, the secular, the less affluent, younger people and among university graduates. Additionally, the authors noted a patriotic decline through the generations: compared to their elders, younger generations expressed less willingness to sacrifice themselves for Israel and/or to remain in Israel, especially if emigration would significantly improve their economic standing.

Other research that explored Israeli patriotism demonstrated that Jewish-Israelis are expected to adjust to life under the constant threat of terror and understand that "life must go on." That is, they need to acknowledge the risks of living in the country, a central theme in the Israeli collective narrative. This understanding is further accompanied by the feeling that there is shared responsibility to contribute to the homeland in numerous ways (e.g., Litvak Hirsch et al., 2015; Sever et al., 2008).

In April 2017, the Israeli Peace Index asked respondents questions about patriotism. Major results indicated that 86% of the Jewish respondents felt very proud of being Israeli. The proudest supported the right-wing settlers' political party, with the least proud coming from left-wing voters. These findings further mesh with Schnell's study (2017) that showed that Jewish settlement over the Green Line helped establish a blind uncritical patriotism.

Sekerdej and Roccas' (2016) studies compared constructive and conventional patriotism in samples in Poland and Israel. Israeli students negatively associated constructive patriotism with the pursuit of self-interests. The researchers also found that when Israelis wrote texts about contributing to the nation, individuals who scored higher on constructive patriotism wrote more detailed texts than people who scored lower.

In the one study that we found that noted the issue of patriotism/Zionism among *Otef Aza* residents (Litvak Hirsch et al., 2015), some mothers, who were asked about what "home" meant to them, mentioned the patriotic/Zionist significance of the concept (the researchers did not specifically ask them about this connection). One interviewee tied the significance of home to patriotism and Zionism, an ideology she said was emphasized in her childhood home. Another woman stated that remaining at home exemplified her pride in being a strong Israeli and that remaining in her home during war was a price she was willing to pay, in order to demonstrate her patriotism.

Finally, as noted in Chap. 3, Israeli patriotism has been linked to psycho-social beliefs (e.g., Bar-Tal, 2000; Bar-Tal & Ben Amos, 2004), including beliefs concerning military service. The Israeli military is a central socializing factor for patriotism. It is imbued with issues of security and with the national ethos of acts of heroism and sacrifices made for the country's defense (Bar-Tal et al., 2012; Press, 2007; Zamir, 2015).

Zionism

The official birth of the modern Zionist movement took place in Europe in 1897 (Neuberger, 1999). Fifty-one years later, when the State of Israel was established, its Declaration of Independence related to cornerstones of Zionism:

> The Land of Israel was the birthplace of the Jewish people. Here their spiritual, religious and national identity was formed. Here they achieved independence and created a culture of national and universal significance … wrote and gave the Bible to the world. Exiled from Palestine, the Jewish people remained faithful to it in … never ceasing to pray and hope for their return and restoration of their national freedom … [Jews] returned … reclaimed a wilderness, revived their language, built cities and villages … They sought peace, yet were ever prepared to defend themselves. They brought blessings of progress to all inhabitants of the country … the first Zionist Congress … proclaimed the right of the Jewish people to a national revival in their own country … The Nazi holocaust … proved anew the urgency of the re-establishment of the Jewish state … It is, moreover, the self-evident right of the Jewish people to be a nation, as all other nations, in its own sovereign state. Accordingly, we, the members of National Council, representing the Jewish people in Palestine and the Zionist movement of the world … proclaim the establishment of the Jewish state … [it] will be based on … liberty, justice and peace taught by the Hebrew prophets; will uphold the full social and political equality of all its citizens without distinction of race, creed or sex; will guarantee full freedom of conscience, worship, education and culture … We offer peace and amity to all neighboring states and their peoples.

As can be seen from the above, while the Declaration of Independence manifestly ties Israel's establishment to the historical-religious history of the Jews in *Eretz Yisrael* (the Land of Israel) and to the Holocaust, it also connected to values of human rights, equality, democracy, and peace. This declaration, thus, reflected the official approach to Zionist ideology on which the country was founded.

One significant aspect of Zionism is *building*. Chowers (2002) notes the many instances in which the word בניין—*binyan*—which can be a verb (to build) or a noun (an actual building)—permeates Zionist ideology. Since *binyan* relates both to creation and to actual buildings that help form national identity (such as monuments, schools, and cultural centers), the Zionist project is often characterized as *binyan leumi* (nation building). The *chalutzim* (pioneers), who arrived in Palestine in the early twentieth century (Almog, 2000), shaped the Zionist ethos. They saw the biblical land as the foundation for nation-building and the structure as comprised of the waves of immigration and the establishment of the economic and civic organizations, rejuvenation of the national language, and (pre-)state and military institutions (Robinson Devine, 2000).

Another hallmark of Zionism was rejection of everything "Diasporic"—rejection of the Diaspora image of the Jew, rejection of Jewish Diaspora culture—perceived as being at the root of the "Jewish problem" in Europe (Robinson Devine, 2000), and rejection of continued Jewish life in the Diaspora (Auron, 2015). The Diaspora Jew, who was perceived as weak and unable to defend him/herself (Bar-On, 2008), was an image that the Zionist *chalutzim* aimed to change. They aspired to create a "new Jew"—the *Sabra*—who broke with traditional bonds of religion, was physically strong, worked and built the land, and fought for/defended the country (Almog, 2000; Naveh, 2018).

It is important to note that modern Zionism was/is a collection of movements, and not one cohesive, static idea. Furthermore, *within* these movements, there have always been heated debates. In the beginning, this movement was mostly led by *Ashkenazic* Jews and was mainly, though not solely, a national-secular movement (Gaynor, 2006), one that arose as a response to the centuries of discrimination and persecution of the Jews in Europe (Don-Yehiya, 1998). However, it is also important to remember that Jews in the Arab/Muslim countries experienced much less persecution than the European Jews experienced. Hence, the longing of Jews for Zion in the Arab/Muslim countries had a stronger religious-historical basis than a search for a haven for the Jews (Gaynor, 2006).

In its early political form, Zionism called for *aliyah*—immigration to and settlement in *Eretz Yisrael* (Livneh, 1964). *Political Zionism*, the national liberation movement of the Jewish people, was not created in a vacuum: it emerged within the context of the liberal nationalism that characterized Europe in the nineteenth century (Neuberger, 1999). Alongside and based on political Zionism, other forms of Zionism arose. Some have disappeared, some have continued/evolved, and some new forms were created. These are now briefly presented.

Early (Non-mainstream) Streams of Zionism

Two former streams of Zionism were *Cultural/Spiritual Zio*nism and *Brit Shalom* (The Covenant of Peace). Ahad Ha'am ("One of the People," the nom de plume of Asher Ginzberg), was one of the main leaders and philosophers of the cultural stream. He did not advocate for massive Jewish immigration to Palestine, but rather understood Zionism as emphasizing Jewish culture, what he perceived to be at the heart of Jewish identity (Chowers, 2002). Since Ahad Ha'am believed that Jews would continue to live in the Diaspora, he envisioned the Zionist project as the "building of a 'spiritual center' in *Eretz Yisrael*/Palestine that would become the beating heart of the Jewish people" (Maor, 2013, p. 81), living throughout the world.

The second non-mainstream stream, *Brit Shalom* (established in 1926), joined together Labor Zionist ideology (detailed below) with cultural/spiritual Zionism and the belief that agricultural labor created a commonality between the Arabs in Palestine and the Jewish immigrants (Vogt, 2016). Some of the prominent philosophers/leaders of the movement included Martin Buber, Hannah Arendt (for a while—Raz-Krakotzkin, 2011) and Gershom Scholem. *Brit Shalom* advocated binationalism, seeing the Arabs as natural partners in the Zionist project (Maor, 2013, p. 17). The movement believed Arabs and Jews would strive together for national liberation through labor and the creation/maintaining of roots and a joint community in their shared land. Thus, this stream perceived Zionism as the opposite of European colonization, and as a step toward decolonization (Maor, 2013). However, once the UN partition plan was put into motion and Israel was established as the nation-state of the Jews, this Zionist stream disappeared.

Labor/Socialist Zionism

This kind of Zionism was the mainstream ideology until the mid-1970s, in general, but was extremely prominent in the early decades of the twentieth century. *Labor Zionism* emphasized that reclamation of the land was dependent upon massive immigration of Jews, who would engage in cultivation of the land, in collective settlements rooted in a socialist ideology (Zouplna, 2008). The ideologues of this stream included, among others, David Ben-Gurion, A.D. Gordon, and later Yitzhak Tabenkin (Chowers, 2002; Zouplna, 2008). Labor Zionism aimed to create an ideal Jewish society, based on egalitarianism, socialist values, agricultural work, self-sufficiency, and participant democracy (Peleg, 2005).

One of the main pillars of the Labor Zionist movement was *kibbush avoda* ("Conquest of Labor"), which stressed the necessity of Jewish labor for creating Jewish society in the new/old country (Glazer, 2007). As Glazer (2007) notes, "resurrection was another powerful symbol in the context of Hebrew Labor, since the mainstream Zionist ideology viewed Palestine as a dead land, in need of 'upbuilding'" (p. 29). For example, he cites a 1934 manifesto, "Hebrew Labor in the Hebrew Yishuv!" that was issued by the Committee to Strengthen Hebrew Labor in *Eretz Yisrael*. This document declared that by employing Jews in manual labor, there would be a resurrection of the Hebrew language, spirit, and working masses (p. 29).

This Zionist ideology was at the basis of the political-economic power structure until 1977, when there was an electoral "revolution"—the right-wing Likud party won the national elections, in what became known as the *mahapach* (revolution), becoming the dominant ruling party, which was more or less been in power until mid-2021. The Likud—which was/is based on *Revisionist Zionism*—focused on a different kind of Zionist ideology, which became the new mainstream ideology in Jewish-Israeli society.

Revisionist Zionism

In the Revisionist Zionism's founder, Vladimir (Ze'ev) Jabotinsky's, famous article "The Iron Wall" (November 4, 1923), the leader set forth the essence of Revisionist Zionism. While believing that it was "utterly impossible" to eject the Arabs from Palestine, as long as the Jews remain a majority, that was "good enough" for him. Jabotinsky further stressed that the Arabs would never voluntarily relinquish their land. Hence, the only way to achieve Jewish sovereignty over *all* of *Eretz Yisrael* (including Transjordan at the time) was through military force—what he termed the Iron Wall.

In the beginning, Revisionist Zionism—considered the Zionist Right (Peleg, 2005)—differed from and objected to mainstream (Labor) Zionism. This movement saw itself as providing a concrete program of action that rejected the policies of the contemporary (1920s) Labor Zionist leadership (Zouplna, 2008), such as socialism or a willingness to partition *Eretz Yisrael*/Palestine between the Jews and Arabs (Peleg & Scham, 2007). Revisionists, who emphasized the need for massive Jewish immigration, called to extend the borders of what would become the state, and supported urban development and capital investment over agricultural pioneering (Zouplna, 2008).

As Peleg (2005, pp. 129, 132) avers:

> [F]or the leaders and followers of the Zionist Right … Greater Israel was not merely an issue of power interest or even a matter of survival in an anarchic world … "Greater Israel" was for them an article of faith, sacred and unchangeable, an element of "being" … forming the core of Zionism and Judaism itself … Revisionists … dream[t] about the re-establishment of "Malchut Yisrael" [the Kingdom of Israel]. The emphasis … [was] on the renewal of its glorious past, when the Israelite kingdom spread on both sides of the Jordan River … within the Revisionist myth, national power, territory, and identity were inseparable.

After the sudden death of Jabotinsky in 1940 (Peleg, 2005), *Neo-Revisionism* emerged as the most radical, secular version of Israeli nationalism (Peleg & Scham, 2007), led by the *Herut* (Freedom) Party under

Menachem Begin. The Neo-Revisionists, who rejected the 1947 UN partition of Palestine, later supported an assertive, militarized Israeli foreign policy. Since the electoral revolution 1977, the Likud party, which has ruled for most of the years, has implemented a strong settlement policy in the Occupied Territories (Peleg & Scham, 2007) and moved the country from a more socialistic/welfare state base to a neoliberal economic base.

Religious Zionism and National Religious Zionism

Another stream in Zionism was the religious stream, which, before the establishment of the state, related to the return of the Jewish people to *Eretz Yisrael* from a theological, messianic perspective (Gaynor, 2006; Salmon, 1998). The religious Zionist movement took hold in the late nineteenth century, during the period termed *Hibbat Zion* (Love of Zion) (Luz, 1998). The major movement that eventually evolved from this wedding of settlement and religion, in the twentieth century, was the *Mizrachi* movement (Salmon, 1998).

The main ideologue of the modern *religious Zionist* movement was Rabbi Abraham Isaac Kook, who perceived Zionism as reflecting *Halacha* (Jewish law). He urged young religious Jews to immigrate, and urged the secular Labor Zionists not to forsake Judaism. Kook saw Zionism as a part of a divine scheme, which would eventually bring *geula* (salvation)—first to the Jewish people, after it resettled in its homeland, and then to the entire world. This would eventually make it possible for the Messiah to come (Samson & Fishman, 1999).

While there are still religious Zionists who adhere to the socialist stream of Zionism, overall, the movement became more radicalized and is known today as the National-Religious Right (Rabinovich, 2018). The national-religious stream believes that the state should reflect Jewish interests. Therefore, it aspires for a social-political system based on values from the religious world and Jewish legacy, rather than from the secular-liberal-cosmopolitan world (The Rise of the Religious Right in Israel, 2017). The main expression of the national-religious stream has been its push for settlement in all of *Eretz Yisrael*. This ideology emphasizes Jewish religious identity and nationalism, seeing liberal and universal values as detrimental to the Jewish people and the Jewish state (Acosta, 2014). Furthermore, this ideological stance and program of action posits an alternative to the ideology of secular Zionism that has ruled the country since its founding.

If, in the beginning, religious Zionism stressed "Torah and labor" and "Torah and *derech Eretz*" (moral behavior), over time, it shifted its focus to Jewish settlement in all of *Eretz Yisrael*. It was from these circles that *Gush Emunim* (the Bloc of the Faithful) emerged in the early 1970s (Ben-Moshe, 2005). This stream of Zionism garnered more support in direct response to the Oslo peace process, which advocated trading land for peace, and was a response to the growing post-Zionist voices (described below). "The religious right, the main ideological opponents of the Oslo process, believed Rabin was giving up Greater Israel because he and his supporters lacked the will to stay and fight for their beliefs" (Ben-Moshe, 2005, p. 15). Settler adherents to this stream of Zionism see themselves as the new pioneers, who are founding new communities in the "barren dangerous hills of Samaria" (Ben-Moshe, 2005, p. 16). The movement sees control over Greater Israel as a way to preserve not only Israel's physical security, but also its spiritual security (Ben-Moshe, 2005).

Other characteristics of this Zionist stream are a more aggressive approach to Jews' relationship with the world, in general, and the Arab world, in particular. The national-religious perspective focuses on Jews' uniqueness in the world, emphasizes the idea that "the whole world is against us," and perceives the main lesson of the Holocaust to be the need for Israel to be militarily strong, in order to be prepared to fight off potential enemies (Ben-Moshe, 2005).

Post-Zionism

In the late 1980s and early 1990s, many Jewish intellectuals and academics, artists, and journalists began challenging and, in some cases, debunking the Zionist historical narrative. This phenomenon, labeled *post-Zionism*, incorporates numerous critical perspectives concerning mainstream Zionist worldviews (Naveh, 2018). One notable criticism is the call to turn the Jewish state into a state for all its citizens (Don-Yehiya, 1998; Ram, 2005).

In his discussion of post-Zionism, Ben-Moshe (2005) cites Laurence Silberstein's (1999) definition of the term: "It is a set of critical positions that problematize Zionist discourse, and the historical narratives and social and cultural representations that it produced" (Ben-Moshe, 2005, p. 14). Gorni (2003) differentiated between "positive" post-Zionism—which accepts the former contribution and legitimation of original Zionistic aspirations—and "negative" post-Zionism—which negates the legitimacy and essence of the Jewish state.

However, as Ben-Moshe (2005), Naveh (2018). and Ram (2005) point out, post-Zionism has numerous meanings and interpretations. For example, Ram denoted four different perspectives of this stream. (a) The *post-ideological perspective*, which avers that once statehood was achieved, the old ideology became irrelevant, and it became important to move on to a new phase of Israeli life and endeavors. This perspective sees this evolution as normal historical development. (b) The *post-modernist perspective* "regards post-Zionism … as a new … epistemology, which subverts and undermines the linear and essentialist point of view of nationalism. Post-Zionism is the exposition of the multifarious identities that have been repressed under the national banner" (p. 31). In other words, this perspective deconstructs the mainstream Zionist collective historical narrative and problematizes it, such as silencing the actions and practices that have occurred on many state and non-state levels concerning disposition of Palestinians from their land and occupation of the Palestinian territories (Algazi, 2013). (c) The *post-colonial perspective*—a particular case of the post-modern perspective—adopts the Orientalism point of view, from an intra-Jewish perspective. This approach sees mainstream Zionism as mainly a White Ashkenazi project, which silenced other Jewish voices and experiences—mainly those of the Mizrachim. This perspective aims to remedy this discriminatory situation (Acosta, 2014). (d) The *post-Marxist* approach considers economic and social changes to be major factors in the shaping of the political and cultural transformations associated with post-Zionism.

In sum, post-Zionism is comprised of numerous streams, social-political-ethnic-economic ideologies. As a result, perhaps its only common factor is that it challenges what came before and calls for new outlooks, policies, and practices concerning the development of Israeli society.

Chapter Summary

The above shows that there are many perspectives on what it means to be a patriot, in general, and what it means to be an Israeli patriot, in specific. Furthermore, what began as a wide variety of approaches to and movements of modern Zionist ideology evolved into more approaches, perspectives, and movements. As a result, when Jewish Israelis are asked if they consider themselves to be "patriots" and/or "Zionists," it is not surprising to hear different perceptions and understandings of these issues. In the following chapter, we examine what our *Otef Aza* interviewees told us—in their words and photographs. Our interviewees expressed new forms that add to the complexity of these phenomena, hence showing that the debate is far from over.

References

Acosta, B. (2014). The dynamics of Israel's democratic tribalism. *Middle East Journal, 68*(2), 268–286.

Adorno, I. W., Frenkel-Brunswlk, E., Levinson, D. J., & Sanford, R. N. (1950). *The authoritarian personality.* Harper & Row.

Algazi, G. (2013). Zionism in the present tense. In M. Birk & S. Hagemann (Eds.), *The only democracy? Zustand und Zukunft der israelischen Demokratie* (pp. 47–61). Aphorisma.

Almog, O. (2000). *The Sabra: The creation of the new Jew.* University of California Press.

Arad, U., & Alon, G. (2006). *Patriotism and Israel's national security: Herzilya patriotism survey 2006.* Lauder School of Government, IDC Herzilya. Diplomacy and Strategy Institute for Policy and Strategy.

Archibugi, D. (2012). Cosmopolitan democracy: A restatement. *Cambridge Journal of Education, 42*(1), 9–20.

Ariely, G. (2016). Why does patriotism prevail? Contextual explanations of patriotism across countries. *Identities: Global Studies in Culture and Power, 24*(3), 351–377.

Ariely, G. (2017). Evaluations of patriotism across countries, groups, and policy domains. *Journal of Ethnic and Migration Studies,* 1–20. https://doi.org/1 0.1080/1369183X.2017.1319761

Ariely, G. (2018). Evaluations of patriotism across countries, groups, and policy domains. *Journal of Ethnic and Migration Studies, 44*(3), 462–481. https:// doi.org/10.1080/1369183X.2017.1319761

Auron, Y. (2015). *Israeli identities: Jews and Arabs facing the self and other.* Berghahn Books.

Bar-On, D. (2008). *The "others" within us: Constructing Jewish-Israeli identity.* Cambridge University Press.

Bar-Tal, D. (2000). *Shared beliefs in a society: Social psychological analysis.* Sage Publications.

Bar-Tal, D., & Ben Amos, A. (2004). Patriotism as a psychosocial phenomenon: Introduction to the analysis of the Israeli case. In D. Bar-Tal & A. Ben Amos (Eds.), *Patriotism, we love you oh country* (pp. 13–28). Hakibbutz Hameuchad. (in Hebrew).

Bar-Tal, D., Sharvit, K., Halperin, E., & Zafran, A. (2012). Ethos of conflict: The concept and its measurement. *Peace and Conflict: Journal of Peace Psychology, 18*(1), 40–61.

Beck, U. (2011). *Cosmopolitanism: A critical theory for the 21st century.* Hakibbutz Hameuchad. (in Hebrew).

Ben-Moshe, D. (2005). The Oslo peace process and two views on Judaism and Zionism, 1992–1996. *British Journal of Middle Eastern Studies, 32*(1), 13–27.

Cafaro, P. (2009). Patriotism as an environmental virtue. *Journal of Agricultural Environmental Ethics, 23*(1), 185–206.

Canihac, H. (2017). From the German past to the European Union's future. Constitutional patriotism and the transnational making of a European political concept (1988–2008). *Journal of Contemporary European Research, 13*(4), 1377–1393.

Chowers, E. (2002). The end of building: Zionism and the politics of the concrete. *The Review of Politics, 64*(4), 599–626.

Cosmopolitanism (2019, October 17). *Stanford encyclopedia of philosophy archive.* https://plato.stanford.edu/archives/win2019/entries/cosmopolitanism/

Davidov, E. (2010). Nationalism and constructive patriotism: A longitudinal test of comparability in 22 countries with the ISSP. *International Journal of*

Public Opinion Research, *23*(1), 88–103. https://doi.org/10.1093/ijpor/edq031

Deats, R. (2002). The higher patriotism. *Fellowship, 68*(3–4), 3. https://search.proquest.com/docview/209441911?accountid=40474

Don-Yehiya, E. (1998). Zionism in retrospective. *Modern Judaism, 18*(3), 267–276.

Druckman, D. (1994). Nationalism, patriotism, and group loyalty: A social psychological perspective. *Mershon International Studies Review, 38*(1), 43–68. https://doi.org/10.2307/222610

Eckersley, R. (2004). *The green state: Rethinking democracy and sovereignty.* The MIT Press.

Ferry, J. M. (2000). *La question de l'Etat européen.* Gallimard.

Ferry, J. M., & Thibaud, P. (1992). *Discussion sur l'Europe.* Calmann-Lévy.

Gaynor, A. (2006). "Neither shall they train for war anymore": Reflections on Zionism, militarism, and conscientious objection. *NWSA Journal, 8*(3), 181–190.

Glazer, S. A. (2007). Language of propaganda: The Histadrut, Hebrew labor, and the Palestinian worker. *Journal of Palestine Studies, 36*(2), 25–38.

Godwin, I. (2016). Patriotism, political participation and women's rights: A critical analysis of Nigeria's Fourth Republic. *Journal of Politics and Law, 9*(9), 15–21.

Gomberg, P. (2002). Patriotism is like racism. In I. Primoratz (Ed.), *Patriotism* (pp. 105–112). Humanity Books.

Gorni, Y. (2003). Zionism as a renewing idea. In T. Friling (Ed.), *An answer to a post-Zionist colleague* (pp. 457–480). Yediot Achronot (Hebrew).

Grammes, T. (2011). Nationalism, patriotism, citizenship and beyond—Editorial. *Journal of Social Science Education, 10*(1), 2–11.

Gusacov, E. (2019). Am I or can I be a citizen of the world? Examining the possibility of cosmopolitan-patriotic education in Israel. *Ethics and Education, 14*(2), 213–226.

Habermas, J. (1996). *Between facts and norms: Contribution to a theory of law and democracy.* MIT Press.

Jabotinsky, V. (1923, November4). *The iron wall.* http://en.jabotinsky.org/media/9747/the-iron-wall.pdf

Joppke, C. (2005). *Selecting by origin: Ethnic migration in the liberal state.* Harvard University Press.

Kateb, G. (2008). *Patriotism and other mistakes.* Yale University Press.

Kelman, H. C. (1997). Nationalism, patriotism and national identity: Social-psychological dimensions. In D. Bar-Tal & E. Staub (Eds.), *Patriotism in the lives of individuals and nations* (pp. 166–189). Nelson-Hall Publishers.

Kosterman, R., & Feshbach, S. (1989). Toward a measure of patriotic and nationalistic attitudes. *Political Psychology, 10*(2), 257–274.

Lacroix, J. (2002). For a European constitutional patriotism. *Political Studies, 50*(5), 944–958. https://doi.org/10.1111/1467-9248.00402

LaMothe, R. (2009). The problem of patriotism: A psychoanalytic and theological analysis. *Pastoral Psychology, 58*(2), 151–166.

Litvak Hirsch, T., Braun-Lewensohn, O., & Lazar, A. (2015). Does home attachment contribute to strengthen sense of coherence in times of war? Perspectives of Jewish Israeli mothers. *Women & Health.* https://doi.org/1 0.1080/03630242.2015.1022688

Livneh, E. (1964). Does Zionism have a future? *Tradition: A Journal of Orthodox Jewish Thought, 6*(2), 30–41.

Luz, E. (1998). The limits of toleration. In S. Almog, J. Reinharz, & A. Shapira (Eds.), *Zionism and religion* (pp. 44–54). Brandeis University Press.

Maor, Z. (2013). Moderation from right to left: The hidden roots of brit Shalom. *Jewish Social Studies: History, Culture, Society, 19*(2), 79–108.

Menent, M. (2016). A new European constitutional patriotism for Habermas. *Philosophy Study, 6*(8), 496–510.

Morris, D. (1982). *Self-reliant cities, energy and the transformation of urban America.* Sierra Club Books.

Muller, J. W. (2007a). Is Europe converging on constitutional patriotism? (and if so, is it justified?). *Critical Review of International Social and Political Philosophy, 10*(3), 377–387.

Nathanson, S. (1993). *Patriotism, morality, and peace.* Rowman & Littlefield.

Naveh, E. (2018). Israel's past at 70: The twofold attack on the Zionist historical narrative. *Israel Studies, 23*(3), 76–83.

Neuberger, B. (1999, October 12). *Zionism.* Israel Ministry of Foreign Affairs. https://mfa.gov.il/mfa/aboutisrael/state/pages/zionism-%20background.aspx

Nussbaum, M. C. (2002). Patriotism and cosmopolitanism. In M. C. Nussbaum & J. J. Cohen (Eds.), *For love of country? Debating the limits of patriotism* (pp. 2–17). Beacon.

Parekh, B. C. (2000). *Rethinking multiculturalism: Cultural diversity and political theory.* Macmillan.

Parker, C. S. (2009). Symbolic versus blind patriotism: Distinction without difference? *Political Research Quarterly*, 1–18. https://doi.org/10.1177/1065912908327228

Parker, R. D. (2002). Homeland: An essay on patriotism. *Harvard Journal of Law and Public Policy*, 25(2), 407–427.

Peleg, I. (2005). The Zionist right and constructivist realism: Ideological persistence and tactical readjustment. *Israel Studies*, 10(3), 127–153,247.

Peleg, I., & Scham, P. (2007). Israeli neo-revisionism and American neoconservatism: The unexplored parallels. *The Middle East Journal*, 61(1), 73–94.

Press, E. (2007). Death and sacrifice in Israel. *Raritan*, 27(2), 125–143.

Primoratz, I. (2017, Summer). *Patriotism*. The Stanford encyclopedia of philosophy. https://plato.stanford.edu/archives/sum2017/entries/patriotism/

Rabinovich, I. (2018, December 6). Religion and politics in Israel. *The Caravan*, 1820. https://www.hoover.org/research/religion-and-politics-israel

Ram, U. (2005). Post-Zionist studies of Israel: The first decade. *Israel Studies Forum*, 20(2), 22–45. www.jstor.org/stable/41805141

Raz-Krakotzkin, A. (2011). Jewish peoplehood, "Jewish politics," and political responsibility: Arendt on Zionism and partitions. *College Literature*, 38(1), 57–74.

Richey, S. (2011). Civic engagement and patriotism. *Social Science Quarterly*, 92(4), 1044–1056. https://doi.org/10.1111/j.1540-6237.2011.00803.x

Robinson Devine, D. (2000). Zionism and the transformation of Jewish society. *Modern Judaism*, 20(3), 257–276.

Roccas, S., Klar, Y., & Liviatan, I. (2006). The paradox of group-based guilt: Modes of national identification, conflict vehemence, and reactions to the in-group's moral violations. *Journal of Personality and Social Psychology: Interpersonal Relations and Group Processes*, 91(4), 698–711.

Roccas, S., Sagiv, L., Shalom Schwartz, N., Halevy, N., & Eidelson, R. (2008). Toward a unifying model of identification with groups: Integrating theoretical perspectives. *Personality and Social Psychology Review*, 12(3), 280–306. https://doi.org/10.1177/1088868308319225

Sahar, G. (2008). Patriotism, attributions for the 9/11 attacks, and support for war: Then and now. *Basic and Applied Social Psychology*, 30(3), 189–197. *Israel announce agreement on* https://doi.org/10.1080/01973530802374956

Salmon, Y. (1998). Zionism and anti-Zionism in traditional Judaism in Eastern Europe. In S. Almog, J. Reinharz, & A. Shapira (Eds.), *Zionism and religion* (pp. 25–39). Brandeis University Press.

Samson, D., & Fishman, T. (1999). *Torat Eretz Yisrael*. Eretz Yisrael Publications.

Schatz, R. T., & Staub, E. (1997). Manifestations of blind and constructive patriotism. In D. Bar-Tal & E. Staub (Eds.), *Patriotism* (pp. 229–245). Nelson-Hall.

Schatz, R. T., Staub, E., & Lavine, H. (1999). On the varieties of national attachment: Blind versus constructive patriotism. *Political Psychology, 2,* 151–174. https://doi.org/10.1111/0162-895X.00140

Schnell, I. (2017). The impact of occupation on Israeli democracy. *Palestine-Israel Journal, 22*(2). https://pij.org/articles/1773/the-impact-of-occupation-on-israeli-democracy

Sever, I., Somer, E., Ruvio, A., & Soref, E. (2008). Gender, distress, and coping in response to terrorism. *Affilia, 23,* 156–166. https://doi.org/10.1177/0886109908314317

Sekerdej, M., & Roccas, S. (2016). Love versus loving criticism: Disentangling conventional and constructive patriotism. *The British Journal of Social Psychology, 55,* 491–521.

Shapira, A. (2004). The bible and Israeli identity. *Association for Jewish Studies Review, 28*(1), 11–41.

Siegel, D., & Morris E. (Eds.) (2010). *Green patriot posters: Image for a new activism.* Thames Hudson.

Silberstein, L. J. (1999). *The post Zionism debates: Knowledge and power in Israeli culture.* Routledge.

Staub, E. (2003). Blind versus constructive patriotism: Moving from embeddedness in the group to critical loyalty and action. In E. Staub (Ed.), *The psychology of good and evil: Why children, adults, and groups help and harm others* (pp. 497–512). Cambridge University Press.

The Rise of the Religious Right in Israel. (2017). The Jewish People Policy Institute. http://jppi.org.il/en/article/english-shifting-trends-in-the-west-and-their-impact-on-israel-and-the-jewish-people/english-part-2-shifts-in-israel-that-could-influence-the-wests-approach-to-israel-and-the-jewish-peo ple/%D7%94%D7%AA%D7%97%D7%96%D7%A7%D7%95%D7 %AA-%D7%94%D7%99%D7%9E%D7%99%D7%9F-%D7%95%D 7%94%D7%9C%D7%90%D7%95%D7%9E%D7%99%D7%95% D7%AA-%D7%94%D7%93%D7%AA%D7%99%D7%AA-%D7%91% D7%99%D7%A9%D7%A8%D7%90%D7%9C/#.XxAiMigzaHs

Todd, A. M. (2013). *Communicating environmental patriotism. A rhetorical history of the American environmental movement.* Routledge.

Tyler, A. (2011). Encounters with Zionism: A ripened vision for peacemaking? *International Journal on World Peace, 28*(1), 67–84.

Vogt, S. (2016). The postcolonial Buber: Orientalism, subalternity, and identity politics in Martin Buber's political thought. *Jewish Social Studies, 22*(1), 161–186.

Warburg, M. (2006). *Citizens of the world. A history and sociology of the Baha'is from a globalisation perspective.* Brill.

Zamir, S. (2015). Military program as a patriotism-oriented socializing agent among Israeli youth. *International Journal of Arts & Sciences, 8*(5), 443–457.

Zavala, A. G., Cichocka, A., & Eidelson, R. (2009). Collective narcissism and its social consequences. *Journal of Personality and Social Psychology, 97*(6), 1074–1096.

Zouplna, J. (2008). Revisionist Zionism: Image, reality and the quest for historical narrative. *Middle Eastern Studies, 44*(1), 3–27.

9

Otef Aza Residents' Understandings of Patriotism and Zionism

This chapter offers our conceptualizations and examples of "*Otef Aza*-style" patriotism and Zionism, based on the interviews and the photographs. We present the results of these two concepts in one chapter since most of the interviewees (21 people) said that Zionism is the Israeli version of patriotism, and they often used the terms interchangeably. Furthermore, even for those residents who differentiated between the two, the concepts remain connected to one another, on a theoretical level, since they are both ideologies and relate to the essence of attachment to Israel and to the *Otef* region. However, since most people talked more about patriotism than Zionism, we will present more examples from the interviews and photographs that emphasize the patriotic discourse than those that focus mainly on Zionism.

We begin by noting that most of the interviewees voiced a very deep, if not existential, fear that connected to their perspectives on patriotism/Zionism. The residents expressed that the years of living under terror attacks and wars have taken their toll, emphasizing that their and their grand/children's lives are in constant danger. The exception to this finding was among the religious-national interviewees, who expressed their belief that God promised the Jewish people the Holy Land and that,

© The Author(s), under exclusive license to Springer Nature Switzerland AG 2022
J. Chaitin et al., *Routine Emergency*, https://doi.org/10.1007/978-3-030-95983-8_9

ultimately, all is in God's hands. In their interviews, we did not find signs of existential despair. Therefore, the context of the patriotism/Zionism for most of the secular interviewees is one of existential angst, while the context of the patriotism/Zionism for the religious-nationalist interviewees is a religious belief that appears to give them a sense of wellbeing and completion.

Otef Aza-Style Patriotism: Our Conceptualizations

While some of the kinds of patriotism expressed by our interviews reflected conceptualizations from the academic literature, we found more nuanced and/or different understandings than the kinds described in the literature. Furthermore, we often heard interviewees state that they had a difficult time "connecting" to the concept, and/or that they did not tend to think in terms of patriotism in their everyday lives.

We do not perceive the types of patriotism expressed by the interviewees as being conceptualized in a linear fashion, but rather as discrete, qualitatively different modes of love of and attachment to country/region that usually showed complexities. Overall, we found seven categories of patriotism: (a) 11 *constructive* patriots—who stressed patriotism to the country, the *Otef Aza* region and their community, sometimes mixed with aspects of *constitutional* patriotism, and what we termed *Jewish-cultural-historical patriotism*, and *creative/originator* patriotism; (b) nine *conventional* Zionist patriots, who expressed such aspects as the importance of volunteerism, a special feeling for one's community and *Otef Aza*, deep respect for the country's symbols and importance of the army; (c) four *critical* patriots, who were very unhappy with governmental policies and actions, yet did not talk about engaging in activism; (d) three *fighting* patriots, who engaged in volunteer security work of the community and region or *hasbara*; (e) three *religious* patriots—whose patriotism was rooted in their religious beliefs; (f) three *lapsed* patriots, which included one *anti-patriot* and two *shaken* patriots; and (g) one interviewee, who could not identify with the term, but loved the country and was dedicated to improving the local and national *environment*.

It is important for us to note that we did *not* find instances of *blind* patriotism. While there were interviewees, who at first glance, appeared to reflect such a patriotism, when we delved into their interviews, we discerned either existential fear or deep religious beliefs, as noted above, which, in our opinion, explained their seemingly unwavering support of the governments' and IDF's actions and policies, and non-acceptance of critics. In other words, the term *blind* did not seem to capture the root of the ideology. As a result, we understood these perspectives as better capturing the essence of their patriotism than the label of blind patriotism. Concerning *cosmopolitanism*—as we will briefly discuss below—we saw a few signs of adoption of this notion, mainly in the words of the anti-patriot, but also hints of such adoption of some of the values in the words of others.

Examples from the Interviews and Photographs

Given the length, breadth and depth of the interviewees' reflections of patriotism and Zionism, we present some longer examples of the different kinds of perceptions, rather than short quotes from everyone, which, in our opinion, would lead to the loss of the depth that we found. By presenting and discussing longer quotes and some photographs, we aim to provide more of a "feel" of the person concerning her/his perspective on patriotism.

Constructive Patriots

As presented in the preceding chapter, constructive/democratic patriots feel love and attachment to their country/region, while questioning and criticizing practices they perceive as harming democratic values and, ultimately, the nation. Furthermore, such patriots are also activists, who work for the rights for all. Eleven of our interviewees reflected such patriotism. We present three such examples—each one with a different twist.

Yael, a 21-year-old left-wing woman from Sderot, expressed constructive patriotism, mixed with characteristics of constitutional patriotism and cosmopolitanism, some criticism of "typical" Israeli patriotism, and some inner conflict concerning what it means to be a patriot. This may be why she struggled, at times, with putting into words how she understands the concept:

(Patriotism) is first of all love of the place where the person lives, the country, some feeling of responsibility concerning what happens here and activism, it's a feeling of responsibility and actually doing something with it, to make the place you live better … Israeli patriotism is also a bit tricky because … there's something in patriotism that is solely Israeli, that doesn't look at the entire picture … if I'm only an Israeli patriot and want to improve … Israel and Israeli society … then I'm ignoring part of the population and … one of the biggest and most important problems in our society, the Israeli-Palestinian conflict, so if I only … sanctify Israel … I may even be doing harm … I see a lot of good people who want to do good things, but … there are so many conflicts between populations here … I have encountered so many good, smart, intelligent people, motivated to do [good], but they simply see only one part of the picture … it's amazing that they take action but … it's a bit of a shame that they don't aspire perhaps to get to know other perspectives of the matter, I feel that, at times, there is some degree of shutting down in the society toward other opinions. I'm not succeeding in formulating what I want to say … let's take the "New Guard",[1] they are very strong "Israeli patriots" and they help the country … and educate for values of loving the country and these things are amazing and beautiful, but they too only see a certain part of the picture … I'm not pretending to say that I see the whole picture … if only I could … I would like there to be patriotism toward people's lives, Israel is very

---

[1] According to the organization's website, the New Guard works to: "safeguard its lands and maintain the Zionist connection between those lands and the people of Israel… [since] agricultural crime has become epidemic in scale and… a complete disconnect has developed between the people of Israel and their roots. We… engage in agricultural and forestry work alongside educational initiatives that strengthen connections to the land" (Our Mission, The New Guard, 2020). However, according to DeMalach (October 25, 2019), the New Guard is seen by some Israelis as engaging in "soft racism," by mainly targeting Arab Bedouins and by calling agricultural crime—"terror."

important to me ... but human life is more important to me ... I can define myself as a patriot of values or something that I believe in more than the country, I really love the country and am attached to it, but I don't want this love to cancel out or decrease ... peace, human life, justice, equality ... I can connect to the concept of patriotism, but can't say that I'm completely sure that I'm a patriot ... I did a year of national service[2] ... in the army, I served in the lookout unit ... and boy did I ever contribute to the defense of the State of Israel's border in the most direct fashion there is and I'm planning that part of what I will do in the future will relate to helping people ... so according to my definition, that defines me as a patriot.

The second example comes from Zohar, a 65-year-old man born in Morocco who came to Sderot as an infant. He self-defines as a left-wing socialist. Zohar's conceptualization of constructive patriotism had a special twist: he has spent most of his life creating cultural and academic programs and institutions in Sderot and at the Sapir College. Zohar sees patriotism as tied to creation on the local level, and he expresses ongoing dedication to making his hometown a city full of many innovative cultural outlets. Zohar was one of the interviewees who talked about patriotism and Zionism together. He said:

[T]he border between being a patriot and a nationalist is very thin ... patriotism is loyalty to a group, the city, the region in which you grew up, to be loyal means that you're also willing to forego chances to leave to another place, to know that you'll pay a price if you stay in the area and invest in it ... I see creativity in the region as an expression of patriotism, of investing in the region's development ... all human creativity is social creativity, nature doesn't sprout movie theatres, theatres, and a pub ... patriotism is loyalty to the path that you chose and are sticking with ... this is where I grew up, this is my home ... this region lets your creativity fly ... [it's] like a blank canvas, for instance, if I stand you in front of a painting and ask you to be creative, this painting will take away your creativity and harm it, but in a place where there aren't many activities, that is [where] you give freedom to your thoughts to create together with people ... in the 1970s, we had a dream that Sderot would become a student city ... we're

---

[2] A year-long program for high school graduates to engage in volunteer work with diverse populations, throughout the country, before their military service.

happy that this is taking place and today Sderot is considered a leading culinary city, in addition to music … the students who chose to live here founded restaurants and projects … they could create them since they are unique … I'm the director of a Sderot singing group "The Vocal Chords," a group that …won first place in Israel … it's the masses that create the development … here, everything that you create has a dimension of being the first … patriotism is first and foremost loyalty to yourself, to create, in the place you live … the things you love … establishing the Cinemateque in Sderot was connected to difficult battles … during the first years they (Sderot residents) accused me … of serving the *kibbutzim* … there was someone running the local movie theatre and he didn't understand the idea of the Cinemateque, for him it was "crazy people bringing us the *kibbutzim*",[3] today … he's the operational manager and I don't think that he would agree to go back before there was a Cinemateque, but each change is a battle … I think of myself as a patriot, but it needs an explanation … I define myself as a Zionist, but not a nationalist Zionist, [I'm] searching for how to bring together a Jewish state and a democratic state and make into a pluralistic state, inside and outside the country … Miri Regev[4] can continue to say she's a Zionist, to wear an "appropriate" Zionist dress[5] … in her … stance against groups in Israel, she's not a Zionist … there are people who say that if you're Zionist because of the Jewish component, then you can't be a liberal, but that's not true, you can be a liberal, that's precisely the Zionist challenge, how to combine liberalism, pluralism, Zionism, values, such as peace and equality … I wasn't raised with a perception that we were born to rule over others … my Zionist patriotism is realization of the idea of a Jewish home for the Jewish people in *Eretz Yisrael*, but not in all of *Eretz Yisrael*, you can work for peace … Zionism is to make culture, productions, and art accessible, loving the other in the wide sense of the word … I'm also a member of Other Voice that keeps up contact with people in Gaza … patriotism means to continually search for the formula that connects you, as a member of a specific culture or religion

---

[3] There have often been bad and hostile feelings between Sderot and the (*Ashkenazi*) kibbutzim. The former sees the latter as exploiting (*Mizrachi*) residents for cheap labor and as being condescending toward them. The kibbutzim have been aware of these (justified) feelings for many years, and have never really succeeded in creating good, equal relations with Sderot residents.

[4] A Likud minister at the time, considered very right-wing.

[5] In May 2017, when Regev was the Minister of Culture and Sport, she wore a dress to the Cannes Film Festival that had an illustration of Jerusalem around its entire hem.

to be capable of relating with respect and equality to other cultures and religions.

The final example in the constructive category comes from Daniel, a 68-year-old religious, left-wing man who was born in France and immigrated to Israel as a young man, eventually settling in a religious *kibbutz*. Daniel is a member of two peace groups—one religious and one secular—that focus on Israel-Gazan relations. His perception of patriotism combined aspects of constructive, constitutional patriotism, and cosmopolitanism. This appeared when he talked about his feeling of connection to Europe, more so than specifically to France, and when he noted that he feels "solidarity with the human race." Daniel's approach to the concept appears to be mixed with Jewish religious-cultural-historical roots, while rejecting glorification of the nation's symbols. Daniel said:

[S]eeing the flag doesn't do a lot for me ... the national anthem does something to me because of the words of *Hatikvah*,[6] the hope of 2000 years touches me, but ... I wouldn't have a problem giving up this anthem since twenty percent of this population ... can't relate to this anthem ... I feel solidarity with the human race ... patriotism is being part of a family ... because, all in all, people speak the same language, have the same memories, the same landscapes that they know, perhaps that is the ... reason that a person feels closer to people who live near him ... in the same country ... nationalism is a very recent concept in human history ... as a French citizen, I see myself as European ... Europe is a very important thing and came before France ... French nationalism and patriotism ... came about much, much later ... after the French revolution ... long beforehand there was a kind of European identity that was very significant ... I can define myself as a Jewish-Israeli patriot, I feel close to the Jewish people because of the history and I received a Jewish education ... I don't have any sentiments for the stones of ... Israel, I have no feelings for the rocks of Samaria or the Judean mountains ... I feel emotionally connected to the people ... here in Israel ... people came from such different backgrounds and cultures and tried to rebuild this people together, I connect to this and perhaps this is what is meant by patriotism ... there's an amazing human richness

---

[6] *hatikva* = the hope.

here ... when I hear about ... *Ashkenazim* who are against their son or daughter marrying a *Mizrachi* or an Ethiopian ... I feel a bit angry, but mainly incomprehension because the possibility to enrich our culture by encountering people from different backgrounds, is the most wonderful thing ... I'm aware ... that when I say "the people", there's a problem with the population that isn't Jewish, we must find the way to build cooperation and integration between us ... the fact that there are Palestinian Arabs ... I think that this is an experience that God is giving us to see if we are capable of fulfilling the lofty ideas in the Torah, in our culture, "love of the stranger" ... the Torah actually obligates us to integrate the stranger within us and give him all rights ... today we have the opportunity to achieve them ... patriotism is our culture, and our culture embodies these things ... some of the religious leaders' battles are the worst thing that could be ... and the most anti-Jewish[7] ... during the Shoah, nobody wanted us as refugees ... and we are still scarred, so how can we do this to others? In our Jewish culture, loving the stranger, helping the stranger is such a basic thing that how is it possible to treat them this way and call them "cancer?" ... we need to be glad that we have the possibility of supporting and helping helpless people, perhaps that is also part of Israeli patriotism ... concerning military service ... there's no doubt that we need to protect ourselves, I've been through a number of wars, I was in the army and my children were in the army ... I'm a bit uneasy about sanctifying the army the way it is sanctified today ... I think it's excessive ... there's talk about ... finding other ways to serve the country ... I'm open to all of these ideas ... there's a certain trend in the Israeli public to sanctify the army ... that's excessive in my opinion.

In summation, when we conceptualize constructive patriotism expressed by *Otef Aza* residents, we see that it is comprised of love and attachment to the region and Israel, love of diversity and pluralism, activism, innovation, Jewish historical-cultural roots, and empathy for the Palestinians. For these residents, being a patriot in a warzone reflects an unwillingness to accept the status quo, an aversion to xenophobia and exclusion, and a need to dedicate their lives to making their community, region, and country a place that emphasizes humanity and creation.

---

[7] Referring to some Israeli religious leaders who called to deport the non-Jewish, asylum seekers.

Conventional Patriots

The conventional patriots in our sample expressed love of and attachment to the country, reflective of the conceptualization found in the academic literature. However, here it had a Zionist twist—that is, their Jewish-Israeli conventional-style patriotism was rooted in basic Zionistic ideology of Jewish connection to the land and army. Although, at times, they criticize government policy or actions, or public behaviors that they see as negative, they do not stress activism for change. Here is one example of such an interviewee.

Sa'ar, a 47-year-old left-wing man from a kibbutz, moved to the area after he remarried. When asked about patriotism, he talked about Zionism; for him, the two are interconnected. Sa'ar expressed nostalgia for a world that he believed existed once, but has since disappeared—when Jewish-Israelis worked the land and fought the Arab enemy, in order to build the country. In addition, he expressed signs of glorification of the country's symbols, as noted in the literature. Throughout his interview, Sa'ar differentiated between *kibbutz/moshav* education and city education—with the former being highly valued, and the latter being something he "hates," as he perceives it as empty and based on personal gain and/or consumerism. Family connection to agriculture, the land and military service in combat units infuse this entire section of his interview. He said:

> Patriotism is the home, the education … the tradition that one received from his father and mother … it's from my grandpa and grandma, it's love of the country, love of the land, love of the *moshav*, I was raised on my grandparents' stories of the *Palmach*[8] … I see how the *kibbutz* infuses patriotism and Zionism into the [children's] veins, "be combat soldiers", "contribute, do something" … in our family, all of our kids do national service, that is patriotism to contribute a year of your life to the country … for everyone, for Zionism, for patriotism … my two big sons live in the city … there's no connection to the country, to patriotism … my boys didn't know

---

[8] The *Palmach* (Strike Companies) was the elite brigade of the *Haganah*—the military of the *Yishuv* (Synopsis of Palmach History, Palmach Organization. Retrieved from http://palmach.org.il/en/history/about/)

that there was such a thing [as national service] … here if you don't do it, you're the exception … My sons … from the moment they get up till they go to sleep, they're on their I-pads and their phones and games … I see the difference between kids who grew up in the city … here on the *kibbutz*, they were nursed on patriotism and Zionism … I'm full of esteem for *kibbutz* education … they go on hikes and to the baby animal farm once a week, it's amazing … it connects to the fields, to the land, to our country … my big sons are city kids and mall kids and **I hate this** … they all wear name brands … my little ones from the *kibbutz* walk around barefoot … they're not afraid of the land and dirt … my youngest son understands what the army is and he wants to be in the *Oketz* Unit,[9] he wants to be a combat soldier … when [my grandparents] were in the *Palmach*, my grandma operated a *Davidka*,[10] and my grandpa was the area commander … that's Israeli patriotism … there was an ideal to build the country, to really fight, my grandpa said that the hardest time in his life was now, because once there were ideals … he did a ton of reserve duty, up to the age of 70, and he was an agricultural advisor … my grandma milked the cows with the children and worked the farm … today, what *kibbutznik* or *moshavnik*[11] works in the cow barn? Workers from Thailand work there, the times have changed … today there aren't [young people] establishing a new *kibbutz* … unfortunately, I can't live in my grandpa's and grandma's historical period, but the fact that I'm here in a *kibbutz* and get attacked by rockets, that is part of coming full circle with my grandpa and grandma, I feel that I owe them … I'm **very** much a patriot, I love the country very much … I have a lot of pride in the country, but in recent years, I'm ashamed of many things … today there was Naama Issachar's appeal[12] … Who you made into a national hero? The girl **smuggled drugs**! … she should pay for it … Why am I bringing this up? Because they turned her into a cultural hero … something here has completely gone nuts … the government hasn't functioned for a year and nobody cares about the old

---

[9] The *Oketz* Unit is the independent canine special forces unit of the IDF.

[10] The *Davidka* was a homemade Israeli mortar used in the 1948 war.

[11] A *kibbutznik* is a person who lives on a kibbutz and a *moshavnik* is a person who lives on a moshav.

[12] An Israeli woman was charged with smuggling narcotics into Russia, when making a flight connection from India to Israel via Moscow. Nine grams of cannabis were found in her checked baggage. Issachar was arrested and sentenced to seven years in a Russian prison. After Netanyahu and Putin held negotiations, she was released in January 2020 and allowed to return home (Ilyushina et al., January 30, 2020. CNN: https://edition.cnn.com/2020/01/29/europe/naama-issachar-american-israeli-pardoned-russia-intl/index.html)

people in the [hospital] corridors … in the Resilience Centers,[13] it's nuts … the psychologists and social workers haven't received salaries for three months … I should have been born in the 1920s, during the *aliyot*[14] … For me, patriotism is the army, pride in the army unit … when I see an army ceremony, I'm full of pride … when I see an army plane fly over and bomb with all the craziness that is here, I idolize those guys.

The second example comes from the interview with Alice, an 80-year-old center, traditional woman who lives in Sderot. Alice emigrated from Morocco in 1964 and has lived in Sderot ever since. Alice only speaks of her love for the country, appearing to see it as the best and the only place on earth where she wants to live. While she had a good life in Morocco, her deep Zionist and religious beliefs led her to want to live in Israel. Alice said:

When everyone in my family began coming and my parents, may their name be for a blessing, came, and my sister came and there was a nursery school teacher who left and my husband … said "So, our people are no longer here, that is, my friends that I would visit. They've gone! It's not simple." Afterwards, we made *aliyah*, thank God, I'm not complaining. Everything is good, God should help them. This place should be the very, very, very best that it can be, thank God, we are lacking nothing. I am happy here! … I really wanted to live in Ashdod, I agreed [to come to Sderot] because of my sister … because a big half of my family is in Ashdod. They told me that meanwhile there are no **places**, no apartments, they're just beginning to build. And, that's it and that's it and that's it, "Go to Sderot" so I came to Sderot and my sister, may her name be for a blessing, we had a good time, we lived across from one another … we had **fun**! Slowly, slowly everything changed, **we grew, we learned**, everything was **good**! It's fine, thank God! We lack nothing here, thank God, He should keep the **soldiers safe** and all the Jewish people, **Amen**! This is our place … my husband didn't want to come, "I'm returning to Morocco." "Go back; I'm not moving from here. Because you didn't give your love the first day we came to Israel!" And I, my heart, I fell in love … I want to tell you,

---

[13] Centers that provide psychological services for people suffering from trauma.

[14] The plural of *aliyah*—the period when the main founders of the state made *aliyah* to Palestine/*Eretz Yisrael*.

before I studied Hebrew … I loved this place; I loved the place as if God gave me a present! From since I came, and up until today, I love it. I only want a small place in my Israel. **I will not go** anywhere else, why would I? Thank God, thank God, that we **have our place!** Not to go to here and here and here; it's unnecessary! … wherever I go, I see Jews around me. I can go to have fun; I can go out to **have a good time**; I'm not afraid! There is no way that a Jew would kill another Jew **without a reason**. I would go to see a movie. I would go everywhere, yes, nothing will happen to me, that's it. We got used to it very fast. We got used to it **very quickly!** **I got used to it and I met people and I helped, and I did everything!** … I would go help people **with all my heart, with all my heart** … because I love helping, from today until tomorrow … God willing, we will have quiet here in our Israel, this place is wonderful, since I came, up until now ((she laughs)) … thank God! We have a **wonderful life, we are lacking nothing**, we have everything, we can buy what we need. **We have what to eat**. We have where to go to have fun and we are happy.

Critical Patriots

Four of our interviewees reflected *critical patriotism*. On the one hand, they were very unhappy with the government and the political leaders, and with some characteristics of Jewish-Israeli society, while, on the other, they did not speak of engaging in concrete behaviors against such policies and actions. In spite of their disappointment and anger, they had not lost their love of and attachment to the region and the country, and they differentiated between their feelings toward the leaders and certain sectors of the population—such as the settlers—and the deep feeling that *Otef Aza* and Israel remained their home.

One such patriot was Ofra, a 58-year-old center-left woman who was born and raised on a *kibbutz*, and moved to a *moshav* as an adult, both in *Otef Aza*. Ofra is an artist, who paints and sculpts. In order to demonstrate her expression of patriotism, we present one of her photographs (see Fig. 9.1).

In this photo, Ofra captured two symbols of *Otef Aza*—the *Kassam* rocket and the anemones—which represent the life-threatening danger and unique beauty of the region. When Ofra was asked how she connects the photograph to patriotism, she said:

Fig. 9.1 Ofra—*Kassam* and Anemones (December 2018)

My husband … is a pipe contractor … one day, in the fields of a *kibbutz*, he sees the *Kassam* and he brought it to me as a souvenir … a normal man brings flowers, and he brought me a *Kassam*, now this *Kassam* is so primitive … you could die from laughing … they made it from an irrigation pipe, welded wings on it … it's from Cast Lead, and I added the ceramic anemones so that it would be the bad versus the good, the *Kassam* is the bad because it comes … to kill me, to destroy me and the red, it's always optimistic, growth, beauty, there is both … during the last round, my father was very bored in the *mamad*, so he counted [the rockets] and reached 150 and he said that they also shot a rocket into his *kibbutz* … he said he'd never heard such a big explosion like that in his life … and I said: "Daddy, why do you continue to live on the *kibbutz*? … Come here, it will be more pleasant," and he said: "No, Ofra, this is my home, I don't have another home, this is what … my soul chose, whatever will happen." And, you can't argue with him.

This photograph is further interesting since it was taken inside—as were all Ofra's photographs. This was in spite of the fact that *Kassam* rockets are shot from Gaza fields, this one was found in a *kibbutz* field, and the anemones, a natural wonder, turn the brown/grey Negev into huge, lush "carpets" of flowers, when they bloom. However, here, the metal sculpture looks dead, and it is hard to see the optimism, growth, or beauty of which Ofra speaks. The sculpture is further shot against a brown/grey wall and tiled floor—colors, which do not usually signify life, but rather the opposite.

It appears, therefore, that what Ofra is (also) trying to say with this photograph, is that the *Kassam* rockets have not only destroyed people, but also turned the outside into a dangerous, dead space. Moreover, by bringing it inside, death and dread invade one's home—the place "the soul chose." Therefore, in her interview, even though Ofra is critical of the government, especially since it has not worked for any political solution to the Israel-*Hamas* conflict, she remains in love with and attached to Israel and *Otef Aza*—her home and soul.

Fighting Patriots

Three of our interviewees, who at first were seen as *blind* patriots, were later classified as reflecting what we termed *fighting patriotism*. The elements of such a patriotism included a very steadfast support of Israel, with little to no criticism of the Israeli government or policies, alongside a fierce need to protect Israel from its internal critics (left-wing Jewish-Israelis, Palestinian citizens of Israel, etc.) and external critics (the Palestinians, the Arabs, BDS supporters, etc.). These residents either volunteered for security units that protected their communities and/or the region or engaged in *hasbara*.[15]

We begin with Shuki, a 55-year-old right-wing man from Sderot who was born in Brazil, moved to Israel, when he was 13, spent a few years as an adult in Argentina, but moved back to Israel 25 years ago. Shuki said:

---

[15] *Hasbara* literally means "explanation," referring to either information or public diplomacy/relations. However, it also has the negative connotation of spin and propaganda. It is commonly used to describe Israeli attempts to present Israel in a positive light in the world.

What makes a person a patriot? (8) ... in the example of *Otef Aza* ... there are two kinds of people who come [here], one who comes because of economic problems, because, in reality, there are benefits, or someone who is escaping some place or someone, very few people come to strengthen the place ... during Protective Edge, come to our area, you'll see what's happening, then go to Tel Aviv, it's a completely different world, they don't feel what's happening here, a grad [rocket] fell in Tel Aviv, everyone's nervous, here we get up and continue to work, that's why I say that in Israel there are those who complain, I'm willing to take them to the Ben Gurion airport, I'll pay for it, so that they'll leave Israel and won't come back ... whoever complains shouldn't be here ... he should go somewhere else ... no one's keeping you here ... if something happens ... I go wherever it's needed, if it's to do a shift in the Border Police or *Mada* (*Magen David Adom*[16]) ... an Israeli who wants the country, you can connect it more or less to patriotism ... someone who wants to remain and is ready to accept everything he goes through, but still waiting for someone from the government to come help us, to stop everything happening on the fence ... they love Israel, they love the *Otef*, they know that if they won't be there, instead of lobbing [rockets] three kilometres from the fence, they'll begin firing farther ... for years they would fire *Kassams* and mortars and people remained ... like I always said about evacuating *Gush Katif* ... I say that it wasn't right that we stay there, because there were a number of soldiers on each resident, in order to hold on to the place ... I knew that the moment we left ... we'd begin suffering from the mortar shells, because they couldn't fire them anymore on *Neve Dekalim*[17] ... so they fired them to the east ... when things heat up and you have to evacuate people, you see on Facebook "Come, I have a room here" ... there are people who love Israel, but don't live there, everyone can't live in the *Otef* ... I think I contribute, but I don't contribute enough, I wish I could contribute more ... take the army, here there are percentages who enlist or volunteer for elite units ... there are more young guys who want to volunteer ... there are those who don't want to do army service ... but if you don't do army service that says you don't love our country, because without the army, you can't exist ... (Elad: Do you think of yourself as a patriot?) I believe so, I'm not willing to leave this place ... I've been there for 22 years ... I remain here in spite of the

---

[16] The Israeli Red Cross.
[17] One of the main settlements in *Gush Katif*.

situation, I also love the country and am willing to contribute, not money, but rather hours to people in need, because you don't know where the money goes … and as a small business-owner, it's not simple, the Border Guard are angry at me for not giving a shift this month in Eshkol … I wish I could give more … when I arrived here [from Brazil] and saw what the country gives people, in other places, you don't have this … free education … social security or all of the small things … I'm not willing to leave the country … I know that Israel is my place … in Argentina you don't know who your enemy is … this is my place … my work is in the area, my family is in the region, I could have moved 10 kilometres to the east or get out of the line of fire, but I'm there on purpose, because I feel that I need to be … if we begin leaving … we'll lose this place, like when we left *Gush Katif* … they'll ask for another kilometre and another kilometre and it's not right … so today we take it, all of the fire … because it's ours and we need to remain there … people who complain all the time bother me, in terms of budgets, and even if the money doesn't come out of my pocket, it's a budget that someone else or someplace else can get … so, if he doesn't like it here, he shouldn't be here.

The second example of a fighting patriot comes from the interview with Ziona, a 71-year-old secular woman from a *moshav* who self-identified as holding center-right political views. After analyzing her words in depth, we found Ziona to be motivated by a very deep-rooted existential fear that drives her to find a way, from her perspective, to ensure the lives of the Jewish people and the Jewish state—as evidenced perhaps in her extreme statement, which reflects existential angst: "*One hundred million Muslims will enter [the Palestinian state] … they won't need any rockets … they'll finish off everybody with knives.*"

Ziona, an artist and poet, spends much of her time fighting people and organizations she sees as being anti-Israeli—be they left-wing Jewish-Israelis/organizations who criticize the IDF, and/or Palestinian citizens of the country, who are opposed to Israel being a Jewish state. She fights through *hasbara:* in 2010, Ziona created a power point presentation that exposes, in her opinion, the hypocrisy of the existence of UNRWA, and also tries to prove that there is no Palestinian people. At night, she reads through op-eds and posts on the internet and Facebook, writes talkbacks, and sends her power point to people, trying to convince them of what she sees as Israel's morality and legitimacy versus the Palestinians' lies and immorality. From Ziona's perspective, patriotism means dedicating your life to combatting the lies levelled against it. Here are some of her words:

I think I'm a patriot ...I love the country ... I think it is righting the history, the Zionist movement and settlement and existence of the State of Israel is a correction of history of unending injustices that happened and will happen again ... therefore, it's so important that our country exists as a state of the Jewish people. Now, whoever accepts this is like a brother and friend for me ... I invest a lot of time in *hasbara* ... a long time ago, I understood that there is some injustice here, something isn't right, that there are two UN organizations that talk about refugees in the world ... I did a doctorate without getting the degree ... on UNRWA and UNHCR ... there's so much material ... you really need to do a doctorate in order to understand all this material ... I prepared a power point presentation of 11 slides ... that compared UNHCR to UNRWA ... and I began publishing it, it was before Facebook, but there were media talkbacks on the Internet and I sat for days on end and put it into the talkbacks ... I sent it to ... newspapers in English, later on when Facebook appeared, I began running it there ... I did it because, according to the comparison between the organizations, you see the big bluff ... of the Palestinian people and of the Palestinian refugees and how the UN is an organization that was established in order to bridge conflicts and prevent war and how this organization, via UNRWA, reinforces war against the Jewish people and the only state of the Jewish people and the moment that you read the presentation, you understand the organized evil ... before Trump was chosen by the Republican party and afterwards during the general elections, I sat for days and nights and sent it to Fox News, every time something is mentioned about the Palestinian refugees ... and the biggest pleasure was to hear the things that I say about UNRWA come out of Trump's mouth—**that was an unbelievable pleasure** ... *hasbara* is very important ... we don't need to lie ... we need to stick to our truth, they can deal with their lies ... my patriotism is expressed in my poetry ... because it comes from the soul ... for someone who lives in the center, if God forbid, Israel doesn't settle in Judea and Samaria, they'll get hit the hardest—to establish a Palestinian state? One hundred million Muslims will enter it ... they won't need any rockets ... they'll finish off everybody with knives ... (Elad: What makes a person a patriot?) ... loving the other, relating to tradition, connecting to the people … to the land, to the culture … worrying about the soldiers … opinions differ, but everyone is like ants, each one does his thing … so that life will be normal for everyone … if an Arab is loyal to the country and he … wants life to be good for everyone … from my perspective, he's a patriot … the moment that he doesn't weave schemes against the existence of the state … whoever lives here and does not abide by the three parameters of demonization, delegitimation and double standard, is a patriot from my perspective … we can argue all night long, but the moment that his actions and behavior are free of these things, he's a patriot … demonization is … to tell lies … apropos *Btselem* or Breaking the Silence[18] … they lie … they turn IDF soldiers into demons, turn Israel into apartheid, **which it is not**, that is demonization … delegitimation says that we don't have rights to this land and the double standard says that the IDF needs to act differently than the United States army—why? … I'm very, very happy that we examine everything under a microscope, but we examine too much … because at some stage we're abandoning our sons' lives due to all this examination … I get the creeps when … Benny Gantz[19] say that he prefers that our soldiers die, the main thing is that Gazans won't be harmed—excuse me! You prefer that my son? A hundred Gazans should die so my son won't die, let them do any inquiry afterwards, he should go to jail, but not die, so that's a double standard … and all of the UN behavior is a double standard, human rights … what I do is undertake a mission … to tell the real story of *Eretz Yisrael*, settlement in the country, of belonging, of the demonization of the Jewish people, of the lie of the Zionist occupation, it's an obligation, it takes a lot of energy, to cope with the lies … they have an industry of lies … now, criticism is criticism, I have what to critique … but the moment there's nullification of Zionism, what are you doing here? … Are you here only to invite the *Hezbollah* or Haniya to destroy everyone? … I'm dying in the morning, to lie in bed another hour and read a book, go to bed early, not to sit up at night and send out the materials … it takes a lot of energy.

---

[18] Two Israeli human rights organizations that document and publish human rights violations undertaken by settlers and/or soldiers against Palestinians.

[19] Former Military Chief of Staff between 2011 and 2015—during Pillars of Defense and Protective Edge. He founded the *Kachol-Lavan* (Blue-White) political party, and serves as the Minister of Defense.

In summation, the fighting patriots expressed their need to combat Israel's enemies—via volunteering for security organizations that protect the border or via *hasbara*. "Enemies," from their perspective, are defined as people (including Jewish-Israelis) who complain too much, or shirk military obligations, or take more than they give, or tell "lies," or delegitimize the Jewish state, or denigrate the soldiers, or hold Israel to a double standard. These patriots appear to see life in black and white terms and, therefore, tolerate very little criticism of the government and/or political leaders. These are activist patriots—they not only express their opinions, but also devote much of their life to fighting these internal and external enemies. The motivation behind their words and actions appears to be an existential fear that if they are not constantly "on guard," the Jewish people and the Jewish state is in danger of extinction.

Religious Patriots

The three *religious patriots* in our sample presented their patriotism as rooted in religious beliefs. Like many of the other interviewees, they equated Israeli patriotism with Zionism. For them, the reason that they are in Israel and in *Otef Aza* is because they are trying to act according to God's will. They believe that He gave the Jews this land and wants them to settle *Eretz Yisrael Hashlema* (Greater Israel). Furthermore, these interviewees aver that they try to fulfil His will in order to help hasten the coming of the Messiah. As noted above, they did not appear to experience existential despair, but rather expressed that their religious beliefs provided them with comfort, confidence and meaning in their thoughts, feelings, and behaviors connected to patriotism.

Here, we present one example, from the interview with Sarah, a 49-year-old religious woman who had lived in *Gush Katif*. She now lives in one of the villages in Eshkol that was established mainly by people who used to live in the Gaza Strip. Sarah described herself as "the most right-wing woman you will ever meet." Here are some of her words:

> I'm a patriot, but since I am patriotic, I don't like the word patriotic, because it's not in Hebrew and I ask myself, how do you say patriot in

Hebrew? A Zionist, with values, a nationalist ... I only know that this is something very important to emphasize, the reason is because I'm very devoted to *Eretz Yisrael*, to settlement in *Eretz Yisrael*, to the State of Israel, to the Jewish people, it comes from my religious belief ... I believe that *Eretz Yisrael* was promised to *Am Yisrael* by God and, therefore, we need to be here and settle this country ... this is part of the *mitzvot*[20] ... In the regional council, I'm in charge of the Forum for the Absorption Heads of all the communities ... everyone there ... wants to bring as many people to his community ... in the community where I live ... we called it the *mitzva* of absorption, because for religious people, the most important thing is the *mitzva*, the *mitzva* of observing Shabbat and the *mitzva* of absorption into the community and when something turns into a *mitzva*, you do it ... with all your heart, you're completely devoted to it ... my patriotism is derived from my loyalty to the people and the country and to action and settlement ... there are stupid researchers who think that money motivates people ... or respect, that's completely wrong ... most of the things that we do in our lives are not economical, if in the end we have money, we have children and giving birth to children is uneconomical, afterwards you have money, so you build a house and put all of your money into the house, so once again it's uneconomical ... or you travel abroad ... and you wasted the money, so it seems that what you want isn't money but rather to realize your values ... when something is important to you, you really don't care what people say about it ... you do what's best for you ... people are motivated by their values ... after Protective Edge, people made shirts that said, "We don't surrender Nirim,[21]" they aren't ceding Nirim because God ordered people to settle in Nirim ... for them, settlement is a value, safeguarding the state's borders is something very basic, they're willing to ... give their soul, they're willing to put their lives in danger, they're willing to endanger their children, and that's amazing ... what motivates people is this thing of belief ... we have a people, our people has a state and our state is of value, to safeguard the state, to safeguard the settlements in the country is of value ... from my religious perspective, a Jew who says that he doesn't believe in God, in the root of his soul, does believe in God and his values are derived from this connection ... I believe there is a Jewish soul, which is different from other people's souls ... the *Torah* is seared in the Jewish DNA ... a miracle happened. For 2000 years we were in the

---

[20] The commandments. The singular is *mitzva*.
[21] A *kibbutz* close to the border in which two members were killed on the last day of Protective Edge.

diaspora, Jews from Yemen, Morocco, the Ukraine and America, everyone dreamed about the same land and spoke the same language and prayed in the same direction, I believe that all of the values connect to this topic, I believe that even when a person says that he doesn't believe in God, his values and his DNA were built around this … he still has this Jewish identity … that cannot be denied … if you aren't Jewish, why are you here? Go to New York … if you want peace, go to New Zealand, there's no war there, you're here, you're a Jew … we wasted so much time [debating] the Jewish and the democratic, in the end, that's the root, we're Jews, therefore, we're here, because otherwise it wouldn't be logical and that's the basis of all our values.

Lapsed Patriots

In our analyses, we also found three interviewees who we categorized as *lapsed patriots*—one had become an *anti-patriot* and two were former patriots, who no longer believed what they had when they were young. These three had become disillusioned with the country and the governments after they experienced either trauma, due to the ongoing war, and/ or due to the lack of a peace process that they saw as being the key to a sustainable/peaceful/inclusive reality. This change in perspective concerning patriotism was a slow process, built upon years of disappointment, experiences, which were extremely frightening, and deep frustration with what they saw as the leaders, and often large segments of the Israeli public, as either adopting harmful social-political values, actions, and policies or abandoning residents of the *Otef* to danger, without really protecting them. Here, we offer two examples.

Rami is a 61-year-old kibbutz member who self-identified as secular and left-wing. In March 2018, he established the Lighthouse—an open dialogue encounter group that meets every Friday afternoon to talk about the meaning of the *Gaza Space* (the term that Rami chose for this region, as opposed to the term, *Otef Aza*, which he rejects)—that includes the Israeli area adjacent to the Gaza Strip and the Gaza Strip. On most weeks, the people who come to the Lighthouse hold a video call with people from Gaza, who wish to create peaceful relations with Israelis. This activity takes place in an abandoned sulfur factory, located near the fields and in the forest of his *kibbutz*, which is close to the Gaza Strip. Rami was our *anti-patriot* and the interviewee who expressed the strongest signs of cosmopolitanism, perhaps even to "hard" cosmopolitanism that was presented in Chap. 8.

While Rami identified as a patriot for many years, today he perceives patriotism as a dangerous phenomenon that divides people, rather than uniting them, and as a harmful mechanism that exploits people for governmental goals, rather than providing them with quality of life. Rami expressed cosmopolitan notions when he said: "My mission is to plan and shape the future and create a consciousness and perception of wealth and one big space for everybody," and "We are just a part of a political game … I feel sorry for the Gazans; we're all living in the same space, but my country keeps on separating us"—emphasizing his belief that all human beings should be united, not separated. In addition, Rami tells us that he feels "more Gazan than a Tel Aviv resident," demonstrating his belief in human fraternity and compassion for people who many Israelis consider to be their enemies.

In order to demonstrate Rami's anti-patriotism, we present one of his photographs (Fig. 9.2) and what he said about it:

> This is one of the wonders of the sulphur factory … I've been there for **hundreds of sunsets** … every day in the sulphur factory, there is a sunset that comes from the **west** and our wind comes from … the northwest … there is an ongoing dialogue between this place and where we sit and hold our activities of the Lighthouse, in the **abandoned** sulphur factory and the space, which is to our west, which is the **sea** and the entire Gaza Strip and the wind blows, so we have the sounds, the voices and the smells and these wonderful sunsets, it's some kind of **expression** of this **one space**! The building isn't important! It's blurred, it's in a shadow, everything here is light and shadow! What's important is that there are always sunrises and sunsets … it's an interesting picture, because it shows the **spatial** connection of this place.

In our analysis of the photo, we see an abandoned factory, with its holes, empty windows, and broken walls, which could also symbolize the death of the shared space of Jews and Palestinians that existed before the

Fig. 9.2 The Abandoned Sulfur Factory at Sunset (Rami, February 2020)

state was established. That is, this factory and joint life belong to the pages of history. The sky is very dramatic, providing a massive "halo" to the factory, giving the sense that the factory is holy. It has a spiritual aura to it, turning an abandoned factory, and the surrounding grounds, into something mystical. Through the trees, in the distance, are the outlines of the Gaza Strip—blurred, but part of the magical landscape. Finally, the photo has shades of light blue, greys, blacks, and whites, perhaps symbolizing the moment when the light is about to meet the darkness.

How does this photo connect to Rami's anti-patriotism? We propose that, through this photograph, Rami is saying that this place, which brings together Israelis and Gazans in dialogue, is a holy space. It reminds us that this land has a history of belonging to (at least) two peoples. It reaches up to the sky, connecting the present-day east (Israel) to the present-day west (Gaza). The wind, its sounds, and smells, which come from Gaza, remind us that both peoples are also connected to one another on a visceral and sensory level. Therefore, this place is a reminder of the dangers of patriotism that divides Jews and Palestinians, turning people meant to be together, into enemies. It keeps them apart, instead of bringing them together in harmony.

The second example comes from the interview with Sigal, a 65-year-old woman who politically identified with the center and lives in a *kibbutz*. Sigal has lived her entire life in *kibbutzim*, which were the "epitome of patriotism and Zionism." However, over the years, Sigal became progressively disappointed in and frustrated with Israel's leaders, and with values that characterize Israeli society. As a result, she no longer identifies with the expression and actions of what is considered patriotism and Zionism or the symbols of the country:

> Patriotism is a ridiculous concept ... because patriotism goes together ... with a bit of naiveté, blind faith of something idyllic or a leader ... I once thought that patriotism was very, very important. Today I understand that it is quite stupid, if I go abroad and somehow find myself in a situation that represents the country ... to talk about Israel today, I won't be patriotic if I say that I'm waiting for the moment that Bibi won't be prime minister? That he won't be a figure here at all? So I'm not a patriot? But he's my prime minister ... I think that the moment that I have doubts about my belonging to the person who leads me, I'm in trouble. There were [leaders] that I highly criticized ... Arik Sharon, but I was proud of him when he completed the disengagement [from Gaza], I said—"Only he can ... he's a bastard, but only he can" ... patriotism ... is something very nebulous, which, from my perspective, is very problematic. The settlers think they are very patriotic, I think they're dragging us into war, into loss ... who's a patriot? It's in the eyes of the beholder and patriotism is a word that is very, very problematic for me. I understand that without it, the country has a problem: that is why we're in trouble. There are many citizens in the country, the problem is identifying with what happens here ... I cannot be a patriot of my country ... patriotism is to be in favor of war? ... For me, the word lost the meaning it once had. When I was a child, it was clear, I'm a patriot, it hurt me if you said I wasn't, but today, if I'm opposed to settlements, even according to the Deal of the Century ... I guess I'm not [a patriot], when they're going to extend Israeli law over all of the settlements, including the illegal ones, including the roads ... you can take one narrative

and erase the previous one … there was Ben-Gurion, and now there's Bibi instead, Ben-Gurion said to settle the Negev and Bibi says to settle the territories … everything that the Likud has done in the past years is to erase what was, to erase our heroes, to erase Oslo … You caused Rabin's assassination and you're … saying you're a hero, just "me and my relations with Putin and Trump … and Sarah,[22] Sarah is important, flowers for Sarah" … [we are] a disturbed country, we are completely insane … and Yair[23] is our pet … Is this Zionism? … To settle in Hebron? Okay, Hebron is the City of our Forefathers, the reality is very depressing in my opinion, but I go outside and see that everything is green and there's a guy who comes here from Gaza to work, and there's my friend's father who drives sick people from Gaza to hospitals in Jerusalem, so I say there are good people, and the sick and the evil will pass, I am a patriot of the simple people who contribute and give of themselves … from my perspective, patriotism is a big word that doesn't reflect what's happening today in the country …. I became aware, this was a very hard and painful [process], it took years … the state was established on the shoulders of the *Palmach* and the IDF … I was raised on this … when did things change for me? … Perhaps during the Yom Kippur War … there were booklets … about the fallen soldiers, all of the soldiers I knew … I was a soldier … you understand that there is … a big problem … it took time, until the truth sinks in … perhaps during the First Lebanon War, my husband was in Lebanon … what are they doing there? … my questioning of patriotism … and of the leaders stayed with me afterwards.

In summation, the *lapsed* patriots were interviewees who felt an extreme attachment and belonging and love for their country, coupled with extreme disappointment, despair, and anger at how their country, and its leaders, had evolved. They had come to understand that what they had been taught or believed in as children was either false or harmful. Therefore, they no longer believe in these past values, or in present-day ones. As a result, patriotism is no longer an option for them. These interviewees, however, did not entertain leaving the region or the country, perhaps because, in their everyday lives, they were connected to the natural space and did see small instances of goodness and light—unconnected

---

[22] Prime Minister Netanyahu's wife.
[23] Prime Minister Netanyahu's son.

to patriotism—feeling a deep physical and psychological connection to their home in the *Otef*/Gaza Space.

Zionism in the *Otef*: Our Conceptualizations

As in the case of patriotism, we found instances in which interviewees reflected the kinds of Zionism discussed in the literature, as well as different modes. We found: (a) 13 *conventional, political* Zionists, who mainly expressed the importance that Jews have their own State, due to Jewish history, ongoing anti-Semitism in the world, and hostile Arab nations; (b) seven *proud/fighting* Zionists, who expressed the need to consistently and actively reinforce Zionism, seeing it as still very relevant today, in order to defend Jewish-Israelis from their "enemies"; (c) three *critical/aware* Zionists, who identified as Zionists, but were highly critical of the government and its policies and actions; (d) three *Brit-Shalom*-style Zionists, who emphasized the need for finding a way to live in equality and peace with the Palestinians as an inherent part of their Zionist ideology; (e) five diverse *post*-Zionists, who no longer believed in Zionism; saw it as being irrelevant today; were disenchanted with the meaning that Zionism had acquired—mostly connected to settlement in the Occupied Territories; gave it new meanings—such as settling in the periphery or stressed safeguarding the environment; and (f) three *religious* Zionists.

We present examples of *proud/fighting* Zionists, the *Brit-Shalom*-style Zionists, and the *post*-Zionists, since these understandings add nuances and complexities to the concept usually presented in the academic literature.

Examples from the Interviews and Photographs

Proud/Fighting Zionists

Adele, a 65-year-old center-left, secular woman from a *kibbutz*, was one of our *proud/fighting* Zionists. Adele emigrated from the US during the Yom Kippur War, and has lived in her kibbutz for most of her life. She created and administers a Facebook group called "Life on the Border— Things People May Not Know, but Should," which, as of summer 2020, had over 5500 members. In addition to this page, which she and others from the region update a number of times each day, Adele also created and updates a map of the fires (in Fig. 9.4) that result from the incendiary and explosive kites and balloons launched from the Gaza Strip into civilian areas in Israel. This is a mission that Adele undertakes every night.

Throughout her interview, Adele stresses her devotion to the area and the Zionist ideology, at the basis of this devotion and action. In fact, the first photograph that she shared was a photograph (see Fig. 9.3) in which her youth group met with Ben-Gurion, when they first arrived in Israel.

While Adele also notes that she tries to be empathetic toward the Gaza citizens, she stresses that, for her, the Jewish people and Israel come first, believing that the Palestinians have other places in the world where they can live:

> I very much think of myself as a Zionist, in public and on Facebook I write that I'm a Zionist, I say that it's not a curse, because for a lot of people, it's a "red flag" … the Jewish people have roots here of thousands of years and we needed it because of anti-Semitism and we need to have a home and a place that we know is ours … all of the *hasbara* that I do, all of the *hasbara* … I try to be empathetic toward the other side, but with all the good will, if it is me or them, I choose me, because there are many Arab countries … many places that Palestinians can live. I'm in favor of two states; I'm in favor that Gaza and Judea and Samaria, I'm in favor that they will also have a country, but it can't be on my account … I don't believe in God, but I believe in the Jewish people and I believe that the belief in God kept the Jewish people together … we are stepping here on ancient history, we're

Fig. 9.3   Adele—Group Photo with Ben-Gurion (2018)

breathing it in … I'm also proud of my people who don't live here and sup-port us—it is an amazing asset … the fact that Jews from abroad support Israel, spiritually, financially and from every aspect, they sent me to Switzerland twice and to the US twice and a tour from coast to coast once to talk about life here and to make direct contact between Jews and the Jewish people, who live abroad and the Jewish people who live here.

The second example of a *proud/fighting Zionist* comes from the inter-view with Yoram, a 51-year-old center, secular *kibbutz* member. He moved to *Otef Aza* about 13 years ago, from the center of the country. Although he had no *kibbutz* background, he fell in love with the style of life and the area. Since his arrival, he has been part of volunteer commu-nity and regional security groups who are trained to respond immediately when there is a security threat (see Fig. 9.5). Throughout his interview, Yoram emphasizes his connection to his volunteer work with different

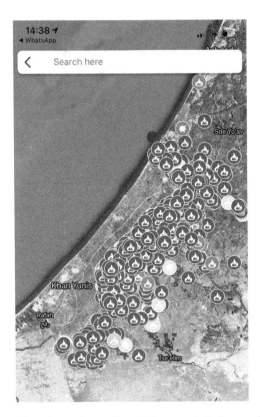

Fig. 9.4 Arson Map from Incendiary Kites and Balloons (Adele Raemer, August 2020)

volunteer armed security groups, who are on call day and night to protect the *Otef Aza* communities and borders. In the first part of his interview, he relates to this in a very romantic way—comparing it to the missions of Israel's early Zionist pioneers. Yoram said:

Patriotism is that you were born in Israel and love your country … or you love the region where you live, like I love my region … Zionism is something that you have to connect to … when you go abroad, for example, you're an Israeli, you're a Zionist, you go to one or another country, there are guys there that will welcome you and there are guys who won't … so you need to go with the feeling and not be ashamed of it that you are a

Fig. 9.5 Gear and a Weapon for the Community Security Forces (Yoram, April 2019)

Zionist ... that's the deal really, because perhaps ... I'm glad that I experienced a little bit of anti-Semitism in Prague ... because it opened up my mind about where I live and that this is my country and nobody can take it away, I'm a proud Israeli, I'm a proud Zionist and I will pay the price and I will even pay with my life, if it's to protect my family or my community and if an ordinary citizen, all of a sudden, faces a security situation and I'm called to defend [him] and I run with my weapon and storm the terrorist ... who is coming to harm my family or the residents ... so, yes it does something that I'm proud that I'm a Zionist and an Israeli, in my opinion they are connected to one another.

Brit-Shalom-Style Zionists

Three of our interviews expressed that their brand of Zionism was connected to peacebuilding and finding concrete ways to create equality and social justice for all Jews and Palestinians in the region. While none of them suggested giving up the Jewish homeland, they were very clear concerning their dream of Jews and Palestinians living together in peace in what they see as a homeland that belongs to both peoples. That is, they did not view Zionism as an ideology that negated the Palestinian other; they saw Jews and Palestinians as equal partners in this homeland.

One such interviewee was Roni, a 75-year-old left-wing, secular woman from a *moshav*. Roni is a highly committed peace activist who is in daily contact with Palestinians in the Gaza Strip. She works on helping them get permits to cross into Israel to either travel abroad or receive hospital treatments. Roni is simultaneously an ardent Zionist and an ardent peacemaker. In her interview, she further states, "My life's mission is to help the Gazans, to communicate with them and let them know we are here to help them"—an inkling that she believes that her attachment is not only to Jewish-Israelis, but also to Palestinians, with whom they should share the land as equals, reminiscent of cosmopolitan values:

> I definitely think of myself as a Zionist, while I have my definition of Zionism, which is a definition that I didn't invent, but I see in documents, this is a country of all of its citizens and there need to be citizens with equal rights and equal opportunities. I'm a Zionist in spite of the fact that I feel that there is another people who belong to this land, I don't think it makes me less Zionistic … for example, I was in Germany for a series of lectures and somebody stood up and began yelling at me—"Tell us, are you a Zionist?" I told him "Yes", but that it depends how you define Zionist. If you think that defining Zionism is that only Jews can live in this land, that there's no place for anyone else, I alone have full rights to this land, then no. But if I think that Zionism is to think that this is my country, but that another people also has affinity to this land, then I really don't think that this makes me less of a Zionist.

Post-Zionists

Five of our interviewees were classified as post-Zionists. Similar to how this term appears in the academic literature, these interviewees also presented a range of post-Zionistic understandings—from thinking that once the state was established, Zionism became irrelevant, to the need to create and realize new Zionistic goals. We present two examples from this category.

The first comes from Shalom, a 46-year old center, secular man from a *moshav*. While he says that he is "definitely a patriot," from his words, we learn that for him, the term, Zionism, lost its relevance, once the state was established. Shalom understands Zionism to be a "longing for Zion" and as having been relevant for people who longed to create a state and home before there was one. He appears not to be able to relate to this term in any other way and, as a result, even when asked about it from different angles, Shalom repeated that the word/ideology has no meaning in his present-day life:

> The term Zionism is a deceptive term … I think that what was defined as Zionism in the past, in the days of the aspiration for a state … is different today, because then, a person was a Zionist because it was derived from the longing for something, today it doesn't exist … because the moment that the state was established … I think that the term changed a bit, because what is Zionism actually? What is the meaning of Zionism today? What differentiates a Zionist from a non-Zionist, or let's say that you ask someone if he's a Zionist and he tells you "no", can he explain what isn't Zionism, does it negate something? … Zionism today gets a bit swallowed up and I would tend more to use the term connection or patriotism and not Zionism because it's a term that … is less relevant, it's lost its essence … I can't define myself as a Zionist, not yes a Zionist or not a Zionist, but I guess I'm not not a Zionist ((he chuckles)) … I don't see a connection between patriotism and Zionism … because Zionism loses its validity, I think you can be a patriot … Zionists will have to explain to me what the meaning of "these non-Zionists" are … you can still be a patriot without being a Zionist … we still haven't completely clarified what the meaning of Zionism is or someone who is a Zionist, what that means in practical terms … when I say Zionist … [it] reflects people who dreamed about this country, who

wanted to come here, who acted so that a country would be established. That was the stage that was at the seam of the establishment of the state and a few years afterward, but from some stage, it shifted, it became another concept. That is, Zionism is partially derived from the longing for Zion, but if you're in Zion, you're here and you no longer have the longing for Zion.

The second example comes from the interview with Noa, who presented herself as a "Stage 2" patriot. This is a different kind of post-Zionism than the kind described by Shalom:

I've actually been thinking quite a lot about … Zionism, in recent years, I belong to a *Beit Midrash*[24] here, so it's something I've been thinking about, I think that Zionism is a word that is no longer current, it's no longer relevant because Zionism, from my perspective, it reflected … the aspiration to be here in Israel, to speak about Zionism …. It's a sin, it's a bit like a mother who is infertile and always undergoing fertility treatments and she wants to have a child … and then she has a child and she is always talking about that she is infertile and undergoing fertility treatments, it's like, come on, we're here, we have a Jewish country … let's get to work. I think that we need to change this word. I'm not against Zionism, I think we need to update it. I see Zionism as a movement that … [says] *Eretz Yisrael* belongs to *Am Yisrael* and I believe this … *Eretz Yisrael* is the country of the Jewish people, you can argue about its borders, but we don't have any other place, this is our place … today the concept of Zionism needs to be changed … I would change it to the mission to create a just, fair, worthy, good society … this is our generation's mission, to turn this into a place that has justice, that is moral, has mutual responsibility. So today, if you ask me if I am a Zionist, yes, I'm a Zionist … but in 1948 Zionism ended, that's it, enough, now we're already in Stage 2. Today I'm a Stage 2 Zionist … in the Israeli narrative, patriotism and Zionism are highly connected and I feel that we're missing the mark when we put them in the same category because … Zionism is the past story and today patriotism is the present-day story … there are still stories of people who immigrate and blah blah blah, so they're still in the first stage. We need to advance to Stage

---

[24] A House of Learning—typically for young Jewish men who are studying religious scripts and commentaries. Today there are many types of *Beiti Midrash*, open to both men and women, who study different Jewish texts in relation to social-political issues of our times.

2 … it's important for me to say that I don't hold a post-Zionist perception, I don't negate Zionism, I think that we simply need to take it up a
level … to say that everyone needs to be culturally diverse, that's not me at
all … Israel belongs to the Jewish people first of all, we need to understand
what we should do with all of the minorities who live here, but it's our place.

Chapter Summary

As can be seen from the above, we found diversity in perspectives on
patriotism and Zionism, ones that, perhaps, upset common stereotypes
held by people who do not live in the region concerning how *Otef Aza*
residents conceive these concepts. That is, often people assume that people who continue to live in a warzone *must* be patriotic and Zionist
because, otherwise, *why* would they continue to risk their lives? What we
learned is that the reality is often much more complex than might be
expected. While we found reflections of "textbook" descriptions of patriotism and Zionism among a number of our interviewees, we also found
kinds of patriotism and Zionism that have not been reported in the literature and/or which provide twists to classical understandings. Another
interesting result was that many of our interviewees shared with us that
they do not usually contemplate if they are a patriot. When asked to
reflect on the concepts, they often needed to "think aloud" about how
they perceived the concept.

How can we summarize our results concerning these concepts? We
aver that since life in the *Otef Aza* region is so complex and dynamic, it is
not surprising to find complex and dynamic definitions/perspectives of
patriotism and Zionism. The ongoing security threat, which continuously evolves, requires people to constantly re-think about the meaning
life has for them. A sense of belonging and love of the community/region/
country is one such topic. We further hypothesize that their definitions
and perspectives are far from being complete, and that if the dangerous
security situation continues, it can be expected that their perspectives on

patriotism and Zionism will continue to evolve. In terms of cosmopolitanism, we found a few signs that a few residents think a bit in cosmopolitan terms. However, there were relatively few people who expressed such beliefs. As a result, we do not (yet) see this perspective as being a dominant one in the *Otef*.

We now turn to our interviewees' perspectives on the Gaza "other"— their neighbors across the border.

10

Otef Aza Residents Talk About the Gazans

Toward the end of the interview, our interviewees were asked: "When you think about the Palestinians in Gaza, how do you see them?" When Gal, a 35-year-old secular woman from Ashkelon, shared her perspective, she said:

Gal's They-poem
Most of the residents in Gaza
are under the rule of a terror organization
They are in a prison
with a very tough regime
I wish they could find
a way to escape
they're only trying
to care for their families

Since Israel and the *Hamas* have been at war for two decades, and, to the best of our knowledge, no psycho-social academic work has explored how Jewish-Israelis from the region view their Gazan neighbors, we were very interested in learning how they perceive/conceive their neighbors. A second reason for this interest was, as we noted in the first chapter, that,

© The Author(s), under exclusive license to Springer Nature Switzerland AG 2022
J. Chaitin et al., *Routine Emergency*, https://doi.org/10.1007/978-3-030-95983-8_10

in the past, many Jewish-Israelis and Palestinians from Gaza used to be in close contact with one another. Therefore, we felt that it was (past time) to gain knowledge and understanding of how Jewish-Israelis, whose lives are intertwined with the Gazans, even though the two peoples can almost never physically meet now, perceive their neighbors. We believed that such knowledge could shed more light on how the *Otef Aza* residents understand the intractable conflict that is the context of their daily lives.

What did we find? Similar to Gal, overwhelmingly, the residents said that the Gazans were unfortunate people, who were suffering at the hands of a cruel, terrorist regime. Our interviewees expressed their empathy for the suffering of the ordinary Gazans, who were presented as innocent victims of a regime that wanted to destroy Israel. This is not to say that our interviewees did not exhibit some inner conflict concerning their perceptions, but all in all, their words reflected compassion and caring.

It was only in the interviews with right-wing interviewees that we found deviation from this perception, though this was usually expressed between the lines, perhaps reflecting that the interviewees were uncomfortable expressing clear disdain or hatred for the ordinary people living on the other side of the border, who are caught in a multi-level humanitarian crisis. In fact, from the entire sample, only one interviewee—Ziona—noted her fear and hatred of the Palestinians and did not express some level of empathy for the Gazan residents.

In order to illustrate the ways in which *Otef Aza* residents related to the Gazans, we present residents' words concerning these perceptions through their I-, We-, and They-poems. We begin with examples from interviewees who self-identified as center or left-wing, and then present interviewees who self-identified as right-wing.

Perspectives of the Gazans: From the Center and Left-Wing

We begin with Eli's We- and They-poems. Eli, a 65-year-old man, lives in a *kibbutz* quite close to the border. His grand/parents came from Iraq, and it is clear from his interview that being from a family that lived for centuries in a Muslim country influenced the connection he feels to his Arab neighbors. In his poems, we see an inner conflict between feeling very close to the Palestinians and feeling distant and wary of them. On the one hand, he sees (some of) them as being immature and hateful, while, on the other, he sees Israelis and Palestinians as "pawns" in the leaders' game. At times, his emotions reflect anger and disappointment, while, at others, they reflect the belief that the Jewish-Israelis and the Palestinians are not only the "same people," but even more so, "brothers." Even though he vacillates between the extremes of good and bad, victimizers and innocents, his poem ends with the reiteration that "they are good people" and "they are my brothers."

Eli's We-poem
Every time we have a siren
We kill someone on their side

...
We feel
That we're pawns in a game ...
We're the same people
We're the same people
We're the same people
We love similar things
Why did we actually get into to this situation?
We don't treat them badly
We wouldn't prevent them from having things

...
We're much closer to them than to Europeans

Eli's They-poem
The Gazans,
They need to take control of their lives
And do something with it,

...
They shoot from there
They shoot sometimes
A man from Gaza

Works here on the kibbutz
A man who is trustworthy, honest, nice
He does odd jobs for people
...
They elected the *Hamas*
And they didn't vote for *Fatah*
...
The Palestinians were distancing themselves from us
95% of them are people like us
They want to work
They were born here
They could have gotten an education
They are people
There is the percentage
Who wants to argue with us
They come here to the hospitals
They come here
A small part of them, to work
The man in charge of growing strawberries in Gaza
Comes into Israel every day
A man after my own heart
If he was my neighbour
All he wants to do is work
When will there be people like that?
And less people who want to lob *Kassams* at us?
Why are they like that?
Why were they born to be like that?
People want freedom
People need to manage
They don't have to act like a seven-year-old
who doesn't know how to channel his anger
That's what they do
Of course, only part
People will mature somehow
Grow up, a bit
Their leaders are not mature enough
They are stuck in their ways
...

A woman's fingers were burned in Gaza
She came for treatments
They put explosives on her
I don't say that she's guilty,
She went along with it
An Arab worker who works here
He drove the tractor into the fire
He passed through it
And he tried to stop it from reaching the bushes
They are good people
They are my brothers
They are my brothers

Zohar, a secular left-wing man from Sderot who has worked for years in the local college and helped found the Cinemateque, talked about the Gazans as workers, students, and filmmakers—people with whom he was in personal contact. He also notes that the Palestinians in Gaza, who shoot rockets, have "nothing personal" against him: the Palestinians who shoot the rockets do so, so that others—in Israel and other countries—will become aware of their (the Gazans) problems. He expresses understanding, and even, empathy toward the rocket shooters, seeing them as "having no choice." In fact, he was the only interviewee who expressed this thought. However, like other interviewees, Zohar differentiated between the *Hamas* militants, seeing them as a small minority, and the innocent general population, which was "held hostage" by the *Hamas*. Furthermore, he expresses criticism against the Israeli government/military when he states that the Gazans learned ways of being violent "from us."

Zohar's They-poem
Laborers from Gaza worked in Sderot
Students from Gaza studied here
Hundreds of rockets were fired at the area
They are suffering
Out of two million people,
30 thousand are in the *Hamas* service
They're holding a big group hostage
A group of filmmakers from Gaza

who love film came here
The residents there don't have anything personal against me
They don't shoot because of me
They shoot because this is the biggest urban community
They also understand
That they have no chance
They shoot to make their problems known
They released a bird with a weapon
They learned this from us

The next example comes from Tamar, a 50-year-old center, secular woman from a *kibbutz* who headed social services in one regional council in the region. Her They-poem can be divided into two sections. In the beginning, she uses single words to describe the Gazan civilians, beginning with "compassion." She then moves on the frustration that the Gazans and the Israelis feel about the ongoing war situation. Here, she speaks of missed opportunities and of helplessness. She even states that Israelis do not know the depths of the suffering of the Gazan people—one of the strongest statements that we heard from the interviewees concerning concern for the Palestinians in Gaza. Tamar, furthermore, calls for an open border between the peoples. In the second part, when Tamar moves on the *Hamas*, however, her poem changes noticeably. Here, she does not express compassion for the *Hamas*, but rather "curses" them and talks about their cruelty.

Tamar's They-poem
Compassion
Sadness
Frustration
A feeling of missing the mark
Of helplessness
They are miserable
They suffer terribly
We don't understand how much they are suffering
There should be an open border
So we can visit there and they, here
I curse them

I don't curse the Gazans
I curse the *Hamas*
They now released the safety catch and shot at me
On the other side of the fence
A war is happening
With horrendous intentions of harming us
They don't succeed in reaching us

The next excerpts come from Micha's I- and They-poems. Micha is a 55-year-old left-wing, traditional Jew who lives in a *moshav*. Micha talked about the Palestinians from Gaza from the beginning of his interview. His words reflect the different perceptions that he has held of the Gazans over his lifetime—beginning from the time that he was a child, when the "Arabs were part of my daily life" and Gazan Palestinians watched over him. Later, as a young adolescent, he developed fear of the Palestinians. This fear, and perhaps hate, intensified, when the rocket barrages became a deadly threat, especially when one of his students was killed by a mortar shell. Today, however, when he talks about the Gazans, he emphasizes the many ways in which *Otef Aza* residents are terrorized by the *Hamas* and the compassion he feels for the Gazans, who are experiencing "great pain." His words conjure up an image of a yoyo, and it is clear that he finds such behavior problematic: "yes, closure; no closure"; "there are permits; there are no permits." Therefore, we see that in spite of the major impact that *Hamas* terrorism has had on Micha's life, he has come (almost) full circle concerning his perception of the Palestinians, who have always been part of his personal, family, and social-political life.

Micha's I-poem
What I remember about being close to Gaza
I remember the Arabs were part of my daily life
I would shop in the "Gazan Market" in Sderot
I remember the open border
I would go with my mom to her Arab doctor
I felt so safe on the busiest street in Gaza
I would wait for her by the falafel stand
I don't need to be wary of an Arab
...

I began feeling there was some enemy here
...
I remember the [Gaza] Strip, from being a reservist
I arrived there as a reservist
I experienced the first *Intifada* there
I experienced the crossings between Gaza
...
I remember hundreds, thousands coming out in busses
To work in Tel Aviv
...
I remember the period was pretty confusing
...
I remember endless stoppages
...

I saw this threat
I remember a very, very, very difficult period
...
I have four children
I think it changed my entire experience
...
I didn't understand the significance of ruling over them, as an enemy
...
Will somebody believe me if I talk about this?

Micha's They-poem
The Arabs were part of my daily life
They would come from Gaza
and set out their wares
...
The busiest street in the heart of Gaza
The falafel man would watch over me
the Arabs weren't the enemy
But in '73,
The Yom Kippur War broke out
...

There's an enemy here
It's forbidden to get close to Gaza
The first *Intifada*
...
All the Gaza workers would come back from the center
yes, they can leave
they are forbidden to leave
they were the ones who built our house
they were always dependent on permits
exit permits
yes, closure
no, closure,
they can come out
there are permits
there are no permits
there started being mortars from Gaza
slowly, slowly, that mortar improved
and the *Kassams* started
...
the tunnels began
sub-machine guns that hit houses
Gaza remains
...
The Arabs were everywhere
mainly in the work branches
in the markets
the restaurants
construction
there's no place where they weren't found
they were part of the industry that creates and builds the country
at a certain hour they needed to get on the busses and return home
or into their cars
they also came with their own cars
like the workers for my wife's parents
who all of a sudden became enemies
they connected to all kinds of terror organizations
and the PLO returned
...

busses explode
restaurants explode
girls or women,
who pretended they were pregnant
and carried explosives
all the suicide bombers
the terror organizations
and the resistance
and the weapons they got
the *Kassams* increased
the hate increases
great pain
Great pain
Great pain
They deserve much more
There are children there
There are citizens there
People exactly like you and me
who want to make a living
to fly abroad
to have fun
to enjoy
to succeed
great pain

The next example comes from Arieh, a 55-year-old center-left, secular man from Sderot. Arieh blames the *Hamas* for the attacks on Israeli citizens (e.g., "it's up to them"; "they control me!"), while also averring that it is important to differentiate between civilians and militants. He further notes that Israel has the responsibility to help Gazan residents (e.g., "they are people," "their lives are not simple," "they're sitting in our jail"). Arieh presents the Gazans as people who speak the Hebrew/Israeli language and are knowledgeable about Israeli society. That is, he sees them as having strengths and positive features. He sees Israeli and Gazan lives as intertwined, as evidenced in his words: "they, too, wish to reach an arrangement."

Arieh's They-poem
It depends on them [the *Hamas*]
They are controlling me, in essence!
They simply control me!
What do they want?
What do they think?
They are people, in the full sense of the word,
they shoot at me
they shoot at a population
that's what they're doing
...
They made a living!
They made a living!
the Arabs did,
they worked here
they would come here
and they understand
they understand
they read our newspapers
they were in our prisons
they speak our language
so they know
they know
they also want to reach an agreement

Rami's They-poem
They are our neighbors
They need to live with us
And the Gaza teenagers
They have some **horizon**
The Gazans as **equal** people
The Gazans aren't the problem
50% of them are under the age of 18
Who were born into a situation,
It's not certain that they feel connected to the Negev
...
They're unfortunate people

Who were imprisoned in a miserable situation
The people in Gaza need
They have nothing!

As noted in Chap. 5, Rami, a 61-year-old kibbutz member, established the Lighthouse, a grassroots initiative for peace dialogue between Israelis and Gazans, held in what he calls *Merchav Aza* (the "Gaza Space"). Rami sees the situation in Gaza as a very clear, unjust situation: the Gazans are innocent people—the majority of whom are very young, even children. He emphasizes that they are equal people, who are denied their most basic rights, and that they are the victims of an impossible situation that was imposed on them (by Israel? By the *Hamas?*). The placing of blame (on Israel and the *Hamas*) is further evident when he states that the Gazans "are not the problem."

Rami's poem further emphasizes the need for joint life between Israelis and Gazans. He calls them "our neighbors," and ends with a passionate statement that the Gazans have nothing and need everything, which echoes his earlier statement that "they need to live with us." In sum, Rami's poem expresses the belief that the Gazans have been manipulated and harmed by destructive regime/s, who is/are keeping them not only from their dreams, but also from gaining their most basic rights. His words reflect the notion that the two peoples are joined together, who need one another to realize their dreams.

We now present perceptions of the Gazans expressed by interviewees who self-identified as being right-wing.

Perspectives of the Gazans: From the Right-Wing

As noted above, overall, people who self-identified as right-wing also expressed compassion for the suffering of the ordinary Gazans, though to a lesser extent than those on the center or left. In addition, they also tended to be more judgmental of the ordinary citizens and blamed them for voting for the *Hamas* (in 2006) and for not overthrowing the regime since. Furthermore, some appeared to be indifferent to the Gazans, not appearing to see them as important or describing them mainly as an obstacle to obtaining quiet for the Jewish-Israelis in the *Otef Aza* region. Only one woman, Ziona (presented near the end of the chapter), expressed clear suspicion and hatred of the Palestinians.

Sarah, a 49-year-old religious and extreme right-wing woman, lived in *Gush Katif* for 14 years, before she and her family were forcibly evacuated in 2005. Sarah said that she knows Gazans "very well," better than most left-wing Israelis. She further stated that she knows that many Palestinians want Israel to rule over them, since they see the benefit of such control.

It is interesting to note that Sarah does not use the term, "Palestinians," but rather refers to them as Arabs, throughout her interview. This could reflect her non-acceptance of Palestinians as a defined national group, within the larger Arab population in the world, which claims rights to the land. When we compare her perspective on the Gazans to most of the other interviewees, we see that while, on the one hand, she expressed pity for the Gazans, she asserted that Israel should conquer them and be their rulers. Thus, her words reflected condescension and paternalism and clearly showed how she perceives power relations between Jewish-Israelis and Gazans.

Sarah began by talking about the Gazans as people who attack—a word that she repeats often. She then notes that the Gazans will have a better life when Israel controls them, integrated with her statement that one cannot help but "pity the Arabs" because they are "locked up." However, in contrast (at least) to Zohar, Rami, and Micha, who imply that Israel has, at the least, partial blame for the grim situation in Gaza, Sarah only blames the *Hamas*. Mixed with her pity is her accusation that the Palestinians elected the *Hamas* and that they should revolt against this regime—and this is the only place in the poem where she emphasizes her words. Her final words are "In war, like war," which can be contrasted to Eli's poem, which ends in brotherhood, and Rami's poem, which ends with the cry to help the Gazans, who have nothing.

Here is most of Sarah's poem about the Palestinians in Gaza.

> The Gazans began doing all kinds of attacks
> And throwing rocks on the road
> And the Arabs really exploited this

There were attempts at infiltrating the settlement
Attempts at attacks
Attacks on the roads
There were a lot of attacks
And attacks and attempts to harm,
and mortars and *Kassams*
and the *Kassams* began to reach
there were mortars, there were *Kassams*
attempts to infiltrate
there were attacks

...

[If we live in and control the Gaza Strip]
It's also good for the Arabs
Awwad, who worked for us
Awwad is a "good Jew"
He's an Arab from Gaza
He was nice with us and loyal to us
Hassam is an exceptional electrician
In Gaza live Arabs who are our neighbors
The *Hamas* controls them
Most of the Arabs in Gaza

...

Would want to live in peace with the Jews
Their leaders
And their gangs
The Arabs in Gaza,
When the IDF will occupy the Gaza Strip
They will have it better
They had more hours of electricity
More clean water
And better medicines
Not like the *Hamas*
You can't help, but pity the Arabs
You can't help but pity the Arabs in Gaza
They live in such a difficult reality
Locked up and closed

...

It's all screwed up there

A cruel and fanatic regime
That doesn't take care of them
It's also their choice
Why don't they revolt against the *Hamas*?
Why don't they replace the regime?
They should do everything to do this
They really should do whatever they can
Why does the *Hamas* take all the money
To build tunnels
How much money they spent on tunnels
And on *Kassams* and on Grad rockets
They chose them
They shot one more *Kassam*
'There are demonstrations on the fence
There's escalation here and there
...
What about destroying homes of terrorists?
In war, like in war

Yoni, a 36-year-old man from the religious right, from a village, talked about the wars and terror attacks that his community has experienced, and about the Gazans—the civilians and the militants—throughout his interview. He repeated that "they don't like me" many times, and called the *Hamas* "dangerous." Yoni talked about the *Hamas* terrorism against its own citizens that does not let ordinary people raise their heads and achieve what all people want—to make a living, to have food, to have a life. He describes the *Hamas* as "villainous": they use children as human shields, have raised generations to hate Israelis and fire rockets at a sovereign state. When talking about the Gazan residents, Yoni described them as "smart," saying that they could have attended the local Israeli college and return to Gaza to be professionals and academics.

What is interesting is what is missing from Yoni's words. Like Sarah, Yoni sees them as people who want to live under Israeli sovereignty, arguing that they will have a better life if Israel will rule the Gaza Strip. Moreover, when stating what Gazans want, the words, equality and rights are missing. That is, Yoni appears to see the Gazans as deserving of the things that will keep them alive and able to work in interesting jobs, but does not seem to think of Palestinians as yearning for higher values, such as self-determination and human rights. Therefore, we have a reflection of not seeing Palestinians as equal partners who want/deserve what Jewish-Israelis want/deserve: that is, not only food on the table, but also their human rights.

Yoni's They-poem

...
Terrorists come out of tunnels at Sufa[1]
Before they kidnapped Gilad Shalit
I don't think that he (the *Hamas*) controls us
He will drag us into escalation
The enemy promotes and that gives him power
The *Hamas*
does it in loops
they don't like me
they are dangerous people
they kidnapped Gilad Shalit
...
I don't think they like me
they've been like that their entire life
...
they're really dangerous people
they're being held hostage by a terror organization
that causes them to hate us
the third generation
they hate us
the Gazans are dangerous people
they're really dangerous
there's a group of a few tens of thousands
who are ruling over them
they don't like me
they're dangerous
a terrorist organization that hides behind children
a terrorist that hides
behind a 10-year old child

---

[1] A *kibbutz* close to the border.

they force him to hide inside a building
A terrorist who only wants to kill us
Shehade[2]—one of the biggest terrorists
Some 17 children were killed
they surrounded him with children
they're hostages
a kilometer from here there are a million people
a million and a half people
who are hostages
...
that is a radical, extreme Islamic way
...
the Gazan residents there
they had it good
it will also be better for them
the Gazan, at the end,
what he wants
he wants his life
he wants his livelihood
he wants his bread
he wants his 300 shekel per day
that's what he wants
they aren't illiterate
they're smart people
one hundred Gazans
one hundred academics
they understand this
they won't do anything for this
because they can't
a terrorist organization shoots at a sovereign nation

The next example comes from Shuki, a 55-year-old right-wing, secular man from Sderot. Shuki expressed little compassion for the Gazans. In his They-poem, the word "fire/shoot" appears repeatedly. Therefore, he presents a perception of the Gazans as people who mainly "shoot/fire"

---

[2] Saleh Shahede headed the *Izz ad-Din al-Qassam* Brigades—the military wing of the *Hamas*. He was assassinated in 2002 by the Israeli Air Force.

rockets at the Israelis. Furthermore, he states, as others did as well, that the ordinary citizens are afraid of the Hamas: hence they are responsible for their fate. While he says that most Palestinians in Gaza want peace, Shuki also states that they are doing nothing to bring about peace, since the Hamas kills anyone "who raises his head." Therefore, according to his perspective, since they are not acting, this proves that the Gazans are not really "unfortunate."

Shuki's They-poem

...
(If we had remained in *Gush Katif*)
They wouldn't fire mortars and *Kassams*
What they fire at us
They actually began firing at us
Instead of firing three kilometres from the fence
They will begin to fire farther
They would just fire rockets on our area
They began firing a bit farther
...
For years, they've been firing mortars and *Kassams*
...
Instead of firing to the west,
They fire to the east
They'll ask for another kilometre and another kilometre
They don't need to be there (in Gaza)
They fire a mortar shell or a *Kassam*
...
90% of them want peace
And they want quiet
And they did nothing to achieve this
Because whoever raises his head
They kill him
They don't do anything that's good for us
They sit quietly and are frightened
...
They have responsibility
They could rise up
And do things

They don't do anything
Because they're afraid
That they'll kill everyone who causes them problems
The majority wants to live in peace
They should begin working
They're not doing anything
As soon as they fire a bomb, a mortar and a *Kassam*
And they don't care
They fired *Kassams* above the football field
...
Some cousin[3] fires a mortar
He didn't get paid
He fired a mortar
They don't want to talk to us
As soon as they fire a mortar
They're unfortunate, but not unfortunate

The final example comes from the interview with Ziona, a 71-year-old secular woman from a *moshav*. Ziona's voice was the strongest voice against the Palestinians, including ordinary citizens. Her words reflect fear and hatred of the Palestinians/Muslims (connected to how she also talked about her perspectives on patriotism and Zionism, discussed in the previous chapter). Here is her They-poem.

Ziona's They-poem
They can keep busy with their lies
The big bluff of the Palestinian people
and the Palestinian refugees
80 to 90% of the Palestinians
settled in recent history in *Eretz Yisrael*
they haven't lived here 2000 years
Most of the Arabs, the Palestinians
Came to *Eretz Yisrael* during the time of the British
Arabs who came from Egypt and Syria
They [were treated] as sub-human

---

[3] Jewish-Israelis often call Palestinians/Arabs "cousins," since the Jews see themselves as descendants of Isaac and the Arab Muslims as descendants of Ishmael, who were sons of Abraham.

They escaped from there
from murder in the family
the tribes heard
they need workers
they came as workers
they knew that they would be treated better here
...
one hundred million Muslims will come
they will spread
they won't need any rocket, only knives
and they'll finish off everybody
One hundred Gazans should die, so my son won't die
...
they can keep busy with their lies
because they put it in their heads
that the Jew is a monkey, a pig, and a dog
that's what they teach them from the time they are born
there are not a few communities in Judea and Samaria
where Hitler is their idol
Amin el Husseini had plans
...
to establish an Auschwitz model
they are our partners
...

Chapter Summary

The above examples—which reflected the entire sample—show that, in general, our interviewees expressed concern and empathy for the *ordinary* Gaza residents, not seeing them as enemies, but rather as unfortunates. All the interviewees blamed the terrorist regime and some—on the center and left—said Israel shared responsibility for their terrible situation. Moreover, only one interviewee expressed hatred of the Palestinians/Gazans, while the rest differentiated between militant factions in Gaza and the general population, seeing most people over the border as people who deserve much more than they presently have. This was even partly true for our interviewees from the national-religious stream, who see *Eretz Yisrael* as having been given by God exclusively to the Jews and, thus, did not appear to be overly concerned with Palestinian rights. When they spoke about Gazan rights, they mainly referred to the fulfilling of basic needs, such as food and economic security, and not equality, human rights, or self-determination.

In conclusion, while we cannot claim that most of the interviewees expressed a desire to become closer to the Gazans, we did find that in spite of the intractable conflict, residents do not see ordinary Gazans as an enemy, but rather as a people who, like them, are caught in a situation that puts them in harm's way.

Now that we have presented all the analyses, we turn to Part IV that ties everything together and suggests ways forward—in research and in actions on the ground—for better understanding and dealing with the intractable conflict in the *Otef-Aza*-Gaza region.

Part IV

Summary and Conclusions— Implications for Living with Intractable Conflicts and Thoughts About the Future

This final Part of the book is comprised of two chapters. Chapter 11 presents our summary and conclusions regarding our findings, which we tie to the theoretical concepts discussed earlier in the book. Moreover, we offer our theoretical understandings and models of the meaning of life for *Otef Aza* residents, based on our results. At the end of this chapter, we engage in a short "zoom out" to look at some other intractable conflicts and to situate our study in this larger world of conflicts. The chapter ends with our call for a non-violent resolution of the Israeli-*Hamas* hostilities, rooted in a perspective of positive peace. The final chapter—the Epilogue—presents understandings that we reached after completion of our work, which were derived from the events of May 2021, which saw not only the last Gaza War (as of this writing)—Guardian of the Walls— but also horrific violence that erupted between Jewish and Arab citizens of the country. Here, we offer some thoughts about this enlarged circle of violence, from both a research and an activism viewpoint.

11

Summary, Discussion, and Conclusions

This book discussed and offered psycho-social analyses concerning the meaning *Otef Aza* residents give to their life in this intractable warzone, their understandings of patriotism and Zionism, and their perceptions of the Palestinian-Gazans. Since we could not undertake a comparative study of people on both sides of the border, due to the war relations that exist between the *Hamas* regime and the Israeli government, and since the *Hamas* regime views Palestinian contact with Israelis as betrayal,[1] we were unable to interview Gazans and learn their perspectives about their lives in the war-torn region.

Our research found that life in *Otef Aza* is extremely complex and dynamic. On the one hand, this was not surprising: after all, we *would* expect that living in an intractable warzone—wherever it may be—would lead to numerous complications in life. However, on the other hand, we could not help but take note of all the specifics and the nuances of the complexity that we found. *Otef Aza* residents expressed and reflected on how the ongoing hostilities have impacted their lives on the personal,

---

[1] See, for example: Hamas Arrests Gazans for Holding Zoom Video Chat with Israelis (April 10, 2020). *Ha'aretz*. Retrieved from https://www.haaretz.com/middle-east-news/palestinians/hamas-arrests-gazans-for-holding-zoom-video-chat-with-israelis-1.8755257

© The Author(s), under exclusive license to Springer Nature Switzerland AG 2022   **269**
J. Chaitin et al., *Routine Emergency*, https://doi.org/10.1007/978-3-030-95983-8_11

interpersonal, family, intra- and intercommunal, and intranational levels. Moreover, we found many instances of paradoxes, in which an interviewee would say one thing and then contradict her/himself. As we will detail below, our results also shed new light on conceptualizations connected to the psycho-social meaning of life in a context of intractable war, specifically concerning societal beliefs, cognitive dissonance, patriotism and Zionism, and perspectives on the other/"the enemy."

We further found that the intractable conflict between Israel and the *Hamas* has led the region's residents to often engage in reflection on why they are there, and, for some, to contemplate if remaining is the right choice. They wonder if the "Heaven" of the region *really* overcomes the "Hell" of the region; how the security situation is affecting their grand/children's physical and psychological lives; and their interactions and place within their communities, within the region, and in wider Jewish-Israeli society. They reflect on their position vis-à-vis governmental leaders, Jewish-Israelis from other regions, and the media, and they try to articulate how they think this conflict should be solved, while often not finding or, at least, expressing a definitive answer. What they all *do* agree on is that what has been *cannot* remain.

More specifically we found:

(a) Four main themes were present in the interviews, photographs, and social media materials—routine emergency/emergency routine; I am my others' keeper; the State of the Western Negev versus the State of Israel; life in the *Otef*—it's complicated, conflictual, and paradoxical. Each theme had a number of aspects, which further highlighted the diversity of emotions and cognitions/perceptions both within and between the residents. These themes demonstrated how the meaning of life in the region is rarely simple or clear-cut.

(b) The residents expressed different and nuanced understandings of the concepts of patriotism and Zionism. At times, these perceptions reflected the academic literature. However, they often expanded and challenged these conceptualizations—including interviewees who defined themselves as anti-patriots or anti-Zionists, or who expressed some signs of cosmopolitanism. Furthermore, there were interviewees who had a difficult time relating to the concept of patriotism, asserting that they did not think of themselves in these terms. These are findings that could be considered unexpected, given that these residents choose to continue to live in a warzone, a choice that many might think implies a strong sense of patriotism/Zionism.

(c) Most of the interviewees differentiated between the *Hamas* and the ordinary Gazans, seeing the ordinary people as victims of a cruel regime, who were deserving of sympathy and empathy. They often related to the Palestinians as neighbors, people with whom many had been close, up until the end of the last century. At times, some residents even related to them as extended family, that were lacking basic rights and the ability to have a good life. Interviewees often used terms, such as "unfortunate," "victims," and as being "locked up," through no fault of their own, when talking about the Gazans. In short, most appeared to see them as neighbors—albeit distant ones, with whom they are not in daily contact—and not as enemies. The main difference between our center/left-wing interviewees and our right-wing interviewees, however, was that the center and the left stressed human rights, such as self-determination and independence, while the right tended to stress more basic needs, such as making a decent wage. Furthermore, only one interviewee in our sample expressed hatred of Palestinians.

(d) As to our last research question—"What do residents think will happen in the next few years?"—there was near-complete consensus among the interviewees that the coming years in the *Otef* would be like the 20 before them: "more of the same." For this reason, we did not devote a chapter to this topic, since the responses to this question were short and repetitive. We found them to be depressing—since they reflect a loss of hope—or at least a lack of ability of residents to articulate hope—that the reality of the region would/could change. However, these results were not surprising, since we have often heard such responses from people we know in the *Otef*, unconnected to the research. This finding cut across the entire sample—including those who wanted a non-military solution and those who thought that a decisive war was the answer. Regardless of demographic variables, the interviewees expressed disappointment and anger with Israeli leaders for letting the situation go on and on and on, and for allowing the suffering of the *Otef* residents to go on and on and on.

It is now time to tie our results together with the academic conceptualizations presented earlier in the book in order to present our theoretical understandings of the meaning of life for *Otef Aza* residents. We begin with a "cloud" comprised of the loaded words found in our interviews and in the social media materials that we analyzed, connected to the main themes we discerned in our analyses.

Loaded Words, Themes, and the Meaning of Life in an Intractable Conflict

Figure 11.1 presents a schematic visualization of the meaning of life in *Otef Aza*, a region embroiled in an intractable conflict, based on the loaded words (Chaitin et al., 2017) that appeared in the interviews and social media materials, combined with the four major themes that we found. We use the term "loaded words" to denote words, phrases, and verbal, written, or visual communication that reflect an extremely strong emotional response communicated by the person who used the words, and might do so in the reader, listener, or viewer, as well.

The "cloud" aims to reflect the messy complexity of life for the residents and the contradictions/paradoxes that permeate their lives. The loaded words connect to experiences that often occur simultaneously, or at least, very close to one another. Therefore, they should not be viewed as discrete categories, which are compartmentalized by residents into neat, unambiguous understandings, but rather should be understood to be reflective, overlapping, and contradicting at times.

Fig. 11.1   Life in the *Otef* via the loaded words and themes (color online)

Our Four Themes in Relation to Prior Academic Knowledge

As noted in Chap. 3, Tzachor (2019) found that his interviewees had a deep need to let others know just how abnormal their life in *Otef Aza* was, and how on edge they usually were, due to the proliferation of rocket attacks and incendiary balloons that were a part of their daily lives. The interviewees shared with Tzachor that they often felt abandoned by the Israeli governments and other, ordinary Jewish-Israelis, living outside the region. Their feelings of constantly having their lives disrupted, their frustration and anger, partly due to the feeling that others expected them to return quickly to normality after each escalation in hostilities, and the psychological scarring they saw happening to them and their children made them extremely unhappy with these others. This unhappiness was with both those who were supposed to solve the conflict—government leaders—and those who they expected to sympathize and empathize with them—Jews from other parts of Israel.

When we compare Tzachor's findings to ours, we see similarity concerning two themes—the theme of routine-emergency and the theme of the State of the Western Negev versus the State of Israel. Our interviewees, as well as residents/activists who posted materials on social media, were extremely concerned with the constant moves they were made to make between routine and emergency, which has taken its toll on them over the years. We, too, found that residents talked about the quick switches they had learned to make, and were expected to make, because the situation left them no choice but to adapt to a continual transition from war to temporary calm.

Our results also echoed Tzachor's results concerning the feeling residents had of living in a "State" of their own. Interviewees in Tzachor's book talked about the differences they experienced between "the State of Tel Aviv and Gush Dan versus the State of the Negev and the Galilee." This referred to and reflected the difference between the lives of Jewish-Israelis in the central, metropolitan areas and the lives of the people in the southern and northern peripheries, who have/had suffered from the Hezbollah in the north or the Hamas in the south. Whereas *Otef* residents saw the people from the center of the country living "normal" lives—that is, free of constant war—they saw themselves as being denied such a normal life, and even worse, facing apathy by those in the center— both governmental decision-makers and the geographical-social-economic center of the country (Tel Aviv/Gush Dan).

Based on these similar results, it appears that the themes of routine emergency and the feeling of separation and invisibility experienced by *Otef Aza* residents toward the rest of the country, including alienation from the government, provide two solid bases of the meaning of life for *Otef* residents. Therefore, our first major theoretical understanding is that *Otef Aza* residents understand their lives as being bound up in two negative experiences: (1) the routinization of hostilities between Israel and the *Hamas* regime, and (2) the disconnect between them and others in the country. In other words, we hypothesize that residents of this region are caught between a rock and a hard place. On the one hand, they experience violence from an external enemy, and, on the other, disregard from the internal, social-political entity, which is supposed to embrace them and keep them safe. This, thus, leads to a strong sense of frustration among *Otef* residents concerning achievement of a good resolution of the conflict.

Figure 11.2 presents a schematic picture of this finding in which we added our two additional findings—"I am my others' keeper" and "Life

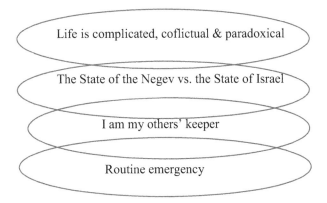

Fig. 11.2 The four-tiered shaky foundation of life for *Otef Aza* residents

is complicated, conflictual, and paradoxical." Beginning with the theme of complexity and paradox—we see this as both being a separate base and permeating the other three themes that shape the context of residents' lives. When looking at routine emergency, the State of the Western Negev versus the State of Israel, and life is complicated/ paradoxical together—we see that three of the four bases are negatively, emotionally charged. They reflect separation, physical and psychological danger, marginality, and ambiguity—feelings that are hard to withstand over time. In other words, much of the meaning of residents' lives centers around ongoing, extremely difficult challenges.

However, in addition to these difficult foundations, there is also one base that is positive—the base of mutuality, solidarity, and giving of one-self to others. As a result, this positive base provides a contrast to the other three, which, perhaps, might explain, not only the ability, but also the desire, of *Otef Aza* residents, to continue to live in such a danger-ous area.

We symbolically shaped the bases in the figure as ellipses, as opposed to "solid" rectangles, since we understand these foundations to be some-what unsteady, reflecting the instability of *Otef Aza* residents' lives. Furthermore, we see them as being dynamic and elastic: if the *intractable* conflict were to become *tractable*, or if the situation were to worsen—this could decrease or enlarge the size of (each of) the "balls" on which resi-dents are precariously balanced. However, currently, their world is shaky and unpredictable. Nevertheless, due to the positive theme of volun-teerism, we propose that while there is despair, disappointment, anger, and alienation, there is also agency, strength, and resilience. These psy-chological states occur either simultaneously or very close to one another—another sign of the paradoxes and/or cognitive dissonance felt by residents. Taken together, then, this combination offers one explana-tion of the complexity of life that we discerned in our analyses.

Now that we have conceptualized the shaky ground upon which resi-dents of *Otef Aza* construct the meaning of their lives, we look at the connection between our results and Bar-Tal's conceptualization of the Ethos of Conflict, in order to expand upon the foundation.

Ethos of Conflict (EOC) in the Perceptions of *Otef Aza* Residents

We found that we could connect all eight societal beliefs, which comprise the EOC (e.g., Bar-Tal, 2000, 2007, 2013), to our results. However, since we dedicated a specific part of our research to understanding patriotism and Zionism, we first relate to seven of the societal beliefs and detail this eighth belief afterward. While we observed connections between Bar-Tal's conceptualization and ours, at times, his notions differed from ours in surprising and sometimes contradictory ways. As a result, we now explore how each belief in the EOC specifically relates to the context of life in the *Otef Aza* region. In short, while we see Bar-Tal's concepts as relevant for explaining how residents understand their lives at times, they need to be extended or viewed differently in other instances. Let us begin.

Justness of goals—since all but one of our interviewees did not question Israel's manifest goals of maintaining a Jewish-democratic state and of having the right to live in peace in their homeland, we see this societal belief as relevant for the context we studied. However, it is important to note that for most of the interviewees, this meta-goal was *not* a topic emphasized in their narratives. In other words, it appeared to be a given, and, perhaps, for that reason, the interviewees felt no need to reiterate the obvious: a country has a right to exist and when an entity proclaims that it should be destroyed or engages in acts of war/terrorism—defending yourself is logical and justified.

In our analyses, we did, however, find differences between the center/left interviewees and the (religious) right-wing interviewees concerning "the goal." The latter emphasized the importance of the Jewish characteristic of the State, while not emphasizing the democratic aspect. It was not so much that these interviewees overtly negated democratic principles, but rather that referral to these values was absent from their interviews, and we found their absence telling. These interviewees from the right appeared to conflate Israeli life with their understandings of Jewish (religious) life, and was reflective of the notion of the ideology of a Greater Israel (e.g., Acosta, 2014; Ben-Moshe, 2005).

For example, overall, the Palestinian Gazans were either absent from their interviews, until we asked them specifically about them, and/or, when they did talk about the Gazans, presented as "background." At times, this background was more prominent, and moved somewhat into the foreground when it was represented as causing deep problems, such as terror attacks. At other times, the Palestinian background was mainly presented as being unimportant—or at least, much less important—than the Jewish-Israelis. When the right-wing interviewees were asked to share their perceptions of the Palestinians in Gaza—as were all the interviewees—and they spoke about Palestinians' desires, they attached only basic needs to this Palestinian "background." That is, they noted that Palestinians wanted to make a living, to live in quiet, and be able to take care of their children. What was missing from their words was the perception that Palestinians also have higher aspirations for independence, self-determination, and other human visions and dreams that go beyond the fulfillment of basic human needs for a decent survival.

It is important for us to note, however, that, in almost all the cases, this message was latent, appearing between the lines. Perhaps this was due to social desirability—that is, the reticence to be politically incorrect that would put them in a bad light—and/or perhaps this was due to their need to emphasize Jewish-Israeli needs, not Palestinian ones. In any event, the Palestinians were presented by these interviewees as background to the Jewish-Israeli, *Otef Aza* foreground, in which the Palestinian other was presented as ranging from unimportant to dangerous. Furthermore, in comparison, the center/left interviewees expressed that while the state needed to provide a safe and democratic home for Jews, they did not express—either manifestly or latently—that they thought such a state should violate or ignore Palestinians' rights.

In sum, therefore, overall, while we see our results as echoing Bar-Tal's understanding, most of our interviewees did *not* dwell on the justness of maintaining a Jewish-democratic state. While usually stating that they believe in such a state, when discussing patriotism and Zionism, the interviewees did not expand upon what this means in terms of the Israel-*Hamas* hostilities. The justness of this goal, therefore, was implied as a given, not as something that needed to be emphasized. Moreover, when it was stressed, our interviewees—from all backgrounds and orientations—maintained that the status quo of the intractable conflict has *not* furthered attainment of this meta-goal. Therefore, we propose that in the *Otef Aza* context, this societal belief simultaneously echoes Bar-Tal's understandings while presenting an alternative perspective.

We found *importance of security* to be *the* most prominent belief expressed in our interviews and in the social media materials. Of course, this could be expected: after all, approximately one quarter of a million Israelis who live near the Gaza border have had to literally run for their lives, hundreds to thousands of times. We understood this belief to be a reflection of the existential fear that pervaded almost all the residents' stories that we studied—again reflecting Bar Tal's overall conceptualization. We assume that the reason that security was found to be so important to the *Otef* residents is because the threats evolve all the time, and have become more diverse and dangerous as the years go by. Furthermore, there is no real "down time" in the *Otef*: the tense security situation is an unpredictable and ongoing presence in residents' lives, which makes it very difficult for them to put existential fears to rest. This finding also ties directly into three of the four major themes that we discussed above, that point to difficulty. That is, the high importance of security connects directly to the themes of routine emergency, the State of the Western Negev versus the State of Israel, and life as a paradox. This is our second major theoretical understanding.

In sum, our findings mirrored Bar-Tal's conceptualization, but can be understood to represent the extreme pole of the concept. Security is not only a central societal belief in the *Otef Aza* context; it is an all-consuming one.

Delegitimation of the enemy—this belief was mainly heard in the interviews and reflected in the social media materials with the right-wing—both the secular and the religious—and was only explicitly emphasized by one interviewee. With that said, it is important for us to note, that even among some of the right-wing group, this belief was not emphasized. Furthermore, we found that *Otef Aza* residents usually saw the opposite as being true, especially when they talked about the Gazans. Nearly across the board, residents expressed sympathy and empathy with the ordinary Gazans, clearly differentiating them from the Hamas, who they *did* clearly blame for the terror attacks and the ongoing war. The interviewees, as well as the residents/groups who posted in the social media materials, stated that the *Hamas* often had some control over their lives, were responsible for the terror and destruction, and kept all residents of the region—Gazans and Jewish-Israelis in the *Otef*—hostage. On the other hand, the ordinary Palestinians were usually portrayed as victims of the *Hamas* cruelty and not as an enemy.

Therefore, our findings contradict Bar-Tal's emphasis on this belief. The totalitarian, Islamic-based regime in Gaza was the enemy—who was definitely delegitimized—whereas the Palestinians living there, most of the population—were not. They were categorized as being on a scale from "victims and unfortunates" to "brothers." However, when we compare the perceptions of the Palestinian Gazans held by the right-wing interviewees (Palestinians as background) to the left-wing and center interviewees (Palestinians as people), we propose that there are two parallel scales that can capture these perspectives—with the center/left-wing seeing the Palestinians in Gaza as ranging from *unfortunates—brothers/sisters* and the right-wing seeing the Palestinians in Gaza as ranging from *unfortunates/unimportant—dangerous/terrorists*.

Furthermore, there is another result that we found that connects both to the theme of the State of the Western Negev versus the State of Israel and to the importance of this societal belief, delegitimation of the enemy.

The *Otef Aza* residents, regardless of political stance and/or religious belief, spoke about two adversaries. In addition to the *Hamas* regime, the interviewees and activists, who posted on Facebook and YouTube, also identified the Israeli government as another type of opponent. We are *not* at all claiming that they related to their governmental leaders as an enemy, in the sense of the *Hamas* regime in the Gaza Strip, but rather as an antagonist that has not brought the hostilities to a resolution and, hence, has extended residents' suffering—either through avoidance of engagement in a total war or through avoidance of negotiating a political agreement.

The residents feel invisible, forgotten and unimportant in the eyes of their elected leaders. They speak about the government in negative terms, protest against them, create posts and video clips that attack or make fun of government officials for ignoring their plight—hence stressing in different ways how the State of Israel is not only often oblivious to the State of the Western Negev, but more so, acting *against* the State of the Western Negev. Therefore, while we find the term "enemy" to be too strong a word to describe residents' perceptions of their government leaders, there is *no* doubt that *Otef Aza* residents view the Israeli government as being located on a continuum that runs from apathy/indifference—as they continue to avoid *seeing* the *Otef Aza* population—to exploitive—when the government relates to the residents as "pawns in a war game," turning them into the "bullet-proof vest of the country" (in the words of residents). In order to relate to both these antagonists, in Fig. 11.3, we symbolically note the *Hamas*, who is a delegitimized enemy, with a capital "E," and the Israeli government, who is a delegitimized antagonist, with a lowercase "a."

In short, in light of our findings, in our opinion, Bar-Tal's conceptualization of delegitimation of the enemy does not fully capture the understandings of *Otef Aza* residents. It is not only the *Hamas* that makes residents' lives so terrible, who is identified as an Enemy, but it is also their *own government* that is perceived as an antagonist, since residents experience the leaders as ultimately keeping them in their bind, and constituting another major factor for their ongoing suffering.

Furthermore, when we connect this finding to our four major themes, we can better understand why three of the four bases of meaning are emotionally negatively charged, making life so difficult for people in the region. That is, the residents need strength to live with the dangers not only from the outside (the *Hamas*), but from the inside as well. They continue to live with feelings of disregard and alienation from their own government and, at times, other Jewish-Israelis and mainstream media.

Fig. 11.3 The perceived Enemy (capital E) and antagonist (lowercase a) of *Otef Aza* residents

They are, thus, fighting battles on *two* fronts, which is, objectively, extremely draining.

Therefore, our third major theoretical understanding is that the unexpected antagonist that comes from within is a major source of the residents' expression of disappointment, anger, and frustration, perhaps more so—or at least, not less so—than the source of the external, *Hamas* Enemy. Furthermore, since the center and left-wing interviewees perceived the ordinary Gazans as unfortunates, who suffer terribly, this may be another root of their deep frustration: residents may feel that if it were not for the Enemy and the antagonist, the conflict could be solved.

A *positive self-image* was mainly expressed by interviewees in relation to their volunteering and engagement in activities and initiatives for their own communities and for the wider *Otef Aza* community/region. This positive self-image could also be discerned from the sympathetic and empathetic ways in which they spoke about the Palestinians in Gaza, noted above. During the interviews and when undertaking the stages of analyses, we discerned that these feelings were heartfelt and authentic. However, we also hypothesize that by talking about the Gazans in such a way, the interviewees wanted to project the image that they are good, moral people, who wish the ordinary people in Gaza no harm. By expressing such a perspective, therefore, they are further able to see themselves in a good light.

Nevertheless, while our findings, overall, meshed with Bar-Tal's conceptualization on this point, we did find some differences.

Firstly, our interviewees did not appear to connect their positive self-image to a negative image of the ordinary Palestinians, noted by Kelman (2004, pp. 119–120) as one of the characteristics of intractable conflicts, in his concept of negative independence of identities. Secondly, as noted in the theme of "the State of the Western Negev versus the State of Israel," the interviewees and residents who posted on social media, often disparaged their Israeli leaders, as we just discussed above, thus, not claiming that "our leaders are moral/good—theirs are not." That is, the positive self-image appeared to be connected to the ordinary people, but not to the national leaders.

Thirdly, we also had interviewees who talked about their disappointment, frustration, and anger at how Jewish-Israeli culture and society has evolved and how Israel is at least partially responsible for the suffering of the Gazans and the impasse in the greater Israeli-Palestinian conflict and in the specific Israeli-*Hamas* conflict. These interviewees were highly critical of the leaders and/or settlers, who live in the lands that were occupied after the 1967 war. These interviewees saw the settler population, and the leaders who supported these settlements, as disturbing the peace, not helping it. That is, these groups did not reflect a belief of a positive self-image. Fourthly, the emphasis on *Magia lanu (?) (!)* (see Chap. 6), which we found in a number of interview and social media cases, connected to the considerable economic benefits that *Otef Aza* residents receive for living in the region. As a result, there is an implication of greediness. Thus, this, too, puts the residents in less than a positive light.

In sum, when connecting this societal belief to our findings, we see that, on the one hand, residents express strong signs of a positive self-image, while on the other, at times, this positive image becomes muddied, turning even into a poor self-image, both concerning themselves and their leaders. Therefore, in the context of *Otef Aza*, we propose renaming this belief to a *critical self-image*, seeing it as an aspect of intractable conflict, but not a clear-cut positive belief, since it has both positive and negative aspects. In this way, we extend Bar-Tal's original conceptualization when trying to capture the perspectives of *Otef* residents.

Concerning the sense of *victimization*—this belief was often apparent in our interviews and social media materials, most specifically, of course, when residents focused on their experiences during the terror attacks and wars. Victimization also appeared in the interviews in which residents talked about volunteering for *Tzachi*, as ways to help their fellow victims, or among the interviewees who talked about volunteering for the civilian security teams that protected their families, communities, and the *Otef* from rockets and fires. Furthermore, most interviewees and post/videos alluded manifestly or latently to the victimization, even among residents who rarely noted this aspect of their lives—for example, implying that the feeling of being a victim mainly characterized their children, but not themselves. Victimization, thus, could be understood as part of the identity of *Otef Aza* residents, even though there was a range of intensity of this feeling, with some interviewees completely denying its appearance.

When we take an overall look at this societal belief, we find that *victim-ization* appeared in cognitions and emotions expressed by residents and, thus, can be understood to be a part of the residents' societal beliefs' framework. However, in addition to the caveat noted above about the interviewees, who avoided presenting themselves as victims, when taken together with the perceptions concerning *delegitimation of the enemy* and a *positive self-image*, our study also exposed a small number of voices that stated that, in this conflict, the victims were the Gazans, more than the Jewish-Israelis.

Furthermore, by focusing on all of the volunteering and enlistment in activities for the common good, we discerned signs of an identity not rooted in *victimization*, but rather in strength, creativity, and develop-ment. That is, while no one claimed that the terror attacks and wars did not turn Jewish-Israeli citizens living close to the border into victims of cruel hostilities, we understood that residents tended to believe that one could, simultaneously, be a victim while also being strong and capable. Perhaps this was another indication of the paradoxes of life expressed by our interviewees and in the social media materials, discussed in Chap. 7.

Therefore, if we tie our residents' nuanced perspective on identity and victimization to our themes of life as a paradox and I am my others' keeper, we reach our fourth major theoretical understanding that the meaning of life, in terms of identity, for *Otef Aza* residents is found in the tension that exists between victimization and agency. These understand-ings integrate with one another, as opposed to reflecting parallel concep-tualizations that do not meet. Figure 11.4 presents a visualization of our understanding of this complex identity.

The societal belief of *unity* was reflected in the residents' stories con-cerning their experiences connected to solidarity and a strong sense of community, *within* the *Otef*. However, as evidenced by the theme, the State of the Western Negev versus the State of Israel, we found that this was not usually the case *outside* of the *Otef*. Here, we found many instances in the interviews—but especially in the social media materials—that reflected strong negative emotions of frustration, disappointment, and anger with the Israeli government(s), and, at times, Jewish-Israelis in the country, who either did not know what was happening or did not appear interested or sympathetic to residents' ongoing stress and trauma.

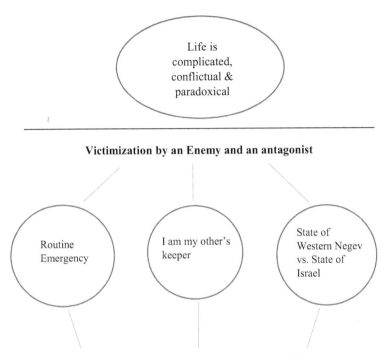

Fig. 11.4 Conceptualization of identity, together with the four themes: victimization by an enemy and an antagonist agency, creativity, and personal and community resilience

Residents also noted that the media often failed to report terror attacks against *Otef* communities. Therefore, residents appeared to be asserting that the feeling of solidarity among Jewish-Israelis, in general, in their struggle against a common enemy—the *Hamas* and the splinter groups in the Gaza Strip—was often more of a myth than reality.

In short, when relating to Bar-Tal's societal belief of unity, we understand it as being partially correct—reflecting life within the *Otef Aza* region, but not within greater Israeli society. This finding, furthermore, adds another layer of support to the points we noted above, concerning the disconnect that residents often feel with others who are supposedly part of their reference groups—Israeli governmental institutions, the media and fellow Jewish citizens.

Finally, concerning the connection between our research and Bar-Tal's societal belief that only one's side in the conflict *wishes for peace*, we found that *Otef Aza* residents tended not to talk about a utopian-type peace that might evolve one day, but rather, appeared to be desperate for the minimum of *quiet*, as evidenced in our finding concerning the recurring motif of *Tnu ligdol b'Sheket*.

In the academic literature, quiet, is conceptualized as negative peace (Galtung, 1996)—a concept that reflects the absence of war, but not much more. The residents also shared their ideas of the different paths to this negative peace—it could be a decisive war, or it could be a long-term *hudna*,[2] for example. Unfortunately, even this seemed to be a very distant possibility, as we noted above concerning responses to questions about what would happen in the area in the coming years.

In summation of this societal belief, our analyses showed that our interviewees did not express the belief that it is their society that yearns for peace, while the other side does not. At best, there was referral to a desire to reach a negative peace; at worst, residents expressed that in future years, what had been would be what was to come—also due to their government's in/actions.

This lack of hope, furthermore, also ties into the three emotionally challenging themes noted above. In other words, residents might feel hopeless when thinking about the foreseeable future, since they are fighting battles on two fronts, against the *Hamas* and against their own government. Therefore, residents have very little room to maneuver, let alone believe that their side is doing what it can to achieve peace. Our fifth major theoretical understanding, therefore, is that *Otef Aza* residents lack hope in their society's desire for peace. Their years of experiences with their governments, and with what they hear from other Jewish-Israelis and the media, has led them to the understanding that such a desire, in this particular case, does not exist.

---

[2] Arabic for a long-term truce/ceasefire. It does not necessarily reflect a treaty that includes positive aspects of the peace.

In Table 11.1, we present the intersections of the four main themes and the perspectives of the Palestinians in Gaza, with these seven societal beliefs.

Based on the above concerning the relation between the four main themes, the main perception of the Gazans, and seven of Bar-Tal's societal beliefs, we conceptualize that these beliefs in the *Otef Aza* region can be anchored, on the one end, by *importance of security*, the most important belief, and that their side is the only side that truly *wishes for peace*, as the least prominent (see Fig. 11.5). Since Bar-Tal did not rank the importance of these beliefs, but rather presented them as comprising the EOC, in general, we propose that this semi-hierarchy reflects understandings of *Otef Aza* residents. Between these two societal beliefs, we find perceptions of the other beliefs that, at times, overlap with Bar-Tal's conceptualizations, and, at times, deviate from them. Since justness of goals is elusive, it surrounds the other six beliefs. As in the case of the four bases of meaning noted above, this proposed hierarchy is perceived as being dynamic, and, of course, subject to change depending on what happens in this intractable conflict.

This is our sixth major theoretical understanding.

Conceptualizations of Patriotism and Zionism in the *Otef*

In our analyses, we found a number of understandings concerning the essence of patriotism and Zionism[3] among our interviewees—some which overlapped with the academic literature and some which did not. Participants offered understandings and adoption of patriotic and Zionist beliefs that ranged from anti-patriotism, with a touch of cosmopolitanism, on the one hand, to fighting patriotism, on the other, and from anti-Zionism and irrelevance—two sub-types of post-Zionism—to fighting and religious Zionism. While there were interviewees who appeared to reflect understandings reminiscent of Bar-Tal's assertion that patriotism

---

[3] This concept was not directly included in Bar-Tal's list of societal beliefs, since he conceptualized a universal EOC for people/societies living in an intractable conflict.

Table 11.1 Combination of themes and perceptions of Gazans with societal beliefs

Societal Beliefs →	Themes and Perceptions of Palestinian-Gazans Among *Otef Aza* Residents				
	Routine Emergency and Wars	Others' Keeper	Negev Versus Israel	Life Is Complicated	Perception of Gazans
Justness of goals	Because of dangers of terror and war, we must protect our right to live in our homeland	Our goals of building, maintaining high-quality communities is also based on importance of helping one another	We understand importance of living by border and strengthening communities; this exacts a high price—others don't appear to understand importance of goals	Should I stay or should I go? It's Heaven and it's Hell	We're brothers; we used to visit Gaza and Gazans came/ worked here. We're in this together (left/ center wings); This is our land— Palestinians need to accept this (right-wing)
Importance of security	No security—no routine, mainly, emergency and war; ongoing existential threat on personal, family, community levels	*Tzachi*, creating cultural institutions; volunteering to fight fires/terror	Government, other Jewish-Israelis and media don't understand/are apathetic to the dangers we face	The *mamad* keeps us safe, but not for the long term. What is the solution—war or peace?	Our lives = their lives. If it's bad for them, it will be bad for us; *Hamas* is the enemy—not ordinary Gazans

Themes and Perceptions of Palestinian-Gazans Among *Otef Aza* Residents

Societal Beliefs ↓	Routine Emergency and Wars	Others' Keeper	Negev Versus Israel	Life Is Complicated	Perception of Gazans
Delegitimation of enemy and antagonist	The *Hamas* often controls our lives	*Hasbara*—against *Hamas*, against Palestinians who want to destroy Israel, against UNRWA	The Israeli government is our antagonist—we're "pawns in their game." They, too, are responsible for our suffering	We're fighting adversaries on two fronts—making life very complicated	The *Hamas* is our Enemy, the ordinary Gazans are not
Critical self-image	Ability to switch quickly between emergency and routine; to make "normalcy" out of danger; to keep our children psychologically and physically healthy	We volunteer, to help others	We are the bullet-proof vest of Israel	We're victims, but we're also initiators, creators, developers and resilient—we're in control.	We're sympathetic and empathetic to the plight of the ordinary Gazans. We're good people—we want them no harm

(continued)

Table 11.1 (continued)

Societal Beliefs →	Themes and Perceptions of Palestinian-Gazans Among *Otef Aza* Residents				
	Routine Emergency and Wars	Others' Keeper	Negev Versus Israel	Life Is Complicated	Perception of Gazans
(Anti-) Victimization	There are no "drops" of rockets; there ARE injuries and damage, even without physical damage	We're active. We volunteer and act in order to take control in a war situation, over which we have no control	*Magia lanu (?) (!)* We're pawns in the leaders' game	We're victims, in despair, while also strong, creative and committed. The *Otef* as Hell	We and the ordinary Gazans are all *Hamas* victims
Unity	During war, solidarity—within the *Otef* and with other Israelis. During routine-emergency—solidarity mainly within the *Otef*. *Tnu ligdol b'sheket*	Doing for others, creating a high quality life. Heaven	Lack of unity/solidarity with government, the media, and Jewish-Israelis from other parts of the country; invisibility	Should I stay or should I go? The Heaven versus the Hell	*Merchav Aza*; they are "my brothers." We visited them. They came and worked here. No unity with *Hamas*
Wish for (negative) peace		Peace activism—peace and rights for Jewish-Israelis and Gazans	Invisibility will never bring peace/quiet. *Tnu ligdol b'sheket*	There's no peace process, only intractable war. Trying to create normalcy in an abnormal, toxic context.	Our lives = their lives

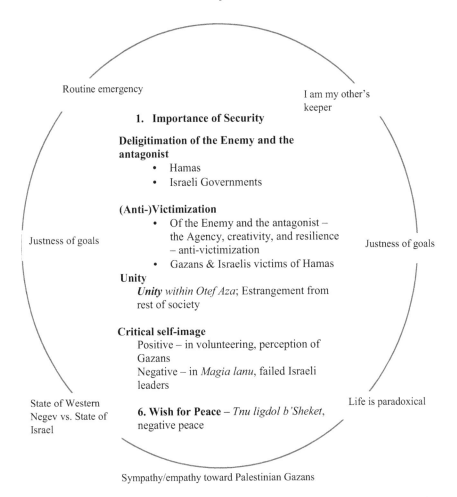

Routine emergency

I am my other's keeper

1. Importance of Security

Deligitimation of the Enemy and the antagonist
- Hamas
- Israeli Governments

(Anti-)Victimization
- Of the Enemy and the antagonist – the Agency, creativity, and resilience – anti-victimization
- Gazans & Israelis victims of Hamas

Unity
Unity within Otef Aza; Estrangement from rest of society

Critical self-image
Positive – in volunteering, perception of Gazans
Negative – in *Magia lanu*, failed Israeli leaders

6. Wish for Peace – *Tnu ligdol b'Sheket*, negative peace

Justness of goals

Justness of goals

State of Western Negev vs. State of Israel

Life is paradoxical

Sympathy/empathy toward Palestinian Gazans

Fig. 11.5 Hierarchy of societal goals, themes, and perception of Gazans in the *Otef Aza* region

is associated with fueling of the conflict, due, for example, to people's willingness to sacrifice themselves for their country and/or the emphasis that some residents placed on *hasbara* or settlement in all of *Eretz Yisrael*, we saw that the picture is more complicated than presented in the EOC framework.

We believe that one reason for the differences is that we not only specifically asked residents to share their understandings of patriotism and Zionism, but did so using very open-ended methods of collection that made it possible to hear specific and nuanced perspectives on these concepts, that are much harder to obtain in closed-ended questionnaires. Furthermore, we asked participants to take and share photographs that represented what patriotism meant to them. These methods, thus, opened up a large window into residents' understandings of these concepts, making it possible for us to obtain a better idea of the variations concerning the essence of patriotism and Zionism held by *Otef Aza* residents.

Below follow two continua that visually present the kinds of patriotism and Zionism that we discerned in the interviews and photographs. While we have placed these kinds on continua, each continuum should not necessarily be viewed as ranging from less to more, but rather as presenting the discrete concepts that constitute the range of perceptions of *Otef Aza* residents concerning these societal beliefs/ideologies. Furthermore, it is important to remember that all of these kinds cut across the sample and the four themes. That is, it was not that lapsed patriots or post-Zionists did not give of themselves to others (expressing "I am my others' keeper") or that fighting and religious patriots and Zionists did not see the Israeli government as an antagonist—with a lowercase "a." In other words, people from across the board gave of themselves and felt abandoned by their leaders, and at times, by other Jewish-Israelis, as well, regardless of their particular patriotic or Zionist stances (or lack of).

Our results point to the understanding that life in this intractable conflict region has also produced, or at least has succeeded in maintaining, types of patriotism and Zionism that at times challenge traditional conceptualizations of patriotism (e.g., as proposed by Adorno et al., 1950; Kelman, 1997; Primoratz, 2017; Press, 2007; Schatz & Staub, 1997; Zamir, 2015). For example, our additions included anti-patriotism—with a touch of cosmopolitanism—and shaken patriotism and fighting patriotism.

In terms of Zionism, a similar picture emerged. We had interviewees who said that they saw Zionism as being irrelevant, or who talked about their disenchantment, or even opposition to this ideology. Therefore, these non-conventional forms challenged and, at times, contradicted the more commonly heard perceptions of Zionism presented by researchers in the academic literature (e.g., Chowers, 2002; Gorni, 2003; Zouplna, 2008). Figures 11.6 and 11.7 present these continua.

Putting It All Together: The Meaning of Life in the *Otef Aza* Warzone

This book explored the meaning of life for *Otef Aza* residents—people who live in an ongoing warzone. When we combine our results with the academic literature on the topics of intractable war, societal beliefs, cognitive dissonance, and patriotism and Zionism, we offer our major theoretical understandings (summarized in Table 11.2) and a holistic conceptualization (represented in Fig. 11.8).

Turning to our holistic conceptualization, we propose the following. The meaning of life in this region of intractable conflict is rooted in four precarious foundations. Furthermore, this world is also framed by the perception that ordinary Gazans are deserving of sympathy and empathy, while the Hamas is identified as the Enemy. Finally, the frame of meaning of the *Otef Aza* world is comprised of feelings and sense of self/identity/community that occur simultaneously, though they are also contradictory: *stress and trauma* alongside *sense of agency and resilience*. These perceptions comprise the psycho-social world in which residents live. Within this context, we find (a) concrete *behavioral mechanisms* that residents have created/adopted for turning the abnormal situation into a "normal" situation, including the residents' ability to live with ongoing internal and interpersonal *cognitive dissonance*; (b) positive and negative *emotions*

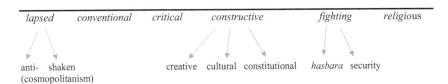

Fig. 11.6 Range of perceptions of patriotism in *Otef Aza*

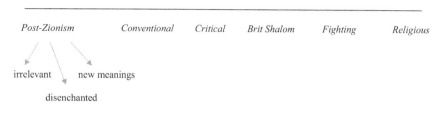

Fig. 11.7 Range of perceptions of Zionism in *Otef Aza*

associated with life in the *Otef*; (c) a range of conceptualizations concerning *patriotism and Zionism*—some which even oppose these ideologies; (d) the *ideological framework of* the Ethos of Conflict, which is an amended hierarchical version of the *societal beliefs*—these beliefs further reflect complexity. (e) The model, thus, comprises emotional, cognitive, ideational, and behavioral levels. Furthermore, it is proposed that these levels have a strong impact on the personal, familial, community, and regional levels.

The Israel-Gaza Conflict and Other Intractable Conflicts

Intractable conflicts, unfortunately, continue to be a part of our world, with the *Otef Aza*-Gaza conflict being just one sad example. We now undertake a short "zoom-out" and relate to other intractable conflicts. The reason for doing so is that while we must be careful not to conflate all intractable conflicts into one homogeneous entity, expecting that understanding one such conflict means we understand all, we need to also be careful not to lose sight of the elements in intractable conflicts share (e.g., Coleman, 2006). By looking at the commonalities, we acknowledge that we have a global problem—one greater than any regional conflict. This give us a better chance to identify and treat the toxicity of such insidious conflicts that negatively affect many more people than those directly affected by the violence.

As we presented throughout our book, Bar-Tal (often with colleagues) delineated eight universal beliefs, which comprise an Ethos of Conflict,

Table 11.2 Summary of main theoretical understandings of meaning of life for *Otef Aza* residents

Topic of Theoretical Understandings	Essence
Major themes of meaning	4 major themes that comprise shaky foundation of residents
Identity	A complex identity—victimhood/pawns in the war, intertwined with creativity, development, and agency
Perceptions of Enemy/ antagonist, themes, and emotions	Residents' lives are bound up in two negative experiences: (1) the routinization of Israel-*Hamas* hostilities and (2) disconnection between them and Israeli others (government, ordinary people, mainstream media). The resulting perceptions: frustration/despair/anger concerning non-resolution of the conflict.
Societal belief combined with themes	*Importance of security* and *wish for peace* connect to themes of routine emergency, the State of the Western Negev versus the State of Israel, and life as a paradox. Positive self-image connects to "I am my others' keeper."
Hierarchy of societal beliefs	Societal beliefs among *Otef* residents are hierarchically positioned. *Importance of security* is the most important and *wish for peace* the least important. These serve as "anchors" for the other beliefs. Justness of goals is elusive.
Societal beliefs in specific *Otef* context	Often extends/revises Bar-Tal's conceptualizations
Negative emotions, perceptions of Israel and *Hamas* regimes, and lack of hope in resolving conflict	The internal Israeli social-political antagonist is a major source of disappointment, anger, and frustration, alongside external, *Hamas* Enemy. Center/left-wing residents perceive ordinary Gazans as unfortunate, suffering neighbors. Residents fighting battles on two fronts. The combination of the *Hamas* Enemy and Israeli antagonist keeps conflict going.
Conceptualizations of patriotism and Zionism	Many different forms—from patriots to anti-patriots, and from Zionists to anti-Zionists—connected also to religious/secular and political orientations

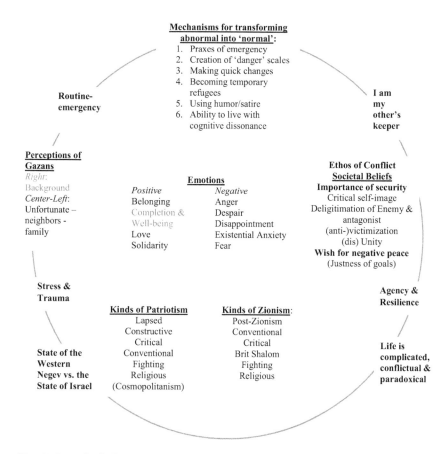

Fig. 11.8 A holistic representation of the meaning of life for Jewish-Israelis in *Otef Aza* (The grey font represents the understandings of the right-wing interviewees)

and we demonstrated how these beliefs are reflected in the context we researched. Furthermore, we found four themes that appeared to comprise the issues around which *Otef Aza* residents construe their lives. We see our context and understandings as also connecting to other conflicts—those ongoing and those that have been formally resolved. Here are some examples.

In a study recently undertaken by Bar-Tal et al. (2021), in which Protestants and Catholics from Northern Ireland were asked for their views about their side and the other, results showed that even though this conflict formally ended in 1998, with the signing of the Good Friday Agreement, young adults still view their social-political life through the EOC lens. Other research has also shown that the centuries' old conflict between the Protestant unionists/pro-British and the Catholic national-ists/republicans has not completely disappeared. Protestants and Catholics live in separate neighborhoods, there is fear/hatred and mistrust of the other (e.g., Byrne et al., 2012), and each side continues to hold the sectarian belief in the justness of its past goals (Griessler, 2021).

As we noted above, the lack of hope concerning a sustainable resolution of the conflict that we found among our residents, appears to continue to be a reality for Protestants and Catholics in Northern Ireland—even among young people. That is, signs of the conflict continue, negatively impacting lives of the "former enemies."

Other examples come from the wars that erupted in the former Yugoslav Socialist Federation in the 1990s (Spini et al., 2019; The Conflicts, n.d.). As Spini and his colleagues noted, the fratricidal dissolution of Yugoslavia resulted in horrendous atrocities, including genocide (Srebrenica, 1995, in Bosnia-Herzegovina (BiH); Hessle, 2020). In Slovenia and Croatia, after their declarations of independence in 1991, ethnic minorities, who had lived side-by-side, and even intermarried, suddenly were categorized as "enemies" by their neighbors/ families, which led to dehumanization (Hessle, 2020).In her study of the tactic of rape employed during the Bosnian War (1992–1995) and the Kosovo War (1998–1999), Hessle (2020) noted that all the gross human rights' violations—rape, constant sniper shootings on the streets, and the Serbian destruction of almost all mosques in BiH—directly tied into interethnic conflict, between Muslims and Catholics, and Serbs and Croats. These animosities, which had been swept under the rug for years, especially during Tito's rule, erupted with horrific force once the federation dissolved. Most alarming is that the perpetrators often staunchly supported their actions, reminiscent of the EOC's beliefs of justness of goals and delegitimation/dehumanization of the other.

These wars resulted in the separation of communities, huge waves of exodus and resettlement—in former Yugoslavian countries and in other places in Europe—massive destruction of human, cultural and religious life, and a surge in intergroup prejudice and nationalistic claims (Hessle, 2020). All this made reconciliation difficult, after the signing of the Dayton Agreements in 1995 (Zenovic, 2020). Furthermore, this legacy lessened inhibitions toward engagement in violent behaviors. As Zenovic (2020) notes, therefore, while the wars ended, many dire consequences continue, impacting peoples in the region, as well as in Europe and beyond.

Cyprus is an example of an intractable conflict that has been simmering on a low flame. As Killian and Agathangelou (2018) recount, after Cyprus gained its independence from Great Britain in 1960, the Greek Cypriots (78% of the population) and the Turkish Cypriots (18%) struggled to attain power in the government. As a result, violence between Greek and Turkish Cypriots erupted throughout the decade. In 1974, a nationalist coup d'état, supported by Greece, was followed by an invasion by Turkey. This led to the internal displacement of approximately 275,000 persons from both communities and to the division of the island into two sections. Since then, UN security forces secure the buffer zone between the Greek and Turkish regions.

While the two communities no longer shoot at one another, attempts to redress the conflict have not resolved the issue of displacement of refugee families and their dispossession of their lands and homes (Killian & Agathangelou, 2018). From a psycho-social aspect, the conflict involves issues of identity—with both Greek and Turkish Cypriots believing they are the victims. They hold prejudices and mistrust the other, and hold contradictory collective memories concerning the history of the conflict (Psaltis, 2016).

For example, Burke (2019) explored the meaning of loss of home, and compared the contents of the Turkish Cypriot Museum of Barbarism—located in the house where a Turkish family was murdered by Greeks—and a Greek Cypriot elementary-level schoolbook—which emphasizes neither forgetting nor forgiving atrocities committed by the Turks against the Greeks. Burke found that the two narratives of loss of home were mirror images of one another, with each side perceiving the other as murderous and evil.

When we compare these findings to ours, we see a difference: most of our interviewees did not appear to view ordinary Palestinians in Gaza as the enemy, but rather as neighbors who have/are suffering terribly from the ongoing violent hostilities. The enemy is the *Hamas*, or the other splinter militant groups—but not the men, women, and children who live in the Gaza Strip. Here, therefore, we have an example of differences in intractable conflict contexts, thus, emphasizing the need to remain aware of the uniqueness of each context.

Other examples of intractable conflicts come from Africa, which continue to reflect delegitimation/dehumanization of the enemy. For example, in South Africa, during the Apartheid era—White South African society brutalized the Black population, using legally adopted mechanisms to do so (Mandela, 1994). This oppression not only affected the direct Black victims, but has had intergenerational effects. As Adonis (2016) found, children of victims exhibit signs of secondary trauma: they speak of suffering from harsh socio-economic problems and feeling powerless and helpless. Therefore, even though Apartheid officially ended in 1994, it continues to be psychologically present. Furthermore, there is still widespread, deep racism, geographical separation in residence between Blacks and Whites, economic gaps between the rich (White) and the poor (Black), interracial relations remain tenuous, and national unity often appears beyond attainment (Malala, 2019, October 19; Smith et al., 2007).

In the 1994 Rwandan genocide, between 700,000 and 1,000,000 Tutsis and 50,000 politically moderate Hutus were murdered in 100 days, as a result of the severe dehumanization of the Tutsis by the Hutus (O'Reilly & Zhang, 2018; Staub, 2006). The perpetrators in this government-organized violence also included ordinary people. As Staub (2006) notes, this was an "intimate genocide, with neighbors killing neighbors, and people in mixed families killing family members … even their own children" (p. 869). This genocide had its roots in a long history of conflict and violence, and Tutsi dominance (the numerical minority of the population—about 14%) over the majority Hutus (about 85%). This conflictual history intensified under Belgian colonial rule, after a 1916 white paper outlined the racist ideology the Belgians had developed, averring that the Tutsis were a superior race (Mamdani, 2002). Even though the genocide ended nearly 30 years ago, and even though the country engaged in a traditional reconciliation process—Gacaca courts, which heard over 100,000 cases (O'Reilly & Zhang, 2018)—deep scars and trauma still remain between the groups.

When we compare our findings to these examples from the African continent, we see similarity in terms of the long-term scars caused by the wars and oppression. In our *Otef Aza* case, the war has lasted, so far, for over 20 years—which is one generation. Our residents spoke about the deep desire *l'gdol b'sheket* (to live in quiet), and questioned whether *magia lanu*—we deserve it (?/!)—when referring to the ongoing traumas of war, rockets and fires. Here, it appears that generations of South Africans and Rwandans are also still grappling with these issues, even though their conflicts and oppression officially ended. Hence, we see that the imprint of intractable conflicts is deep, wide, and long, and that we cannot assume that formal resolution translates into healing and reconciliation.

These are just a few examples of intractable conflicts that have harmed our world. The above demonstrates that such conflicts have extremely long "shelf lives," continuing years after they have officially ended. The *Otef Aza* context, to which we now return, fits into this depressing "puzzle" of intergroup bloody conflicts and emphasizes the need to reach a sustainable resolution that can shorten this universal shelf life.

A Call to Decision-makers to Work for the Creation of a Sustainable Reality for *Otef Aza*

> I went back to managing kibbutzim, so you also have free time to manage these projects. Today, I'm trying to help, to volunteer for projects with Gaza, planning from the civil aspect … not from the political one. To bring investors and connect them, to get them to see the agenda and what you want in order to try to help these processes, so that more people won't be

post-traumatic, so that more people won't be where you are. I really don't want them to be (like me); here it will be a place that blossoms, and not only like it is blossoming today, but rather much more. Or, in simple language, I always said that the day that there won't be rockets and there'll be an agreement, then most likely there won't be more (economic) benefits. The day that there won't be benefits any longer, that will be the sign that we reached our objective, the objective is not benefits, it's to arrive at a place that there aren't any benefits ... because you're not being bombarded by rockets. (Haim, 62, *kibbutz* resident)

For two years, we listened closely to *Otef Aza* residents' voices, found in their interviews and photographs, as well as in their Facebook postings and YouTube video clips. We undertook several analyses, in order to gain in-depth understandings of what residents were telling us, first looking at the individual level, in each interview, and then at the collective level, when we examined the social media materials and compared all of our materials.

During our work, we heard many important messages, ones that influenced us not only on the cognitive-academic level, but also on the personal/emotional level. From our perspective, the most important message was the residents' deep need for this unbearable situation to end. Therefore, we feel that it would be doing our interviewees a grave disservice to ignore this call and end our book without relating to this call.

While the interviewees knew that our research goals were to gain knowledge and understanding about how they perceive their lives, as opposed to offering/promising concrete help, over the course of the study, we realized how we wanted to end this book. Therefore, we are calling upon governmental officials to take concrete steps to end this intractable conflict. We believe that no peoples should have to live in a toxic war environment with no end in sight.

The interviewees and the residents who posted on social media repeatedly stressed how they feel "invisible" and "abandoned," like "pawns in a game," that they are the "bullet-proof vest of Israel," and that there is "the world of there and the world of here." Not only as researchers, but also as citizens of Israel, this was extremely difficult to hear. There is no nice way to put it: most people in the *Otef* often feel that they are on their own. The most they dare to envision is a negative peace that might last a few years, and that would offer them a short reprieve. This is unconscionable and is a situation that not only characterizes *Otef* adults, but has also been transmitted to the children and grandchildren, who have never experienced healthy, sustainable relations with their neighbors in Gaza. As time goes on, there is the real risk that the feelings of abandonment and disengagement from the rest of Israeli society, and lack of faith in national leaders, felt by many *Otef Aza* residents, will only grow. This is a very dangerous situation, in any society, and certainly in such a small country as Israel.

Therefore, we call on the Israeli government and decision-makers to concretely work to end this intolerable situation. *Otef Aza* residents have suffered enough. The Gazans have suffered enough. It is time to develop a sustainable plan that can change this dangerous reality. While we are neither political scientists nor politicians, we know that there are many possible ways to achieve this goal. From our perspective, as long as the agreement provides both populations—the Israelis in *Otef Aza* and the Palestinians in the Gaza Strip—with a real and sustainable light at the end of the tunnel, this intractable conflict can be solved.

It is time to find the way to reach such an agreement, which will require help from partners from the Middle East/Arab world and/or with other world leaders, who will dedicate time and resources to move a sustainable plan forward. Such an agreement is not an idea worth considering—it is an imperative. Furthermore, it is not enough to settle for a negative peace. Rather, there is a need to fashion an agreement that will lead to a positive peace (Boulding, 2000). Only a positive peace can bring about sustainable change—and put an end to the conflict, which continues to unnecessarily destroy so many lives, both psychologically and physically.

Concluding Remarks

Our book focused on the context of *Otef Aza*; however, it is only one of many, other intractable conflicts.

On the one hand, as presented in the few examples we offered above, each intractable conflict has its own history and evolution, and connects to weighty issues regarding specific cultures, religious beliefs, political systems, ethnic/race relations, borders, and economics, just to mention a few factors. Moreover, as we demonstrated, one size of Ethos of Conflict does *not* fit all. Nevertheless, we propose that our conceptualizations—such as the notions of an identity comprised of combined victimization and agency and/or the understanding that people in intractable conflicts adopt and create behavioral mechanisms in attempts to turn their abnormal situations into somewhat "normal" ones—may also be relevant for understanding other contexts of intractable conflict. Our findings, therefore, could be helpful for understanding how other people, who have experienced/are experiencing intractable conflicts, perceive the meaning of their lives.

In order to turn intractable conflicts into conflicts that are perceived as having solutions, there is first a need to document and understand how people living through such conflicts understand their lives and experiences. These ordinary people are our experts: they provide invaluable knowledge concerning the impacts of such conflicts on the personal, interpersonal, family, community, and societal levels. It is essential, therefore, that we elicit their stories and listen deeply to their voices, that we explore their creations (e.g., Rami's complex photograph; see Fig. 11.9), and that we use this knowledge and understandings to work toward an end to these deadly conflicts that have harmed societies around the world, generation after generation.

Otef Aza was described by our interviewees as Heaven that often suddenly turns to Hell. Our deep hope for residents of this region—on both the Israeli and the Gazan side—is that this Hell will disappear, leaving both peoples with good and meaningful lives that hold the promise of a sustainable future, in which both peoples can thrive. After all, this is what all peoples deserve.

Fig. 11.9 Rami—*Merchav Aza* (The Gaza Space) (2020) (color online)

References

Acosta, B. (2014). The dynamics of Israel's democratic tribalism. *Middle East Journal, 68*(2), 268–286.

Adonis, C. K. (2016). Exploring the salience of intergenerational trauma among children and grandchildren of victims of Apartheid-era gross human rights violations. *Indo-Pacific Journal of Phenomenology, 16*(1–2), 1–17.

Adorno, I. W., Frenkel-Brunswlk, E., Levinson, D. J., & Sanford, R. N. (1950). *The authoritarian personality*. Harper & Row.

Bar-Tal, D. (2000). *Shared beliefs in a society: Social psychological analysis*. Sage Publications.

Bar-Tal, D. (2007). Sociopsychological foundations of intractable conflicts. *The American Behavioral Scientist, 50*(11), 1430–1453.

Bar-Tal, D. (2013). *Intractable conflicts: Socio-psychological foundations and dynamics*. Cambridge University Press.

Bar-Tal, D., Trew, K., Hameiri, B., Stevenson, C., & Nahhas, E. (2021). Ethos of conflict as the prism to evaluate the northern Irish and the Israeli-Palestinian conflicts by the involved societies: A comparative analysis. *Peace and Conflict: Journal of Peace Psychology, 27*(3), 415–425.

Ben-Moshe, D. (2005). The Oslo peace process and two views on Judaism and Zionism, 1992–1996. *British Journal of Middle Eastern Studies, 32*(1), 13–27.

Boulding, E. (2000). *Cultures of peace: The hidden side of history*. Syracuse University Press.

Burke, J. (2019). Homes lost in conflict: Reframing the familiar into new sites of memory and identity on a divided island. *History & Memory, 31*(2), 155–182.

Byrne, S., Fissuh, E., Karari, P., Kawser, A., & Skarlato, O. (2012). Building future coexistence or keeping people apart. *International Journal of Conflict Management, 23*(3), 248–265.

Chaitin, J., Steinberg, S., & Steinberg, S. (2017). Polarized words: Discourse on the boycott of Israel, social justice and conflict resolution. *International Journal of Conflict Management, 28*(3), 270–294.

Chowers, E. (2002). The end of building: Zionism and the politics of the concrete. *The Review of Politics, 64*(4), 599–626.

Coleman, P. T. (2006). Intractable conflict. In M. Deutsch, P. T. Coleman, & E. C. Marcus (Eds.), *The handbook of conflict resolution: Theory and practice* (2nd ed., pp. 533–559). Jossey-Bass.

Galtung, J. (1996). *Peace by peaceful means. Peace and conflict, development and civilization*. PRIO.

Gorni, Y. (2003). Zionism as a renewing idea. In T. Friling (Ed.), *An answer to a Post-Zionist colleague* (pp. 457–480). Yediot Achronot. (Hebrew).

Griessler, C. (2021). Divided by national belonging and joint territory: Northern Ireland's national identities. *Studi Irlandesi, 11*. https://doi.org/10.13128/SIJIS-2239-3978-12892

Hessle, S. (2020). Reconstruction of post-war social work: Experience from former Yugoslavia as an inspiration. *International Journal of Social Welfare, 29*(2), 192–197.

Kelman, H. C. (1997). Nationalism, patriotism and national identity: Social-psychological dimensions. In D. Bar-Tal & E. Staub (Eds.), *Patriotism in the lives of individuals and nations* (pp. 166–189). Nelson-Hall Publishers.

Kelman, H. C. (2004). Reconciliation as identity change: A social psychological perspective. In Y. Bar-Siman-Tov (Ed.), *From conflict resolution to reconciliation* (pp. 111–124). Oxford University Press.

Killian, K. D., & Agathangelou, A. M. (2018). *Journal of Feminist Family Therapy, 30*(3), 129–154. https://doi.org/10.1080/08952833.2017.140434

Malala, J. (2019, October 19). Why are South African cities still so segregated 25 years after apartheid? *The Guardian.* https://www.theguardian.com/cities/2019/oct/21/why-are-south-african-cities-still-segregated-after-apartheid

Mamdani, M. (2002). *When victims become killers.* Princeton University Press.

Mandela, N. (1994). *Long walk to freedom.* Little, Brown and Company.

O'Reilly, C., & Zhang, Y. (2018). Post-genocide justice: The Gacaca courts. *Development Policy Review, 36*(5), 561–576.

Press, E. (2007). Death and sacrifice in Israel. *Raritan, 27*(2), 125–143.

Primoratz, I. (2017, Summer). *Patriotism. The Stanford encyclopedia of philosophy.* https://plato.stanford.edu/archives/sum2017/entries/patriotism/

Psaltis, C. (2016). Collective memory, social representations of intercommunal relations, and conflict transformation in divided Cyprus. *Peace and Conflict: Journal of Peace Psychology, 22*(1), 19–27.

Schatz, R. T., & Staub, E. (1997). Manifestations of blind and constructive patriotism. In D. Bar-Tal & E. Staub (Eds.), *Patriotism* (pp. 229–245). Nelson-Hall.

Smith, T. B., Stones, C. R., Peck, C. E., & Naidoo, A. V. (2007). The association of racial attitudes and spiritual beliefs in post-apartheid South Africa. *Mental Health, Religion & Culture, 10*(3), 263–274.

Spini, D., Morselli, D., & Elcheroth, G. (2019). War experiences and emerging rights claims in postwar former Yugoslavia: The role of generalized conflict exposure and collective anomie. *European Journal of Social Psychology, 49*(6), 1173–1189.

Staub, E. (2006). Reconciliation after genocide, mass killing, or intractable conflict: Understanding the roots of violence, psychological recovery, and steps toward a general theory. *Political Psychology, 27*(6), 867–894.

The Conflicts. (n.d.). United Nations International Criminal Tribunal for the Former Yugoslavia. https://www.icty.org/en/about/what-former-yugoslavia/conflicts

Tzachor, Y. (2019). *Life in the shadow of the conflict.* Carmel. (in Hebrew).

Zamir, S. (2015). Military program as a patriotism-oriented socializing agent among Israeli youth. *International Journal of Arts & Sciences, 8*(5), 443–457.

Zenovic, N. (2020). The lasting impact of the breakup of Yugoslavia. *Europe Now.* https://www.europenowjournal.org/2020/06/02/the-lasting-impact-of-the-breakup-of-yugoslavia/

Zouplna, J. (2008). Revisionist Zionism: Image, reality and the quest for historical narrative. *Middle Eastern Studies, 44*(1), 3–27.

Epilogue

After this study was completed, violence between Israel and Gaza flared up again because of friction elsewhere in the Israeli-Palestinian conflict. In April and May 2021, tensions over the planned evictions of Palestinians from homes in the East Jerusalem neighborhood of *Sheikh Jarrah* were exacerbated by religious right-wing Jews who held their annual Jerusalem Day march with a planned route through Palestinian neighborhoods. This intensified riots in Jerusalem and the West Bank, leading to the entry of Israeli riot police on the Temple Mount/*Haram al-Sharif* on May 10. The *Hamas* in the Gaza Strip, who claimed they were protecting the mosque, responded by firing 4360 rockets, four times more than during Protective Edge in 2014, first to the Jerusalem area and then to *Otef Aza*. Over the next few days, it extended its range to more areas in central and southern Israel (Elran et al., 2021). In response to the rockets, the IDF launched Operation Guardian of the Walls.

An especially disturbing aspect of this round of violence was its spill-over *inside* Israel. Palestinian, and Jewish extremists—citizens of Israel—reacted with terrible violence. This included members of the Bedouin-Arab community who blocked roads and threw stones at cars in the Negev,

J. Chaitin et al., *Routine Emergency*, https://doi.org/10.1007/978-3-030-95983-8

before and during the (Jewish) *Shavuot* holiday, which made travel on the busy roads very dangerous. In the center of the country and in the mixed cities, such as Jaffa (the southern section of Tel Aviv) and Lod, Jewish citizens and Arab citizens attacked and terrorized one another. Arab citizens set fire to a synagogue, a school, and Jewish-owned restaurants. There were violent attacks of Arabs trying to lynch Jews, and Jews who tried to lynch Arabs, when they came out in gangs, searching for people who "looked Arab." These violent hostilities led to numerous physical and psychological injuries, even death, and undermined the extremely fragile relations that exist between Jewish and Arab citizens.

The Israel Democracy Institute (Hermann & Einavi, 2021) surveyed Jews and Arabs about their views concerning these internal hostilities. In general, they found that each side thought that the violent extremists from their side came from a small minority while the violent people from the other side represented most of that other community. In other words, the researchers found that Jews and Arabs tended to hold mirror images of one another, perceiving the generalized other as violent.

However, in Israel, life is more complicated than reflected by the above findings and events. Less than a month after the end of fighting, an Arab political party—*Ra'am*—joined the coalition government for the first time in Israeli history. This Islamist party joined parties from the Jewish right, left, and center in order to form a coalition and oust Prime Minister Netanyahu and the *Likud* from their position of power. In order to hold the new coalition together, the new government, headed by Naftali Bennett, promised to maintain the status quo of the conflict. Therefore, while no peace process began, there has also been no further annexation of Palestinian territories, either. Only time will tell whether *Ra'am*'s inclusion is a harbinger of greater Arab political participation and integration into halls of power and if there is (positive/negative) movement concerning a peace process.

These events demonstrate the complexity and interconnectedness of the different conflicts in Israel-Palestine. On the one hand, tensions in one area of the conflict—Jerusalem, the West Bank, *Gaza/Otef Aza*, or within Israel—reverberate violently in other areas. From war to war, the violence escalates and widens. On the other hand, at a time of great interethnic tension, Palestinian citizens of Israel also have more political influence than they ever had before. Therefore, just as tensions reverberate, perhaps there will also be positive developments.

It is our hope that academics will delve deeper into understanding how Arab citizens of Israel perceive their social-political status, the connected conflict(s), including the Israel-*Hamas* conflict, and their thoughts about the future. Furthermore, we hope that peacemakers from the Jewish and Arab-Palestinian sectors will find the strength to turn the tide of this hatred and violence, which endangers more and more people as long as it continues. Therefore, we know that academics and peace-builders have much to offer both Jews and Arabs—be they in Jerusalem, in the center of Israel, in *Otef Aza*, the West Bank, or the Gaza Strip—and that their/our work is critical if sustainable change is to come.

Index[1]

---

[1] Note: Page numbers followed by 'n' refer to notes.

© The Author(s), under exclusive license to Springer Nature Switzerland AG 2022
J. Chaitin et al., *Routine Emergency*, https://doi.org/10.1007/978-3-030-95983-8

CPSIA information can be obtained
at www.ICGtesting.com
Printed in the USA
LVHW081644280322
714606LV00008B/774